Shoot the Puppy

Happy Birthday Bob
This is to keep you up to date!
Love S.

Shoot the Puppy

A survival guide to the curious
jargon of modern life

Tony Thorne

Illustrator: Phil Hall

PENGUIN BOOKS

Published by the Penguin Group
Penguin Books Ltd, 80 Strand, London WC2R 0RL, England
Penguin Group (USA) Inc., 375 Hudson Street, New York, New York 10014, USA
Penguin Group (Canada), 90 Eglinton Avenue East, Suite 700, Toronto, Ontario, Canada M4P 2Y3
(a division of Pearson Penguin Canada Inc.)
Penguin Ireland, 25 St Stephen's Green, Dublin 2, Ireland
(a division of Penguin Books Ltd)
Penguin Group (Australia), 250 Camberwell Road,
Camberwell, Victoria 3124, Australia (a division of Pearson Australia Group Pty Ltd)
Penguin Books India Pvt Ltd, 11 Community Centre,
Panchsheel Park, New Delhi – 110 017, India
Penguin Group (NZ), 67 Apollo Drive, Mairangi Bay,
Auckland 1310, New Zealand (a division of Pearson New Zealand Ltd)
Penguin Books (South Africa) (Pty) Ltd, 24 Sturdee Avenue,
Rosebank, Johannesburg 2196, South Africa

Penguin Books Ltd, Registered Offices: 80 Strand, London WC2R 0RL, England

www.penguin.com

First published 2006
1

Set in 13/15.25pt Monotype Joanna
Typeset by Palimpsest Book Production Limited
Grangemouth, Stirlingshire
Printed in England by Clays Ltd, St Ives plc

ISBN-13: 978–0–140–51580–0
ISBN-10: 0–140–51580–1

In memory of Nana Diana

Contents

Introduction

shoot the puppy

meaning: to dare to do the unthinkable, to grasp the nettle, to bite the bullet

'Can we please align our requirements and promulgate the deliverable through our go-to guy?' asks the senior manager, and of course it's an instruction, not a question. How his subordinates react depends on many things, including how well they know him and whether they think his tongue is somewhere in his cheek. Novel and colourful language sticks in the mind, pretentious and intimidating language sticks in the craw. It isn't always easy to separate the former from the latter; often they are one and the same. A survey of attitudes carried out by IrishJobs.ie recruitment agency in 2005 revealed that workplace jargon is most likely to be used by those in the 30–40 age group. The younger (18–25) and older (50 plus) age groups are the least likely to use this type of language. Sixty-eight per cent find this style of language annoying or very annoying. Exactly the same percentage think that it is primarily used to impress rather than to communicate information. Sixty-three per cent think that 'business-speak' is primarily used to hide a lack of knowledge, while 26 per cent think it is used to intimidate. Sixty-four per cent think it is actually detrimental to communication, but 41 per cent admit to having used such language to impress someone in the context of work. I have carried out my own informal surveys, with BBC World Service Radio and later for King's College, London, and compiled lists of the most prevalent ('penetration', 'b2b' – that's 'business-to-business' – 'ownership', 'downside', 'hands-on', 'synergy', 'ring-fenced' and 'best practice' were all high on the list) and the most disliked ('no-brainer', 'a win-win situation', 'push the envelope', 'seamless' and 'proactive' all featured) jargon expressions and workplace clichés. My findings confirmed the Irish opinions: it's the young and the old who resist and criticize the use of jargon, while mid-lifer professionals accept it with varying degrees of enthusiasm. Whichever camp you find yourself in, the new language of innovation, persuasion and obfuscation (as represented by the extracts quoted here) will inevitably infiltrate and colonize a little part of your consciousness.

We mustn't forget that there is nothing inherently bad about unorthodox language from a strictly linguistic point of view. Inventing and using jargon or colloquialism is taking creative advantage of the conventions of modern English. In any case, 'the cliché', as the French *provocateur* Alfred Jarry once observed, 'is the armature of the absolute', by which I think he meant that it enshrines important truths: our own George Eliot stated (in *Middlemarch* in 1872) that 'correct English is [just] the slang of prigs who write history and essays'. It's context that is all-important, along with the speaker's intention and the listener's reaction.

Much new language is work-related. A client has just phoned to give me, in her words, a **heads-up**, a combined reminder and warning that I need to finalize our agreement. No one is quite sure where this originated; the image is probably either a deer sniffing imminent danger on the breeze, or a wake-up call for someone with their head down, nose to the grindstone. Once you are sensitized to a new expression, you start to hear it all the time, see it in print everywhere, then you become aware that it's used in a different context – a **heads-up display** is a transparent display of data superimposed over another image, on a windscreen or gunsight, for instance – and that it appears in different forms, typically somewhere down the line as an abbreviation or acronym: **HUD** in this case.

Some new terms are heard both within the work environment and in the wider world: a **plus-one** can mean a sidekick, a less assertive or impressive friend or a superfluous member of the group. I think it comes from invitations which name the invitee and add 'plus one' almost as an afterthought. When it means an assistant or a 'gofer', Australian English renders this as an **off-sider**, proof that even in the era of global English some terms don't travel.

Words may submerge and resurface in the public consciousness, and sometimes their meanings mutate in unsettling ways. The 'new' use of the word **gay**, to mean feeble, disappointing or clumsy rather than homosexual, caused a national controversy in the summer of 2006, when it was employed by 31-year-old Radio DJ Chris Moyles rather than by the teenagers who have been using it as an all-purpose term of derision since the end of the 1970s. Although novel and unfamiliar to most, this is not jargon (a category usually reserved for the specialist vocabulary of jobs and technology), but slang, the highly informal code of a subculture.

Other items included in this book are best brought under the catch-all title (it subsumes jargon, slang and other unorthodoxies) of 'buzzwords', terms which are highly topical and which have a resonance in society over and above their actual meanings. The jokey category **metrosexual** (a heterosexual male with 'gay' consumer preferences), treated here together with its offshoots, has just recently been joined by or has spawned **heteroflexible** and **pomosexual**, words popular in the Indian subcontinent. The former denotes an open-minded and presumably 'sexually adaptable' hetero, the latter someone exhibiting 'postmodern' sexuality', whatever that may be.

Just this week the word **freegan**, which has been hovering in the sidelines for a year or so, has been thrust into prominence by a spate of news articles in the English-speaking press. Freegans (from 'free' and 'vegan', although they aren't necessarily adherents of that diet) are boycotters of the profit economy and foragers, mainly for free food, in the excess and waste generated by late capitalism. Also known as **dumpster-divers** or **skip-lickers**, they represent the latest incarnation of the militant counterculture which has been attached symbiotically to consumer society since the late 1960s.

The form of words that constitute a catchphrase or cliché may be variable. A few days ago the former Metropolitan Police commissioner Sir John Stevens, charged with ongoing investigations into the death of Princess Diana, complained that reporters had 'got **under my radar**', from the idea of a stealth fighter-plane sneaking below electronic defence systems, proving that one can be **under**, **below** or **off** the radar as well as **on** it (**not on our radar** is the version preferred in this book).

After writing in these pages about the trendiness of **footprint** (as a noun and verb meaning impact or cover(age)), I have just come across instances in Ireland and Australia of the noun **footfall** used in much the same way, but in a marketing rather than environmental context. Last week George Kearse wrote to point out that **localizing**, which I had recorded with the sense of 'translating into local languages', has different and ominous implications for expatriates when it means 'forcing staff to accept local terms of employment'. **Wipes its face** is the form of the expression that appears as a headword, but just yesterday a friend quoted her bosses declaring of a good idea that **it**

washes its face – in other words it stands up to scrutiny, justifies itself or will make a profit.

Of course where non-standard language like slang and jargon are concerned, no one is in a position to pose as ultimate authority or impose rules and restrictions on use, spelling or pronunciation. The language belongs to anyone who wishes to use it, and will survive as long as it is intelligible. Long-established, orthodox-sounding terms can undergo interesting mutations. One such is the word **leverage**, which in the 1970s was used to mean the degree of debt represented in a company's financial structuring. In the takeover and merger frenzies of that era it often referred to money borrowed in anticipation of resulting profits to finance a buyout. In English there's nothing to stop nouns being used as verbs (Shakespeare often did it) and leverage duly came to mean 'to borrow, or to achieve by borrowing, the necessary funds'. Nowadays the word seems to mean more than the sum of its various senses; it has become iconic, a word to wield. Now denoting something like 'to deploy, negotiate or build upon for maximum advantage', it has undergone what linguists call semantic extension or expansion, in plain English a broadening of its meaning, but it is also invested with an aura of empowerment, a feeling of enablement. Just using it – 'we need to leverage this proposition to impact fully across the delivery chain' – makes you a **mover and shaker**.

Who invents these novelties? Who is responsible for the shifts in their meanings and connotations? The best guess is anonymous working stiffs, whether toiling in an office, a computer suite or a design studio, but also in some cases media commentators, professional trendspotters and futurologists. It is possible for the same expression to be conjured up by more than one person at different times, and this is likely to be the case with **sunlighting**. When I mentioned the word (which in this case means doing another job as well as one's own, by analogy with moonlighting) in an article, Denis Baron wrote in to tell me that he had coined it in 1977, and this is attested by the *Oxford English Dictionary*, but I suspect that more recent instances of it in the USA are independent coinages. Women have complained that so much business-talk has a macho flavour, and it's true that the feminization of the corporate sphere still seems a long way off, but lifestyle terminology, design buzzwords and consumer slang are just as likely to be coined and used by women.

How do you go about coining a new word or phrase? English has various established techniques for forming new vocabulary. The most common is probably compounding – joining words together, either in their full forms, as with **downsizing** or **downshifting**, or by blending – merging – **smirting** from smoking and flirting is an example. It is almost unheard of for a word to be created from scratch; I'm sure that even **stoozing**, one of the most mysterious terms included

here, has a rational derivation. Transfer of meaning –
using a pre-existing word like **staircasing** to mean something else – or coining by analogy as sunlighting.

Less common techniques include what linguists call
'clipping' – an example is cutting 'awkward' down to
awk; changing grammatical function – typically from
noun to verb, as in the case of **solution**; adding prefixes
or suffixes (**re-engineerable**); borrowing from another
language (*cordon sanitaire*); or using another language
to make something unprecedented (**proctoheliosis**)

Shoot the Puppy gathers together a sampling of these
novel and exotic usages, chosen from the mass of new
language recorded since the turn of the millennium. It
is a personal selection and does not claim to be comprehensive since many such terms are already well known
and are adequately described in existing dictionaries,
many others are highly technical and of interest only
to specialists, and still others are intrinsically dull. *Shoot
the Puppy* should not be seen as a dictionary or reference book in the usual senses of those terms. Although
the entries appear in alphabetical order the intention
is not to define as objectively as possible, but to edito-
rialize, to celebrate and sometimes gently to mock, as
well as to explore what theorists call 'intertextuality',
the relationship between the words in front of you
and other words and other understandings of them.

My aim has been to take the insights that language
theory (applied linguistics and lexicology) provides,
but to offer them to the widest possible readership,

avoiding too much of my own specialist terminology, except where it may enlighten or amuse. New and unorthodox language is often dismissed as risible and ephemeral (I've even been accused of making some of it up, but I promise this is not the case), and so it may be, but there is a subtext to this lighthearted lexicon. These expressions are actually to be cherished, as linguistic curiosities, for their formal inventiveness or wit, but perhaps even more importantly for the new concepts and new attitudes they embody. As well as a treasure-house of new words, *Shoot the Puppy* is quite simply a cornucopia of fascinating ideas whose time has come.

> 'The adaptive enterprise engages in a proactive search for self-transformation. It immerses itself in complexity and seeks volatility. Its Digital Leader, eschewing the command-and-control tactics of the "hero boss", actively endorses uncertainty, embraces disruptive technologies and relishes the management of paradox and ambiguity' – insights from a management consultancy.

> 'If we can't get buy-in from all stakeholders and bring the individual players from each cost-centre along, we will have to consider a rationalization and decruitment policy' – a warning from the Director of Human Resources.

'One of the emerging spatial paradigms is that of the network as a system of interrelations between dissipative processes and aggregative structures that shape new patterns and protocols . . . our work focuses in particular on the network model's capacity to facilitate cross-categorical and cross-scalar couplings whereby the initial systems/morphologies are not merely interconnected, but form new hybrid identities' — statement by a design studio.

'Our offer is based on solutions horizontally architected from the ground up, obviating silos by implementing interactive front-ends, visibility-providing infrastructure, intelligent dynamic middleware, context-aware portlets, bi-directional write-back facilities — all within a user-centric framework' — promotion of a healthcare package.

'You will be coming onboard a value-based bioproducts and services sector-leader focused on discovery excellence. A self-starter, you will work within a highly energetic strategic environment in the development and execution of process enhancement and workflow optimization, partnering with customers and suppliers. The role forms the foundation piece at the head of the new strategy to expand on key project success and drive client growth' — job advertisement.

Acknowledgements

Many of the terms that appear in *Shoot the Puppy* were given to me by friends, colleagues or other informants, or were obtained by my eavesdropping on other people's conversations, reading their e-mails or online postings or reports they had written. Some were sent in by readers of my 'Bizword' column in British Airways' *Business Life* magazine or were contributed to my 'Last Word' column, which used to appear in the *Sunday Express*, and to the King's archive (see below). New language may eventually appear in print, in specialist publications, in newspapers and eventually in dictionaries, but by the time that happens the terms in question might have been in circulation for years. I have kept an eye on published sources but have tried to base this work as far as possible on authentic instances of spoken usage, or the 'keyboarded conversations' of the Internet.

I would like to express thanks to my 'ambient resource' – in other words my human informants, both generous language buffs and unwitting donors – and apologize to those whose names I haven't managed to record. I'm especially grateful to Alex Finer, Tim Hulse, Sarah Mower, Patrick Clarke, Ralph Adam, Dolores Hayden, Donata Puntil, Fraser Dean, Tim Greenhalgh, David Loewy, Eithne Treanor, Laurie Armstrong, Steve Ormand,

Sam Sethi, David Murray (who first gave me **shoot the puppy**), Wolfgang Nedobity, George Kearse, Denis Baron, Peter MacAlister Hall, Anthony Fogg, Jan Eisby, Lynsey Hanley, Peter Leeson, George Brown, Helen Akif, Willie Burrell, Gordon Lindsay and Andrew McCracken, Lesley Whyte, John D. Brownlie, Jason Cheskes, Sophie Constance, Lynsey Mailer and Howard James. A special thank you to Reinier Evers of trendwatching.com, and to my agent Julian Alexander, editor Georgina Laycock, Ellie Smith, Elizabeth Stratford and Nigel Wilcockson.

It is a point of honour among lexicographers that they don't lift their data from rival reference sources, and I hope I have never done so. Nevertheless, I have often checked my information against online lexicons such as the Word Spy, Buzzwhack, the Jargon File and *Wired* magazine's Jargon Watch. I would also commend the excellent lexical registers at www.etymologie.info and Michael Quinion's World Wide Words website.

The New Language Archive

The King's College Archive of New Language and Slang is a small library and database of examples of new language and material related to language change. It is a resource aimed at the press, the public and at students, teachers and researchers, and from which reference works and articles are derived. Please donate any examples of new language to the archive by sending to tony.thorne@kcl.ac.uk.

How to Use This Book

Each main entry in the book consists of a 'headword' in **bold** type – actually one or more words or a whole phrase, followed by its definition in *italics*. Then follows the body of the entry in the form of a mini-essay which explores the ideas and themes suggested by the term in question, usually taking in its origins, its usage, its overtones and its undertones. The essay will consider other interesting words or phrases (highlighted in bold type) which relate to the headword, either *semantically* (that is, connected by meaning) or *formally* (that is, resemble it in spelling, sound or grammatical function). Sometimes there will be a reference within the text to another headword or highlighted term discussed elsewhere in the book, and this will be indicated by (q.v.). After the entry itself there may be a cross-reference to expressions appearing elsewhere in the book; preceded by *compare*, if the term in question is an alternative or is used in a very similar way, or by *see also*, if it is more tenuously related.

The terms which are highlighted within entries and in the introduction are also listed in a separate glossary at the end of the book, with a short definition of their meaning there.

al desko

meaning: *without leaving one's workstation*

'I think we'll be dining **al desko** this evening,' quips a member of the team ordered to stay late to complete the boss's pet project. Now established in office slang and popularized by Hilary Price's US cartoon strip *Rhymes with Orange*, the phrase probably originated as a preppie witticism among hard-pressed young workers on US political campaigns of the 1980s. It is of course a play on the well-established expression 'alfresco', meaning in the open air, which seems to have entered English usage via the conversation of sophisticates in the 1940s. Though al desko is a mangling of a foreign language, so, perhaps, is *al fresco*. It's commonly supposed to be Italian, in which language it actually means 'in jail', not out-of-doors which would be rendered by *all'aperto* or *fuori*. And what's more, the Italian for desk is the unfamiliar-looking *scrivania*. *Al fresco* is correct Spanish, though Spanish-speakers hardly ever say it.

Other unorthodox eating habits, by the way, are the early-in-the-office-worker's **deskfast** (a meal, not a fast), **dashboard dining**, snacking while driving or parked (apparently practised by 65 per cent of North Americans), also known as eating **à la car**, and **helicopter grazing**

which involves swooping on an official function just to raid the buffet.

Jocular deformations of other languages are a staple of US campus slang, where the German farewell *auf Wiedersehen* becomes 'my feet are staying', and French *au contraire* becomes 'au Cointreau'. Among professionals the most excruciating example I have heard recently was when a Californian acquaintance mentioned that she was 'suffering from Someheimer's', meaning that she was forgetful part of the time. The pun depends on a mispronunciation of the first syllable of Alzheimer's as 'all', as in 'all of the time'.

awk

meaning: a technical difficulty, obstacle or glitch

The great auk is for some reason renowned as an extinct seabird, and AWK is a programming language named after the initials of its creators, but if you hear an IT or engineering specialist complaining that 'we've hit an **awk**', he (it's probably a he) is referring to a particularly challenging or irritating problem.

This is an example of what linguists and telecom specialists call a 'clipping': a word shorn of one of its syllables and thus transformed into a snappier piece of slang or jargon. Some of these colloquial shortenings like **spec**, **perk**, **stats** and **rep** have long been entrenched in business language. Others only work in context: **apps** may be applications or appointments or appraisals; **ops** opportunities, operations or options.

Some formerly trendy clippings have failed to catch on: the verb to **shroom**, as in 'we've been comprehensively shroomed', an abbreviated version of the old phrase to **give someone the mushroom treatment** (that is, keep them in the dark and regularly dump on them), is rarely heard nowadays. **Pulling a shen** on someone (from 'shenanigans', late-1990s hacker slang for a practical joke or prank) seems to have disappeared altogether.

Clipping is often a feature of someone's private language (in linguistic jargon, their idiolect), or of the quirks of speech developed by a small group (known as a sociolect). Among colleagues sharing an office, for example, it can become infectious as conversations are peppered with 'what's the **diff**?', 'no **probs!**' I've cringed at UK **alpha-geeks** who start nearly every statement with the hideous **unforch**, while in the USA whole phrases are clipped as in **deal!** (short for 'Just find a way to deal with it!'). Jason Cheskes, Director of Sales and Distribution for Ecolab Canada, is fed up with seeing 'I will look into and **follow** with you' instead of good old 'follow up'. Some professionals, either playfully or in ignorance, coin terms that are recognizable but officially don't exist. 'Charlotte's not very **ept**' (derived from inept), 'We've got to try and be more **ert**' (as opposed to inert), and 'Old Dennis is a fairly **scrutable** character' (unlike his inscrutable boss) all have a certain charm as do **gruntled**, **evitable** and **cognito**. People are sometimes taken to task for using **intuit**, on the grounds that only intuition exists, but in fact the verb dates from at least the eighteenth century.

aye aye, shepherd's pie!

meaning: I will comply with your wishes or carry out your orders

What is it about the work environment that causes adult professionals – especially the British it seems – to regress to a childlike state, at least judging by the catchphrases they use?

In the middle of business discussions we recreate the

nursery or kindergarten with triumphant cries of **bish bash bosh!** (meaning roughly 'job well done'). But when the boss exhorts members of the group to **get your ducks in a row** ('get organized, come to an agreement'), what exactly is he up to? Is he (it's usually a he) being patronizing? Is he trying desperately to bond, to flatten the pyramid momentarily so that everyone feels equal? Someone indulging in a fit of temper is said to be **throwing teddy out of the pram** (or **cot**), while something trivial that messes up the system is known as a **sweet-on-book** or **chewing-gum-in-hair** situation. Advertising agencies and film production companies are particularly fertile breeding grounds for this sort of banter. I've been told that many of these buzz-terms (**good plan, Batman!** is another example) are introduced into the office by the service staff, especially electricians and builders, and are then picked up by the **suits**. Some foreigners say that the childish humour favoured by the British is a symptom of social anxiety, serving to smooth over differences in status and stress from overwork, but other English-speakers do it too. The Australian term for a public tantrum is **spitting the dummy**, and **okey-dokey, artichokey!** is apparently a favourite with the very un-childlike senator for New York, Hillary Rodham Clinton. Some baby-talk is actually borrowed from kids – the jaunty **aye-aye** phrase (which can also be followed by **Popeye!**) is one such, along with **easy-peasy, lemon squeezy!** and **Brillo-pads!** (meaning 'well done!' or 'great news').

Other expressions are more obscure: a colleague who is always trying to attract the boss's attention is mockingly referred to as a **window-licker**. Does this describe a toddler trying to distract a parent, or have I misread the imagery here? I cringe when I hear that so-and-so is **not a happy bunny** (both an awful cliché and nearly always a grotesque understatement: s/he is invariably furious, devastated or just-unemployed), but baby-talk can be infectious and I caught myself uttering the very same atrocity the other day.

beer therapy

meaning: the latest health and wellness fad

Waggish drinkers, usually male, have long recommended 'beer therapy', usually in the form of a couple of cold ones to help wind down, and beer shampoos have been on sale for years. Now, however, **beer therapy** of a different sort is for the first time available to consumers of all genders.

The spa culture which has long been prevalent in Central and Eastern Europe has belatedly spread to the UK, USA and Australasia, albeit in a slightly different incarnation. In these countries it tends to be a faddish choice for **luxorexics** (q.v.), particularly female, who indulge (at what are sometimes rebranded as **wellness sanctuaries**) either as pure pampering or as a path to weight loss and beauty rather than as part of a quasi-medicinal regime. Youngish males probably make up the smallest percentage of the regular spa clientele, but this may change with the advent of the **beer spa**. These facilities have appeared almost simultaneously in Austria, Germany and the Czech Republic, where the cellars of a brewery in Chodova Plana in West Bohemia have been converted to provide a comprehensive range of beer bathing, beer massage, beer wraps and inhalations, etc. The silicon and ethanol in beer are claimed to inhibit bone conditions like osteoporosis, while applications or immersions are said to be good for the skin and the whole experience, perhaps not surprisingly, is promised to impart a sense of wellbeing.

In contrast to health-farm practices the beer therapists' is not a puritan approach and clients can drink the brew too, in some cases while they are undergoing the other procedures, after which they are invited to dine on multiple courses consisting of beer-based dishes.

Compare **golden showers**, **home resort**

Bernie

meaning: the sum of one million pounds

The UK financial sector has a robust sense of humour (what is the collective term for a group of bankers? Answer: a **wunch**). The City also has a long tradition of coining (sorry!) colourful ways of talking about its lifeblood, money. It's hard to keep track of all the slang terms in use, from the well-worn like **moolah**,

mazuma, **gelt**, **brass** to the latest novelties, **squids**, **boyz**, **bollers**, **broccoli** and **papes** among them.

Over lunch at the NatWest Tower the other day a trader was boasting that a just-done private deal had netted him 'at least a **Bernie**'. His companion remarked that 'even in today's money that's serious **wodge**'. The first expression is inspired by Formula One supremo Bernie Ecclestone's controversial attempt to donate £1 million to New Labour, while wodge is probably a blend of **wedge** and **wad**, both vogue words from the greedy 1980s.

The City has a long memory and much of its slang is older than users think. **Dosh** (sometimes disguised as **orange squash** or **rogan josh**) derives from **dash**, an African word for a bribe, **ackers** from the name of an Egyptian coin; both were imported in the days of Empire. Even older are **rhino** (recorded in 1670, probably in wonder at London's first rhinoceros), **pelf** (an archaic relation of 'pilfer'), **bunce** (a corruption of 'bonus') and **spondulicks**, often abbreviated to **spon** (originally a Londoners' attempt at *spondylikos*, the Greek name for a seashell used as currency in the South Seas).

Rhyming slang and puns flourish. A fiver has long been a **lady (Godiva)**, and just to complicate things £15 is known in some circles as a **Commodore**, from the Commodores' hit 'Three Times a Lady'. Linguistic inflation means that the same expression (**Hawaii**, for instance, from *Hawaii Five-O*) can refer to different sums – £50 or £500 – depending who you are talking to. If a **monkey** is traditionally £500, the newer term **gorilla** (a 'very big monkey indeed') can mean £5,000 or even £5m. Just yesterday an acquaintance claimed that he had 'dropped half a **bar**', using a word that in the 1960s meant £1 and now denotes the same as a Bernie.

Big Britons

meaning: a new and praiseworthy breed

In the tireless search to uncover and name new social stereotypes, BBC magazines broke fresh ground in 2006 with a survey of 1,000 respondents between 25 and 70 and a series of **focus groups** organized with the help of the Your Future and BMRB consultancies. This limited but apparently statistically sound research overturned assumptions of the importance of **Middle England**, a category made up of middle-aged, middle-class conservatives, to identify a much larger group with quite different preferences and habits and greater spending power and social influence.

The name chosen for these exemplary citizens was **Big Britons**, presumably because they are 'a big influence' and 'it's big of them to be so conscientious', but perhaps also because most of the examples the survey cited were 'big names' like celebrity cook Jamie Oliver, cricket hero Freddie Flintoff and Michael Eavis, organizer of the Glastonbury music festival, and a subtext of the report is that emulating celebrities can have its positive side. Big Britons' defining characteristics (which apply across age groups and regional bases) are that they are dynamic, socially engaged and environmentally conscious; they shop ethically, recycle religiously, protest at injustices, want to better themselves but are motivated by more than simply materialism and self-interest. These conscientious citizens practise what Australians have nicknamed **consumanism** – 'humanist(ic)' consuming. In politics their allegiances are unlikely to be to a particular party but will be issue-based (and 94 per cent of them think that there is too much spin in current public life).

If the survey findings are meaningful, this hitherto invisible constituency will have profound implications for business and society: it is estimated to be 30 million strong – that is, 56 per cent of the UK population – and their collective spending power is around £238 billion per annum.

See also **CSR**

big uglies

meaning: *long-established players in traditional economic sectors*

I was involved in a heated argument recently over the UK government's re-endorsement of nuclear energy. While some of the participants were debating the ethics and environmental issues, an economist was thinking about the implications for financial markets, remarking that it proved his point: investors had been too quick to write off the **big uglies**. The expression he used originated in the USA, where it is a nickname for familiar, cumbersome, apparent dinosaurs like the oil industry, the steel business and mining. These are 'ugly' because their installations themselves are unsightly, but also because they are blamed for despoiling the environment. In normal market conditions, shares in these operations are much less exciting than, for example, **tech stock** (high technology and IT) and so the phrase can denote unpopular shares themselves, commonly known as **dogs**. In fact, as the economist understood, what were dismissed in the 1980s as **sunset industries**, many located in the rundown zones of the **rustbelt**, are an ambivalent investment prospect – relatively unattractive in a bull market, but reliable in a prolonged bear market.

The words 'big' and 'ugly' often come together in colloquial American English: important but unpopular sports teams are also known as big uglies; 'big ugly (fat) fellow' or 'big ugly fat friend' (a ruder F-word may be preferred in final place), abbreviated as **BUFF**, are stock insults on campus and in the armed services. For fantasy author Harry Turtledove, Big Uglies are a race of warriors in his *Worldwar* series, while there is a town named Big Ugly in West Virginia, apparently because the terrain made surveying and building there a nightmare.

Billies

meaning: customers

Colleagues from elsewhere – even from other English-speaking parts of the world – are bemused to hear UK travel reps talking about 'keeping the **Billies** sweet' or airline staff observing that 'the Billies are the least of our worries'. Across Britain the term is still in use in many areas of commerce, from market stallholding through catering to property sales, despite the fact that the allusion is an ancient one. The word is an abbreviation for the rhyming slang **Billy Bunter(s)** which uses the name of the schoolboy anti-hero (the bespectacled 'fat owl of the remove') from Frank Richards' books of the 1930s to rhyme with the equally British and Irish punter, or customer. A rarer alternative is **Normans**, from the eponymous Norman Hunter (that's the legendary footballer Norman 'bites yer legs' Hunter, by the way).

Other derisive nicknames for clients or customers include **mugs**, and **muggles**, the Harry Potter books' designation for mortals with no special powers. Used-car dealers in the UK also refer to Billies, but to **privates**, **civilians** or **wearies** as well; in North American dealers' slang a customer on the lot in person, especially an eager one, is known as an **up**. In the USA 'billies' has a quite different slang meaning: since the 1980s it has been used by younger speakers to refer to money – a diminutive form of (dollar) bills.

Older rhyming slang terms which probably only survive in the patter of British stallholders are **Benny Hill** or **Buffalo Bill**, also borrowing the names of folk icons of the past, for till or cashbox. Market traders still refer to a **flash** when they mean a trader's patch and to the **Toby** which denotes a supervisor or market boss: both expressions are a century old at least.

bitch-fest

meaning: an orgy of criticism

First manifestations of the concept of the **bitch-fest** were **bitch-boards**, online messageboards where criticisms could be posted, set up from the 1990s by employees with grudges, or by corporations themselves to encourage **cyber-venting**. A trendier synonym for the once-trendy **blamestorm(ing)** (see **thought-shower**), the more recent bitch-fest can mean a corporate free-for-all, rarely spontaneous, sometimes staged as part of a training exercise or HR (human resource) strategy, in which participants are encouraged to complain about conditions, colleagues, clients and other corporate frustrations. The phrase is also heard increasingly applied to **podcasters**, who encourage rants, denunciations and feuding by their audiences.

'Bitch' is one of the few formerly taboo insults to be admitted into US daytime television. The free use of the word in rap and hip-hop culture, both pejoratively when applied to women and approvingly in the adjective **bitchin'** (impressive, exciting), has added to its allure: **bitch-slap**, originally administered to a 'bitch' or 'ho' by her pimp, is now widely used metaphorically for a spiteful attack, often unexpected and devastating.

Since the 1980s bitch has been reclaimed by feminists to signify a ballsy, feisty woman, and in the **noughties** as the title of a feminist magazine. The two senses of the word – troublesome female and bitter complaining – come together in US office and campus slang, where a **bitch-fit** (the phrase is used by females as well as males, sometimes diluted to **BF**) refers to a temperamental outburst of the sort characterized in the UK as a **fanny-fit** or **hissy-fit**. Other sorts of bitch-fest with positive intent are the **stitch 'n' bitch** gathering, a new North American ritual where women (trendies rather than frumps) sew or knit while gossiping, and the **bitch 'n' swap party**, a New York fad whereby socialites, **fashion mavens**, etc. get together to exchange unwanted clothes and accessories and **dish the dirt** on one another and absent friends.

The widespread acceptance of this short, sharp, challenging word means that similar terms such as **diss-**

ing sound timid. The old-fashioned terms 'muckraking' and 'mudslinging' seem to have fallen out of favour – the latter is more fashionably rendered by **poo-flinging**, possibly inspired by the excrement-hurling monkeys in the kids' animation *Madagascar*.

the bleeding edge

meaning: the forefront of current development in technology, product design, services, etc.

Obviously a play on those well-known business-world clichés **leading edge** and **cutting edge**, this concept ('**bleeding-edge** sportswear', cyber-games designers 'operating at the bleeding edge') takes us several steps further into the unknown, with the suggestion that we are swimming in uncharted seas where the water is turbulent and sharks may be lurking. When you're so far out in front the cutting edge can cut both ways. In the UK the term is still rarely heard and then almost always ironically (it's used straight-faced, often with pride, in the USA) and in connection with the recent meltdowns in dot.com and telecom markets – what Carly Fiorino, former CEO of Hewlett Packard, referred to in a speech in 2004 as the **tech-wreck** phenomenon. In the USA the nicely overdramatic sound of 'bleeding edge' makes it a favourite with the youngest **upstarters** (start-up impresarios), who are also known in some quarters as **entreprenerds** or simply '**treps** – the vanguard of the so-called **Generation Y** (younger siblings of **Generation X**, the slackers and grunge-fans who entered adolescence in the late 1980s). More seriously, bleeding edge refers to the heady mixture of frenzied excitement and high risk that goes with a rate of hi-tech innovation that is running almost out of control. In areas like product development, industrial design, biotechnology and training, hyper-intense competition means that experiments are often driven from the lab or workbench into the marketplace before they are proven. Even more glaring instances occur with software solutions and web-design, where avant-garde products are outstripping clients' own technical capabilities. In the words of web-designer A. G. Peabody, 'The bleeding edge . . . is what happens when someone pursues the cutting edge past the precipice of sanity and into the abyss.' And just in case you thought that this bizword is unlikely to catch on, consider this: a recent Internet search threw up at least twenty companies, from cybercafés through training consultancies to mountain-bike customizers, using 'Bleeding Edge' as part of their name and around fifty thousand instances of the phrase itself occurring online.

blobitecture

meaning: constructs mimicking shapes and textures found in nature

In the 1990s computers accelerated exponentially, first their technical capacity to configure in macro- and microscale at previously unimaginable speeds, then, drawing on animation and graphic techniques already used in the movie industry, to develop a **digital aesthetic**, using not only shapes from nature but wholly virtual and imaginary patterns derived from chaos theory, fractals and **wave-forms**.

One spectacular result was summed up by the rather ungainly portmanteau term **blobitecture**, used by Californian journalist John K. Waters for the title of his 2003 design survey, referring to a cluster of interesting concepts in design and architecture, some of which had been circulating since the late nineteenth century but which have yet to coalesce into a coherent, universally acknowledged style. The label seeks to characterize toy-like structures and amoeba-shapes in public buildings, and interior design and **accessorizing** based on **soft-edged** as opposed to **hard-edged** forms and/or textures with 'natural' finishes. Blobitecture was originally a mocking usage by those who ridiculed the **blobists** or **blob-meisters** who launched the trend, and were unreceptive to the picturesque language that they tended to employ: usages such as **dimensionless territories**, **utterance without language** or **chimerical forms**.

The related term **blobject**, coined by either academic Steven Skov Holt or designer Karim Rashid, referred to a specific trend from the late 1990s onwards for reshaping household objects, from Philippe Starck's kitchen implements, through electronic hardware such as the Apple iMac to the frog-like Nissan Micra and retro Volkswagen Beetle. **Emotional design**, **cuddletech** and **huggability** were other terms used about curvy, friendly objects.

In design, the pure **blobbiness** of blobitecture is already giving way to a compromise between its organic focus and the more familiar straight lines of modernism, yielding hybrids like the Apple iPod. In architecture, blobitecture is a continuation of an older tradition known as **organic architecture**, a term first seized upon as a slogan by US architect Frank Lloyd Wright and later pioneered by Hungarian visionary Imre Makovecz who has been building for decades using organic materials and shapes inspired by nature and by the folk art of his native Hungary. In Western Europe organic architecture is still a craze waiting to happen despite the influence of Frank Gehry's Guggenheim Museum in Bilbao and the work of Europeans Santiago Calatrava and Will Alsop. Alternative designations for this genre are **natural**, **biomorphic**, **zoomorphic** or **zootropic architecture**, which in turn is closely related to **eco-architecture**, using low-cost sustainable materials, and to schemes for the green- ing of urban environments. In the late 1990s the Belgian architect Luc Schuiten was proposing to humanize the blank façades of modernist cityscapes with 'vertical gardens', grass and trees grown on walls and roofs, while in 2006 German designer Bernd Ötte produced decorative elements made of grass for in- teriors, using a version of the hydroponic technique to grow seeds on hard surfaces, to create what was termed an 'art-meets-eco-trend experience'.

See also **sensory sells**

blood in the water

meaning: (first) visible signs of an adversary's weakness

'Laxey's Tanks on Wyevale's Lawn' announces a 2005 headline in the business pages of a UK national newspaper: elsewhere in only one edition we find 'Dubai Exchange Hires City Guns', 'Kroll's Big Shots Get the Bullet' and 'Mittal's Phoney War with Arcelor'. Images of warfare and violence are nothing new in boardroom conversation or business journalism, as both seek to glamorize the drama of merger and acquisition. Politicians, too, are fond of reporting **tanks on the lawn**, the image being of the first stages of a banana republic *coup d'état* where a rival or usurper has made his (occasionally her) move, shown his hand and staked his claim.

At the UK Conservative Party conference in September 2005, metaphors of bloodshed were used as it became clear during the leadership struggle that young pretender David Cameron was about to oust the favourite, David Davis. The phrase employed most frequently was **blood in the water**, a usage that was recorded in the USA at the time of the Watergate affair and which provided the title of a 1997 book by Frank Partnoy describing fiascos on Wall Street and their aftermaths. The expression evokes the tiny traces of blood that are sufficient to attract sharks to a victim, hence the first signs of weakness in a soon-to-be-doomed adversary.

Of better-known versions of the 'bloodshed' scenario, **blood on the floor** is probably the most familiar, graphically suggesting the evidence of a vicious struggle for supremacy or settling of accounts. There are subtle distinctions, in some professionals' minds at least, between blood on the floor and **blood on the walls** (an even more violent struggle or a mass 'culling'); **blood on the stairs** or **in the elevator** suggest that there has been conflict between those on their way to or near the top of the organization.

Macho and/or military terminology abounds: recently US executives have been talking of **shock and awe**, supposedly what Saddam Hussein's Iraqi army felt when faced with invasion. Now the phrase is more likely to refer to the devastating of North American industry by Chinese competition. **Slash and burn** epitomizes the sort of indiscriminate aggression practised by the US military in Vietnam and since; **crash and burn** means to fail suddenly and visibly. The bold and assertive stick their heads **above the parapet**; their insignificant colleagues, though, are **not on our radar**. I pray that no one **rattles sabres on my watch**, and **loose cannons** are always a problem. When an important player is ejected from a senior post a more sophisticated usage is **defenestration**, a practice popular in the old Czechoslovakia when political outcasts were literally cast out of the windows of Hradčany castle in Prague.

Sometimes political discourse can be both brutal and vulgar (to use an old-fashioned term), even though it may not appear so at first sight. When a UK government spokesman threatened in 2005 that health trusts who were in deficit the following year 'would have to **swallow their own smoke**', he was using a euphemism for a stronger S-word.

blook

meaning: a book derived from a blog

This odd-sounding neologism was probably coined by US journalist Jeff Jarvis in 2002, but achieved prominence only from 2006 when **Anglosphere** publishers suddenly swarmed towards online **weblogs** in the hope of turning the best of them into old-fashioned paper bestsellers. This next big thing was triggered by the novelty of a hybrid literary form and by the fact that it had been tried and tested over four years – giving rise in late 2005 to the Lulu Blooker prize, a literary award.

A **blook** may differ from its hard or softcover predecessor in more ways than one; many were written and posted in chunks over a period of time, thus resembling the serialization of Charles Dickens's novels. Unlike Dickens, some of these authors welcomed the intervention of their readers who were able to suggest changes or adapt the text themselves, and some blooks were free to download while others were delivered simultaneously via podcasts. Before mainstream publishers got involved a few authors had already self-published print editions of their own work, calling the process **beta-releasing**, from the concept of **beta-max technology** – deliberately opting for an obsolete format (betamax videos were ousted by VHS) for reasons of cost, nostalgia or just, in the words of one blogger, so that you have something to take to the beach.

Whatever you think of the concept, for ugliness, the word 'blook' is certainly capped by **bleaders** – the term coined by some **bloggers** to describe their aficionados (those who log on and exchange messages are also, confusingly, called **posters**). **Blogagery** is the new term for the images on the many sites devoted to comic art and graphics, and how about **blogroll** – a register of blogs – a word that cannot have been coined in total ignorance of the British slang for a toilet roll. (This in turn recalls the remarks in early 2006 by German advertising supremo Jean-Rémy von Matt, which he was later forced to retract, to the effect that weblogs were 'the toilet wall of the Internet'.)

Still unrealized at the time of writing but touted, we are told, as the next next big thing to emerge from the **blogosphere** is the **flook** – the film of the blook.

Compare **nanopublishing**, **splog**

boggo

meaning: standard issue, bottom-of-the-range

'It's just your basic **boggo** piece of kit,' says the technical salesman – a Brit – to the utter bafflement of his US
and Singaporean clients. In British conversation the affec-
tionate '**piece of kit**' now denotes any sort of hardware,
from a wrench to a refinery, but what on earth is
'boggo'? Australians may think of Boggo Road, a notorious jail in Brisbane, and fantasy game-players will
recognize Boggo as a male dwarf; but this isn't those;
it's a slang version of the phrase 'bog-standard'. 'Strictly
boggo' denotes no-frills, meat-and-potatoes, *sans* added
value. No relation, by the way, of **BOGOF**, a new item
of UK retail-speak reported by **fashionista** and magazine editor Sarah Mower. This turns out to be an acronym
for 'buy one, get one free': either a statement of fact or
a scornful **dissing** of a rival's product line.

The great majority of bizwords are Americanisms
and it's up to the rest of us to interpret them. However,
some North Americans are beginning to pick up on
UK lingo, as witness a cybermoan by David Chess about
a magazine carrying 'yet another instance of your (ooh,
can I say it?) bog-standard (I love them Britishisms!)
blog article'. **Blog** is of course **weblog**, the last next
big thing, which has given us the new verb **blogging**
(incidentally, why *do* we get so excited about an online
journal?), but the 'bog' in bog-standard is more of a
mystery. The phrase first appeared in the early 1980s

and one unproven theory is that it started out as a mishearing of 'box-standard', that is, just as it comes out of the manufacturer's box and before any modifications. I tend to think that 'bog' is what linguists call an 'intensifier', an essentially meaningless prefix added to give a harsher edge (as in the British vulgarism 'bog-all', which means 'absolutely nothing').

Your piece of kit may be strictly boggo, but that isn't necessarily a bad thing. In this **over-spec'd** world it can actually be an advantage to simplify products and lower prices by removing the **bolt-ons** and all the **bells and whistles** – from computers, digital cameras and cars, for example – a procedure sometimes called a **featurectomy**.

brand damage

meaning: *the sabotaging of a successful corporate image*

Some buzz-terms look straightforward and self-explanatory but are actually freighted with ideas and implications. In 2005 insurance underwriters at Lloyds of London warned the business world that **brand damage** was one of their biggest concerns and a principal cause of massive financial losses. They had analysed the causes of brand damage which included, in their jargon, **customer** or **employee trauma, product incidents** and **undocumented features** (in plain language, product flaws). In simple terms, then, brand damage is bad publicity.

A one-off blunder doesn't necessarily add up to brand

damage: the disastrous launch of the Edsel model by Ford in 1957 has gone down in history, but it didn't actually result in much **collateral** for the company's long-term image. The most spectacular examples of the phenomenon are self-inflicted, often by one key individual. British corporate slang still talks of having **a Ratner moment** or **doing a Ratners**, and poor quality merchandise may be dismissed as **a load of old Ratners**, all referring to the 1991 speech to the Institute of Directors by chairman Gerald Ratner in which he described some of his own (jewellery and silverware) product lines as 'crap'. The company quickly lost £500 million and its CEO shortly thereafter. In 2001 Topshop fashion chain's marketing director, David Shepherd, had to apologize for describing his customers as 'hooligans' while Barclays chief executive, Matt Barrett, did it again in 2003 when he announced that he had advised his children not to use credit cards. *Fortune* magazine coined its own jocular term for this, **SRDS** or 'sudden reputation death syndrome'.

Probably the most memorable example of undeserved brand damage in recent years was the adoption of the luxury fashion and accessory Burberry brand by the UK's feckless, troublesome, shamelessly downmarket **chav** subculture (see **chaviot**). The company struggled – finally by 2006 successfully – to recover from several years of seeing its trademark check motif on baseball caps, shirts and accessories being flaunted by the underclass.

For some reason tyre manufacturers seem especially susceptible to brand damage; witness the massive product recalls of 2000 and the US Formula One race fiasco of 2005. Occasionally companies suffer completely unpredictable misfortune, as Cadbury Schweppes found when its Bali Blast drink was still on shelves days after the 2004 terrorist atrocity in Bali, but sometimes the damage is inflicted by outsiders deliberately, as in the case of Green activists launching negative publicity campaigns against companies held to be polluters or exploiters.

channel-stuffing

meaning: intentionally oversupplying customers

In the business world there are many scams that skim along the border between legality and illegality and test the powers of courts to discriminate between the two categories, practices, for the most part, that those outside the corporate and financial spheres are unaware of. Two intimately related examples illustrate the fine line and how it can become blurred. **Trade-loading**, also called **sales loading** or just **loading**, is potentially illegal in most circumstances: it means deliberately inflating year-end or quarterly sales and profit figures; false results are recorded with the intention of deceiving shareholders and/or creditors. This is often done by **channel stuffing**, aka **stuffing the channel**, which involves pushing unwanted or excess items along the distribution chain (the channel) from producer to end-user so that it looks as if they are part of a normal sales cycle, whereas they are in fact grossly distorting it. By this method sales are entered on the books on what is known as a **sales-in** basis, in other words as if they have taken place successfully; regulators insist that they should properly be recorded under the **sales-through** or **sales-out** headings, thus making it clear that the transaction hasn't completed. What has really happened is that those further along the channel have either been pressured into accepting more items than they need, or have agreed to take the excess temporarily, often in return for a kickback, euphemistically referred to as a **contingent commission**.

Sometimes a massive excess of inventory is not the result of devious behaviour but just bad luck. When **Viking raiders** (q.v.) Atorka withdrew their bid for UK building group Low & Bonar, they left the British company with a huge **stock overhang**. Ordering more than your immediate requirements – **advance** or **forward purchasing** – by customers is not in itself illegal, and it's relatively easy to argue that oversupplying them, too, has been done accidentally or with good intentions. Nevertheless, when disparities become too public shareholders and/or regulators will prepare to intervene. At one point in 2001 customers of SSL International, owners of the Durex condom and Scholl medical footwear brands, were sitting on £63 million worth of oversupply. As the satirical magazine *Private Eye* reported, Aon made £132 million from contingent commissions in 2004, and stopping the practice in October 2005 cost them 750 jobs in the UK.

chasse gardée

meaning: *a private preserve; a no-go area*

Perhaps it's not surprising that despite globalization very few foreign words or phrases have managed to infiltrate the professional jargon of the Anglo-Saxon nations. After all it's a *sine qua non* that English, or rather American, is the *lingua franca* – *par excellence* – of world business, IT and entertainment. But like all languages English has what linguists call 'lexical gaps', concepts that our language hasn't yet found a way of expressing, but others often have. And so we borrow from them: *Schadenfreude* and *Zeitgeist*, for example, sound sharper and neater than 'perverse delight in others' misfortune' and 'intangible spirit of the moment'.

One reason why fewer foreign terms make it into English in the twenty-first century may be that these days a different sort of person is coining new language. A hundred years ago it was poets, ambassadors and international sophisticates, most of them already grounded in Latin and Greek, who had the greatest influence on our vocabulary. Today it's IT specialists, management consultants and financiers, many of whom speak no other language than their own.

But occasionally an exotic borrowing does catch on, and **chasse gardée** is one such. It originally described the private hunting reserve of a nobleman, but in the jargon of geopolitics came to mean a recognized zone of special influence (still with slightly feudal overtones), as in: 'Central America has traditionally been the USA's chasse gardée.' More recently business people have been using it, often when protesting attempts to corner a territory or market: 'We must resist Norsk Techno's attempts to create a chasse gardée in the Baltic States.'

Other recent examples of imports are hard to come by. In South-East Asia the Japanese term for foreigner, *gaijin*, is now applied by many English-speaking expatriates to all 'non-natives', including themselves, and **salaryman**, a literal translation from the Japanese, denotes any middle-ranking corporate wage slave. In the Western hemisphere, US executives are fond of going **mano a mano** – getting down to tough, one-on-one negotiations, from the Spanish for hand-to-hand (combat).

My own current favourite is another of those big German words, one that I have heard a number of mainly North American travellers dropping into their conversation; it's **Fingerspitzengefühl**, which literally means a feeling in the tips of one's fingers, but translates as 'an instinctive grasp', or 'a sixth sense' for business (apparently it was also one of Einstein's favourite words, stressing what was essential to the perfection of scientific thought). Myself, I like to think I have that *je ne sais quoi*, a *Fingerspitzengefühl* for the latest language trends. Pretentious . . . *moi*?

chaviot

meaning: *a tastelessly enhanced cheap car, a 'chav chariot'*

When a new buzzword is embraced by the media and thereby passes into everyday conversation, it often spawns related terms, and so it was with the UK print media's favourite word of 2004. From local slang in the Chatham area south-east of London, the Romany word **chav** (meaning 'pal' or 'kid', originally probably a nickname for a young fox), now used to designate an aggressive member of what used to be called the 'lower classes', quickly spread across Britain, sweeping aside contemporary synonyms such as **townie**, **pikey**, **steek**, **spide** or **pov**. In the UK the word, unlike its equivalents in the USA, **trailertrash**, **the Springer crowd**, or Australia, **bogans**, didn't just refer to an uncultured and feckless underclass, but for some social commentators seemed to carry overtones of a new attitude and perhaps even a new form of consumer behaviour.

Wits characterized as chavs the Prime Minister's spouse Cherie Blair, high-profile football stars and their wives and the **D-list micro-** or **nanocelebrities** thrown up by reality television shows, the implication being that the transition from a society where status depended on nuances of class and education to one dominated by tasteless vulgarity and self-assertion was now complete.

Chav fashion statements and accessories (aka **chav-chic**) acquired their own nicknames: the scraped-back hairstyle favoured by many **chavesses/chavettes** was

known as a **Croydon facelift**, after the unglamorous London suburb; cheap, flashy jewellery as **Argos bling**, or **bingo bling** (incidentally the emblematic **bling**, from US hip-hop slang, is now rendered as **blingage** or **blang** by the truly cool). Cars owned by chavs, so-called **chav chariots** or **chaviots** for short, were often 'customized', sometimes using the check fabric motif of the Burberry brand which had been hijacked by the subculture in a memorable infliction of **brand damage** (q.v.). When disreputable Welsh rappers Goldie Lookin Chain parked their **chavalier** (a Vauxhall Cavalier with Burberry-like tartan bodywork) outside Burberry's London store as a publicity stunt, the company had it destroyed. The cut-price customizing concept, long promoted by **laddish** publications like *Max Power* magazine, was popularized further by the television car-improvement show *Pimp My*

Ride (**pimp my ride** is hip-hop slang for 'embellish my vehicle'), imported into the UK in 2004 and fronted by the street-slang- speaking DJ and 40-year-old bishop's son Tim Westwood.

Even if it had serious implications – and this was arguable – the chav phenomenon was of course also a spoof style label, an ironic joke, and this aspect was celebrated by the website www.chavscum.uk, featuring donated snapshots of chavs – and their cars.

the China price

meaning: 30 to 50 per cent less than your lowest possible price

Veteran consumer activist Ralph Nader used this simple but resonant term in a doom-laden warning of US industry job losses in 2004; a little later *Business Week* described **the China price** as 'the three scariest words in US industry'. Scarier even than **the Internet price**, in fact; sometimes **the China syndrome**, used as the title of a 1979 Jane Fonda movie in which it referred to the threat of nuclear meltdown, is also reinvoked to describe the ubiquitous presence or impending effect of China's power in world markets.

Nader's message was that US industries are being **hollowed out**, when not actually put out of business, by competition from Chinese manufacturing: there's a consensus among other US commentators that what is known as **industrial migration** – **relocating**,

offshoring and **outsourcing** – may transform into **gravitational pull** – sucking capital, people and R&D resources out of the Western hemisphere altogether.

The relationship between the USA, still protectionist by instinct, and its Chinese trade partner used to be a simple case of **knowledge economy** versus **sweatshop economy**. Now that China is competing in more sophisticated sectors, indeed in all sectors, with the support of (the protectionists claim) an undervalued currency, the playing-field surface has tipped alarmingly in America's disfavour. As well as legitimate trading practices there are lingering controversies in play: **pirating** and **bootlegging** may be rather dated terms, **knockoffs** (unlicensed copies) and **dumping** (selling off surplus stock at below-market prices) are not. Now known in business and diplomatic circles simply as **the Mainland**, China confronts the USA with what is described baldly as the **new math**: employing a fashionable Americanism, Fluor Corp president Robert McNamara observes from personal experience, 'When they target an industry to dominate, they don't **mitigate**.' Experts used to talk about market and industry **erosion**, but that hardly seems to do the current landscape justice, suggesting as it does a gradual whittling away. Recently US CEOs have been using the Iraq War jargon phrase **shock and awe** to describe the effect of the **first wave** of what they see as a looming trade war.

chronocentrism

meaning: *a conviction that you live in the best of all possible times*

Formerly restricted to such specialist areas as bioethics and historical teleology (explaining processes by ascribing purposes to them), the quasi-technical and impressively *Zeitgeist*-flavoured concept of **chronocentrism** has emerged into mainstream thinking since 2000. It is seen as a form of discrimination, just like sexism, ageism, **eurocentrism** or **geocentrism**, and describes an attitude which assumes that present-day values are superior to anything that has gone before.

Related but not synonymous is the concept of **presentism** (don't confuse this with **presenteeism** – see **sunlighting**), which itself has two senses. The first and best known is the tendency to apply the standards of the present to other eras, passing moral or social judgements that ignore changing mores and conditions. I can't see how, for example, **queer theory**, the discovery of hidden sexual ambiguities in texts from the past, by now well established in academia, manages to escape this category, sometimes labelled the *nunc pro tunc* (Latin, 'now for then') fallacy. 'Presentism' can also refer to the belief that only the present exists, or is meaningful – a New Age, quasi-Buddhist stance that sits easily with the **consumer-centric** ethos that pervades late capitalism. Certainly if the yardstick by which eras are measured is easy access to new technology and consumer goods, it's hard not to feel somewhat chronocentric.

Senior executives, in my experience, are unlikely to worry too much about the ethical dimensions of chronocentrism — or ego- or Anglocentrism for that matter — but are fond of musing on time's depredations, lamenting, for instance, such phenomena as **corporate entropy** (the inevitable tendency for systems to run down) and **mission-creep** (the way in which a strategy inevitably unravels as **goalposts move** and costs mount). Among their less formal pronouncements two of my favourites (both genuine) are: 'It's déjà vu all over again,' and 'Plus ça change, plus c'est la même merde.'

CLM

meaning: 'career-limiting move', a blunder that could cost you your job

Judging by the response, recent articles I've written on abbreviations struck a nerve. Loved only by a few **jargonauts**, initials and acronyms are either laughed at or loathed by everyone else. Simon Turner of Group 1 Software pointed out that I'd overlooked the most obvious of all: **TLA** ('three-letter acronym'), and apparently some fanatics now actually refer to them as **abs** and **acs**. Most terms reported were everyday functional ones like **ROI** ('return on investment') or **DONM** ('date of next meeting'). Steve Ormand of Teradyne Diagnostic Solutions cited the popular e-mail exhortation to **JFDI** — 'just ***ing do it!' Steve didn't care for **ROW**, a North

American designation for 'rest of the world' which lumps together everything and everyone outside the USA in one dubious category. (The Australian version is **O/S** for overseas). Others disliked **VS**, 'voluntary separation', Human Resources doublespeak for redundancy where we all know that the S isn't always 100 per cent V. **CLM**, another euphemism, was mentioned as being both amusing and ominous. Typical CLMs used to be spilling coffee on the boss's tie or leaving a xerox of your nether parts on the copier; now it's likely to involve e-misdemeanours like bookmarking that Japanese software website or inadvertently copying the CEO in on subversive cyber-gossip.

Colleagues from overseas were frustrated by the chatty shorthand that natives slip into their e-mails; **FWIW** ('for what it's worth') **IIRC** ('if I recall correctly') and **ITA** ('I totally agree'), for example. Even more deliberately obscure are **TIIC** ('the idiots in charge') or, at the end of a tirade, **JHTV** ('just had to vent [my anger/feelings]'). But it's not only initials that irritate; Catharine Hayes of SOGECA France ('I work for an acronym!') objected like many to the appearance of

juvenile txt msgng conventions like CUL8R in e-mails dealing with serious matters.

By now everyone knows that acronyms and abbreviations are old hat – everyone but the European Union, that is. A Eurocrat reader who wishes to remain anonymous reminds us that their online glossary has 42 web-pages of **EMUs**, **EUREKAs**, **TROIKAs** and **TUNICs** – and that's the short version. So a general plea, to you the reader and to the rest of the business community: let's work together to stamp out abs and acs – **EOD** (end of discussion).

See also **awk**, **1661**, **SPOC**

coachee

meaning: an individual undergoing coaching

In only five years, from around 2000 to 2005, the profession of management training, in the doldrums since new technology impacted and corporate funding dried up, reinvented itself under the new banner of **coaching**. Approaches drawn from therapy and psychology (but surprisingly rarely from sports coaching) and pioneered by **life coaches** have been applied in the corporate environment to help professionals set goals and 'discover and exploit their inner resources'. Like any practice keen to establish itself, coaching has evolved its own jargon: **health and wellness**, **takeaway nuggets** (insights), **interflow**, **roadblocks** (obstacles to the former), **synergizable, scalable lifeskills**, and its own sometimes arcane techniques and concepts: **neurolinguistic programming** or **NLP**, **systemic constellations**, **'orders of love'**. The role of the coach has been likened to a New Age therapist, a 'friend-for-hire', a facilitator and enabler, and to 'all of the above' in one, while the person receiving the coaching – formerly the **client** – is increasingly referred to as the **coachee** (by analogy with trainer/trainee and the more obscure **mentor/ mentee**) to distinguish her or him from the **sponsor** (the fee-payer) and the **stakeholder** (a line manager, for example). An additional player emerges in the form of the **role-sitter**, the person who substitutes, fielding e-mails and phone calls, while the coachee is absent. Those who baulk at the free use of the '-ee' suffix may do so because this combining form (as linguists term it) originated as a feminine past participle ending in French. Unsurprisingly, it seems to sit most easily with English words shared with French, like 'address', 'absent' or 'divorce', or words which resemble French like 'appoint' or 'train', and not so happily with 'mentor' (originally a Greek name), 'tutor' (from Latin) or 'coach' (originally from a Hungarian word).

the concrete ceiling

meaning: an impenetrable barrier to professional advancement

When you read a polemic asserting that 'women of colour in the US business world are encountering a concrete ceiling' (the same has been said of women in the film industry in the UK), it's not hard to see that this is a variation on the famous **glass ceiling** of the 1990s, a phrase that first appeared in writing in the publication *Adweek* in 1984. It has always referred principally to sexist discrimination, whereas spin-off terms such as **bamboo ceiling** and **melanin ceiling** describe anti-Asian or anti-'colour' prejudice; **pink ceiling** refers to gays and **silver** or **grey ceiling** to the effects of ageism.

Glass is transparent, so the barrier was not visible, and glass can be shattered, so it wasn't unbreachable either. It was a ceiling because those who imposed it and those who came up against it were still, despite all talk of **flattening the pyramid**, working with old-fashioned vertical hierarchies with their notions of **upward mobility** and **high-flying**. In practice, the glass ceiling was usually located in the upper reaches of middle management, beyond which was an almost exclusively male, in most cases predominantly white, domain.

The concrete ceiling is not only much more difficult to crack, it doesn't even allow you to see the higher reaches of the structure. According to US academics who have adopted the expression for studies of Afro-American women administrators, it denotes 'artificial barriers based on attitudinal or organizational bias that prevent qualified individuals from advancing upward'. Is it working the metaphor too hard to point out that concrete is a workaday material associated with foundations and basements? Those same academics locate the concrete ceiling at a level below even middle management.

conditionate (vb., adj.)

meaning: (to make) conditional upon something

If there's one thing that causes even more **ballistication** (fury – from 'going ballistic') among language purists than the over-use of acronyms, it's the invention of new words by redesigning old ones. A prime example is **conditionate**, as in 'It's our R&D capacity that conditionates our ranking in the global marketplace', or 'We must conditionate our agreement on compliance with industry norms.'

Another current favourite started as **envision**, itself thought by many to be a bastardization of 'envisage' which then mated with 'engineer' and underwent spare-part surgery to give birth to the hugely impressive-sounding **re-envisioneering**. Adding extra syllables is almost *de rigueur*, giving us, for instance, **acceptation**, a trendy – if unnecessary – synonym for acceptance. You may find these novelties ugly or pretentious but it's hard to believe now that there was an outcry in 1977 at the idea of **access** being used as a verb. The 1970s also gave us **prioritize**, followed by **strategize**, then in the 1980s **optimize** and **incentivize** (which has now evolved into the highly fashionable verb to **incent**, by the way). And **solution** has recently become a verb, too, 'Let's solution it' apparently sounding much sexier than 'Let's solve (or resolve) it'.

The psychology behind this is clear: mastery of a new jargon confers prestige and mystique, and – even better – disempowers outsiders. Linguistically speaking, though, it's no crime: turning nouns into verbs, adjectives into nouns and recombining parts of words has a long and noble history in English. Some of these bizwords also fill what linguists call a 'lexical gap'. In standard English there's a noun 'apathy' and an adjective 'apathetic', but we lack a verb or personal epithet to go with them. No problem; marketing and ad-speak have recently adopted **apathize** and **apathist**.

I've managed to uncover the real origins of this particular crop of bizwords. Nearly all of them were coined, not by the business people who now use them (and thus stand accused of mangling our language), but by US behavioural therapists and self-help gurus. It is they who are reinventing English to give us all, they proudly claim, a new vocabulary of self-management and self-mastery.

See also **execute**

copyleft

meaning: (an agreement) to force exclusive rights into the public domain

The anti-globalization movement hasn't given us much in the way of new language so far, but one term that its activists are promoting is **copyleft**, the obverse of copyright, whereby freedom to publish or copy is made available to anybody and everybody. At a time when protecting intellectual property rights is a multi-billion-dollar priority for software and scientific corporations – and for the arts and entertainment industries, too – this is a red-hot issue. Would-be monopolists have pushed for radical extensions of **format-protection**, making it illegal to imitate even the **look-and-feel** of a product or service, simultaneously trying to ensure that the **decryption tools** needed to unlock software secrets are rigorously restricted. Their opponents range from legitimate operators like Michael Stutz, who has posted at www.dsl.org/copyleft an all-purpose copyleft agreement in the hope that it will be universally adopted, to networks of underground **hackers** and **crackers** calling themselves **warez d00dz** who pirate commercial software and distribute it freely across the Web.

Another term from the same source, coined by dissidents but now adopted by mainstream business, is **whitelist**, the opposite of a blacklist. This can refer to a register of companies you approve of or partners to whom you are willing to give free access to information, licences, etc. It's also the name of a new filter system for spam and online hoaxes.

One buzzword that still belongs exclusively to the anti-capitalist **no logo** movement (so named after the title of Naomi Klein's bestselling manifesto) is **ad-jamming**, also known as **ad-busting**, coined to describe the sabotaging of advertisements by altering the real thing or producing subversive spoofs thereof. Typical examples are hard to tell at first sight from the originals, featuring, among others, Ronald McDonald, Obsession perfume and Absolut vodka. The technique is not new. Back in the 1960s the French Situationists (anarcho-leftist agitators) practised what they called **détournement** ('hi-jacking') which meant appropriating images from mainstream publications and reworking them into messages ridiculing conformism and inciting consumers to revolt. Throughout the 1970s advertising hoardings and posters across Australia and New Zealand were creatively defaced and annotated by the **Bugerup** collective; more recently the New Zealand beer-maker Tui's mocking catchphrase 'Yeah Right' has been added by hand to a host of billboard slogans such as 'Supermarkets Care'.

corporate DNA

meaning: the invisible but essential components of a firm's unique identity

Traditional views of business organizations saw them as structures made up of 'pieces' – the Lego analogy is often used. Even innovations like the **BPR** (business process re-engineering) of the 1990s, which sought to replace a **silo mentality** (q.v.) based on physical location and distinct product-lines by concentrating on processes such as distribution and marketing, still treated the company as a set of components. More recent **holis-tic** approaches to management have viewed the company as a complex organic entity with a unique 'personality' operating within a business **eco-system**. Where knowledge and information (the **grey-matter economy**) rather than mechanisms and structures are the key to wealth, management science based on engineering or military-style **command-and-control** tactics may no longer be appropriate. Since the end of the 1990s the idea of **corporate DNA** has been invoked to describe the inherited framework of core values, traditions, attitudes and expertise that reside, in the words of Australian ethicist Simon Longstaff, 'deep within the fabric of the organisation'. Critics of market-based economies sometimes argue that the multinational corporation itself is a victim of its 'genetic code' – the inbuilt, unquestioned impulses that predispose it to monopoly, merger and acquisition, to stress shareholder value above all else, to globalize and to outsource unthinkingly.

By the same analogy individual companies may mutate and hence perish if they don't preserve their DNA by sticking to a code of ethics, by becoming aware of their own essential natures (using for example **knowledge-** and **skills-mapping**, **human inventories**, **value-audits** and **talent management**). Companies, like people, can suffer from **institutional memory loss** when a generation of key workers retires or when a CEO forgets what his team's **core competencies** are.

The genetic metaphor is now bandied about so freely

in the business world that it is in danger of losing its originality as a concept: these days it often functions as a trendier synonym for an organization's 'culture' or 'identity'.

countergoogling

meaning: *using a search engine to investigate a customer or candidate*

Googling, after the name of the dominant Internet search engine, is a well-established tactic on the part of consumers/users, whether to get information, to identify products or to trace friends online (in the worst case to indulge in **cyberstalking**). Now the roles are being reversed and producers are googling their consumers – it's known as **countergoogling** or **contragoogling** – checking out private individuals through Internet searches, in a form of **data-mining** or social **drill-down** in order to improve their insights into **demographics**, identify **niches** and practise highly targeted (**hyperlocated**) sells.

HR (human resource) departments in both private and public sectors now employ the technique as part of the recruitment process: hapless interviewees have been caught out when gaps or falsifications in their CVs have been revealed by a search of their past as logged electronically.

Reverse googling is slightly different: it can mean starting from what is usually the end of a search, an address or telephone number, for example, and working back to gather more extensive information about an individual or enterprise.

CSR

meaning: corporate social responsibility

Acronyms and initials tend to be viewed with suspicion, but some of them stand for beneficial developments. Ever since investors and financiers realized that it is a concept that can actually be **monetized** (that is, has tangible financial benefits) as well as being simply a 'good thing', the three letters **CSR**, for 'corporate social responsibility', have featured in every business magazine and boardroom discussions everywhere.

In 1988 came the formation of **BITC** (a rather unfortunate spelling), or **Business in the Community**, an independent UK charity dedicated to encouraging businesses to contribute to society. Ten years later the same organization established the **CRI** or corporate responsibility index, a means of measuring and publicizing the relative performances of individual companies in areas such as environmental impact (see **footprint**), ethical investing and sourcing, and care of employees. The *Reader's Digest* magazine has also carried out a survey to identify the most trusted brands on a 0–5 scale of perceived integrity.

Signing up to CSR in general and to the CRI in particular (only 131 firms were actually assessed in 2006) is obviously morally laudable, but is also becoming a business imperative, since **stakeholders** – customers, shareholders and outside regulators – not to mention the public and the media, are increasingly demanding evidence of responsible behaviour. Non-compliance is now seen as failing to manage **goodwill**, **brand reputation** and **non-financial risk**. Marketers stress the commercial value of an **ethical proposition**, in other words a public image based on **fair trade**, **sustainability**, health issue-awareness, etc., while at the same time warning against **bragging** or **over-claiming**. The response of many big companies has been to buy in credibility by acquiring small niche enterprises who already have a good social profile, thus the Unilever food conglomerate bought Ben and Jerry's ice cream and cosmetics giant L'Oréal took over Body Shop.

cuddle party

meaning: a tactile but non-sexual get-together

Despite the terror and distaste bound up with taboo sexuality as manifested in paedophile scares, and despite the vastly increased danger of being litigated against over inappropriate touching, slapping and so on, many of today's empowered consumers still hanker for some form of intimacy-on-demand, something as instantaneous as, but a little less individually challenging than, **speed-dating**.

To cope with this demand, a cross between a blind date and group therapy, with hugging as a centrepiece, has been developed in New York City under the name of the **cuddle party**. Groups of strangers can sign up to participate in a stage-managed social bonding at which they undergo what resemble well-established training and therapy techniques such as **huddling** and **mêlée-ing** (a fancy word for orchestrated mingling).

Though packaged as a novelty craze, this reminds me of the 1960s and early 1970s. I recently used an expression from that era twice, once in deriding the proposal for a workshop to mend office relationships, and secondly to describe the cosying up of two organizations toying with the idea of a merger: my reference in each case to a **love-in** was met with blank looks from even slightly younger colleagues, for whom it obviously had no meaning. And was it the ephemeral 1965 dance craze, the Let-Kiss, that involved participants hurling themselves into a great heap in the middle of the dance floor, not unreminiscent of the cuddle-party's **puppy-pile**? No, on second thoughts it was the Bastido. The puppy-pile seems to be a drug-free counterpart of the horizontal gathering of euphoric and exhausted Ecstasy users in chill-out rooms or bedsits, known in slang as a **cuddle-puddle**.

The cloyingly innocuous, touchy-feely cuddle party can be contrasted with the radical **flash mob** craze which surfaced in New York in mid-2003 and was quickly emulated across the developed world. This demonstration of the mobilizing power of e-mail and cellphone brought crowds of strangers to congregate at a prearranged location for no discernible purpose – again, to a **boomer** like me, recalling the free-form **happenings** or **be-ins** of the 1960s. The name chosen for these manifestations was probably inspired by **smart mobs**, as described in a 2002 book of the same title by Howard Rheingold, and **flash flood** or **flash crowd**, Internet slang denoting a sudden and overwhelming rush of loggers-on to a particular website.

I'm sorry, but I can't stop thinking of another – very vulgar, to use an old-fashioned qualifier – phrase from the 1960s; it describes something which a cuddle party emphatically is not: a **group-grope**.

Darren

meaning: *an unsophisticated younger male*

For a long time certain given names have been used in slang and facetious conversations as shorthand for social

types: from the 1960s a **Nigel** could denote a quintessentially middle-class male (usually, as with many
such epithets, with pejorative overtones: implications
of social ineptitude, unattractiveness, etc.), while a
Tarquin or, occasionally, a **Rupert** epitomized a toff.
From the 1970s to the 1990s footballers and football
commentators were collectively dubbed **Brian**. Television
critic A. A. Gill endlessly rails against the **Tristrams**, the
self-satisfied upper-middle-class gatekeepers – producers, editors and directors – of UK television output.

These names are not necessarily those that feature in
the top ten baby names published annually, but are part
of collective folk memory and work because they trigger a predictable response in a significant number of
people. For about a decade particular given names have
conjured up the unsophisticated lower orders – what
used to be called the working class, except that, as a
self-confessed **chav** protested recently, 'We don't bleedin'
work for a living!' Most popular stereotyping names for
males are **Darrens**, **Waynes** or **Kevins**, and for females
Mandies, **Tracies** or **Sharons**. In certain milieux other
names are chosen: surfers and skateboarders tend to
refer to all girls as **Betties**, still harking back, although
they are probably unaware of it, to the character played
by Michele Dotrice in the 1970s television comedy
series, *Some Mothers Do 'Ave 'Em*. In north London Jewish
circles in the 1990s, young girls were collectively **Becks**,
from the common name Rebecca and perhaps from a
favoured brand of imported bottled lager.

It's a curious phenomenon of the **noughties** that the (actually very sudden) end of the traditional British class system, with its immovable certainties and codes based on school ties and subtle differences of accent and dress, has not meant an end to snobbishness, merely that wealth and celebrity have been substituted for upper-class affectation as the benchmarks. Vulgar, feckless, borderline dangerous **townies**, **pikeys** and of course chavs themselves are the butt of mockery by middle-class teenagers as well as by more privileged **yatties** and **poshos**. But Darrens aren't just a pub joke or a figment of the adman's imagination. A survey of UK car-owners by the Churchill Insurance group showed that males bearing this name are statistically likely to drive a downmarket Ford Escort. The same model was favoured by Waynes and Tracies, while Alexanders, Matthews and Adams were more likely to be driving a Renault Clio.

See also **chaviot**

desk rage

meaning: a violent tantrum resulting from workplace frustration

Following on from the high visibility of terms based on 2000's word of the year (according to several mainstream dictionaries), **road rage** (these newly identified lifestyle afflictions included **bike rage** and **trolley rage**, also known as **checkout-** or **aisle-rage**), came their workplace equivalents: first, **computer rage**, a state in which office workers smashed their main-frames or terminals, or threw desktops across the room, then the pummelling or throwing of what were renamed **slaptops** for the occasion, updated to **desk rage** or sometimes **tech rage**. First highlighted in work-related stress surveys in the UK in 1999 and in the USA in 2000, **anger contagion** was identified as a product of overcrowding and oppressive schedules: the answer, naturally, is a course of **anger management**, but the thought of that can itself provoke furious spluttering in many sufferers, myself included. The American poll revealed that 42 per cent of respondents had witnessed yelling and verbal aggression and 14 per cent violence against machines, over and above the widespread practice of **percussive maintenance** (that is, hitting a machine to make it work).

A slightly more recent phenomenon has been the appearance of the **crackberry**, a nickname which is a blend of BlackBerry, the trademark for a highly mobile electronic communicator, and the highly addictive drug crack (cocaine). The typical crackberry, unable to survive offline, can be seen tumbling out of a plane, feverishly grappling with her or his hand-held device: if anyone interferes with it, **BlackBerry rage** will almost inevitably follow.

Among the many irritations of free-market capitalism, automated phone messages and call centres outsourced to the wilder shores of intelligibility rank very high: losing one's temper with these has been dubbed **robot rage** or simply **phone rage**. In the words of the *Evening Standard*, 'We all know the person at the other end of the line is a computer, but that doesn't stop us from shouting down the phone, does it?'

desktop philanthropy

meaning: online sponsorship of good causes

Not given to acts of gratuitous generosity, a corporate lawyer of my acquaintance has become a **virtual angel**, and is happily funding a scheme to provide low-cost cellphone access in rural Africa. This new form of **social capitalism** – there's a term, **redistributionism**, for the philosophy behind it – has also been called **desktop philanthropy**. The practice probably began offline around 2000 in the USA under the name of **microlending**, which then meant making small – typically $200–300 – loans to individuals in low-income neighbourhoods in order to stir up economic activity at street level. **Microloans** or **microfinancing** now usually refer to interest-free online lending by individuals in the developed world to support **minipreneurs** in developing countries, typically engaged in socially responsible projects in deprived areas.

US-based organizations such as Kiva (the Swahili word for agreement), Grameen and ACCION International offer what Kiva calls a 'high-engagement personalised experience', in other words the chance to make a short-term socially responsible investment and track the results via e-mailed progress reports. Lenders are repaid without interest, and the loans, unlike charitable donations, are not tax-deductible, so the onus on the borrower and the profit for the lender are almost entirely moral.

Microlending also encompasses the phenomenon of **P2P** (peer-to-peer or person-to-person) or **community banking**. Pioneered by Zopa in the UK and Prosper in the USA, this involves private individuals lending to and borrowing from each other via an Internet intermediary, but without the involvement of the traditional banking sector. Dubbed 'the eBay of banking', this sort of lending and borrowing exchange matches responsible borrowers with lenders who compete to offer the most favourable terms. **Scamsters** – practitioners of the **Nigerian fraud**, for example – are screened out, **due diligence** is observed and the **predatory lending** practised by some orthodox financial institutions is taboo.

Incidentally, **Zopa**, chosen by a team of former Egg employees as the name for their venture, is itself a significant buzzword. It represents the underlying rationale for the practice and stands for 'zone of possible agreement', in the theory of negotiation the difference between one person's **bottom line** or **walk-away position** and another's **top-line**. As the slogan goes, 'if there's no zopa, there's no deal'. In that case the only alternative to what the theory calls **intractability** is some sort of **fall-back** strategy described by the acronym **Batna** – a best alternative to a negotiated agreement.

diarize

meaning: *to agree a joint schedule*

Correspondent Willie Burrell tells me that, although it's pretty common, he still cringes every time he hears the word **diarize**. It is widespread, employed either intransitively as in 'OK guys, now let's diarize', meaning check and coordinate our agendas, or transitively as in 'we must diarize the meetings', meaning write them down. I have heard **calendarize** used in the latter context, too. The diary or calendar is likely to be in electronic form these days, so, although **pencil you in** is still used for noting a tentative appointment, I'll **enter you (in)** seems set to replace it and a nuance of difference may be lost. Just recently diarize has been proposed with a quite different sense. Steve Allen of Reports Systems Australia Pty is recommending that home-owners diarize their house by keeping a property logbook on the same principle as the car logbooks that document a vehicle's history.

New jargon is invented with two main motives. First for the sake of brevity, as when 'put it in the diary' becomes one neat businesslike word, and secondly in order to come up with something more fashionable, exclusive, impressive and/or intimidating. Hence 'follow up on this' can now be just **follow** and 'what we can take away from this experience' is abbreviated to **take-away**. To impress or intimidate, the empowered professional typically takes a standard term and refashions it into something more exotic and resonant. The ubiquitous noun **parameter** becomes a verb, then a gerund or participle, yielding **parametring** (or **parameterizing** if you prefer). **Solution, mentor, transition** and **task** (a favourite in the public sector and government-speak: 'we have been tasked with taking this forward') have all become verbs quite recently, while **learnings** has become plural and all sorts of things have combined to give us **repurposeable**.

The US Food and Drug Administration has taken to using the word **issuance** when talking about sending out drug safety warnings, creatives and training specialists have replaced brainstorming or **thoughtshowering** (q.v.) with **ideation**, but my personal prize for innovation/pretentiousness goes to the Australian marketing expert who announced that 'the selfish empty-nester scenario simply hasn't **eventuated**', where eventuate simply means happen.

See also **conditionate**

digital leader

meaning: a new breed of corporate boss, reinvented for a new global reality

In hoping to enlighten us, and to justify their fees into the bargain, management gurus and management consultants have generated a whole slew of buzzwords which aim to define models of leadership. Their latest quest is to chase down and name the ultimate winner, the mythical boss who can confront global uncertainty and dot.com meltdown and triumph. Among the categories recently touted by management strategists, we have had the **syndicating chameleon**, the **complement magnet**, the **land grabber** and the **fearless maverick**. But these and earlier models, we are told, are all now obsolete. **Visionaries**, **tribal chiefs**, **techno-savants** and the rest have failed to rescue businesses from economic turmoil, ethical malpractice and **dot.cons**. More and more old-style CEOs (sorry, **CXOs** is more fashionable these days) are going to the wall, defeated by market volatility and disorientated by **noise** (defined as the overwhelming influx of 'essential' data that a manager has to process, together with the mass of conflicting theories on how to do it).

PA Consulting Group's Peter Fisk has seen the future and, he claims, it works. Enter the **digital leader**, a super-being who 'surfs the edge of chaos', 'embraces disruptive technologies', 'actively seeks uncertainty' and 'relishes the management of paradox and ambiguity'.

Wading through a similar jumble of labels for business enterprises themselves, two in particular stand out: **clever old dogs** are outfits like Toys "Я" Us, Walmart and Tesco who have successfully adapted to e-commerce. More progressive is the so-called **adaptive enterprise**, Cap Gemini Ernst and Young's name for the organization which, like its digital leader, is willing to 'proactively search for self-transformation', 'immerse itself in complexity' and 'seek volatility'.

There's certainly some truth in the idea that traditional methods of leadership – the 'command and control tactics' of the 'heroic' boss and the 'mechanical leadership' of the boss who simply does what has come to be expected – are failing, but does this juggling of labels really amount to convincing theory? Isn't it a circular, self-authenticating argument: the new CEO, whatever colourful name we choose for him or her, is not a model but simply an individual who, by luck or judgement, rides out the market cyclones and cyber-storms?

directional (n., adj.)

meaning: (a design that is) avant-garde (if not totally ridiculous)

The fashion business is an intensely competitive hothouse environment with its own code to keep outsiders out and insiders feeling smug. As **fashionista** and magazine editor Sarah Mower explained to me, much of the jargon of *haute couture* consists of snooty euphemisms – important-sounding terms intended to hide their often bitchy intent. **Direction** means stylistic trend, as in 'this season's African-meets-punk direction', but **directional** implies something so far ahead of its time that no one is betting that the public will ever catch up. You may recoil at low-fronted crotch-revealing pants, but Britney Spears is already wearing them. Slightly less radical but supposedly daring ideas are said to be **forward**. Little words become charged with meaning: 'Mmm, Comme des Garçon's three-legged pant, I'd say that's **difficult**', is diplomatic-speak for frankly hideous and unwearable. **Pant**, incidentally, is much cooler than 'pants' (and 'trousers' don't exist), just as **lip** is how you say 'lipstick' or 'lipgloss'. **Look** doesn't mean 'look', but refers to a coveted outfit that has been worn on the **runway** (catwalk). 'Can you get that Versace look sent over after the show?'

Further downstream in the retail outlets, salespersons have evolved another fashion-based slang: **shopgrifters** (from 'grifter', old US slang for a cheat or cheapskate) are customers who buy a product, wear it once to show off and return it for a refund. More bizarrely, **shop-droppers**, the opposite of shoplifters, illicitly add their own clothes to the designer lines on display (the practice itself is called **dropping in**), either to publicize their amateur designs or as a protest against high-price labels. Sales staff may resort to **vanity-sizing**, labelling a garment one size smaller to flatter you into buying, or passing off **carry-overs** – last season's stock – as the **item du jour** (latest **must-have** accessory). If you're a **fashion victim** hoping to pass for a fashion-ista, beware if the sales assistant says you look **kewl!** When pronounced like a cat's miaow it's always ironic. **Nifty!**, **nutty!** or **not too shabby!** means they really approve. If you hear voices swapping acronyms outside the changing-room, it's bad news. **MDL** is 'mutton dressed as lamb', **BLC** is 'bag-lady chic' (not a compli-ment). In UK boutiques unstylish males are wither-ingly dismissed as **catalogue-man, Mr Byrite** (after a cut-price Oxford Street chain) or **man at C&A**.

disaster capitalism

meaning: profiteering in the wake of global catastrophes

Not all buzzwords are concerned with marketing trends or corporate or office life. The globalization debate

and **geo-economics**, for instance, have recently generated a clutch of interesting expressions. A polemic by activist Naomi Klein which appeared in April 2005 popularized the notion of **disaster capitalism**, the dynamic which takes advantage of global chaos to, she alleges, impose Western economic – and political – models on vulnerable societies.

An associated term which has suddenly leapt to prominence is **terra nullius**. The phrase, Latin for 'no one's territory', was a quasi-legal concept first used by the British to justify their colonization of Australia and New Zealand. Then it suggested that the land being occupied did not belong to anyone, or that the locals were nomadic, uncivilized and/or incapable of governing. Today it refers to a location that has been wiped clean by disaster (when this is the result of military action, by the way, the US army refers to it as **area denial**) and now represents a blank slate, ready for **predatory reconstruction** or **re-colonization by**

stealth. Examples are coastal areas of South East Asia devastated by the 2004 tsunami, hurricane-damaged parts of the Caribbean and **post-conflict** regions or **limited-sovereignty** states like Afghanistan and Iraq.

The latest economic theory has already analysed the pros and cons of rebuilding and **stabilization** (a term that may imply a degree of political and **social (re-) engineering)** and the danger that coalitions of outsiders – **for-profit** construction companies, aid agencies and other NGOs – will create effective monopolies within the ravaged regions. The potential damage to locals left out of the deals is described in economists' jargon as **spillage** or **externalities**.

A more futuristic idea is being embraced by some on the left and on the right who hold that globalization is about more than transforming local economies and internationalizing trade. In their view what's taking place – inevitably – is a mutation in our identities: the very concepts of statehood and national economies are obsolete. These self-styled **post-nationalists** already inhabit, they say, a world without meaningful borders or traditional allegiances, in which **global nomads** (a concept promoted by Indian-American writer Pico Iyer, among others) and **travelling cultures** (a phrase coined by Australian cultural theorist James Clifford) will hold sway. Indonesian shrimp farmers, I suspect, may not yet see it that way.

discount diva

meaning: a thrifty but demanding consumer

It was probably in the fashion industry that the phrase **discount diva** was first used (in gentle mockery perhaps, or else in waspish disapproval) of a customer who expects top-level service at bargain-basement prices. The slang phrase has been trademarked by two US shopping gurus who also employ the derived noun **divatude**. Diva, of course (like *prima donna* – literally 'first lady'), is from the Italian (for 'goddess') and denotes the lead female singer in an opera: it has been a favourite term in the camp lexicon since the days of disco and movie 'divas' like Donna Summer and Liza Minnelli.

Airlines in particular have taken note of the **thrifter** mentality and embraced the discount diva nickname, incorporating it into their internal literature. They cunningly adapt their planes by, for instance, strategic **odorizing** (see **sensory sells**), placing flowers in toilets and installing hydraulic toilet seats, gimmicks which impart a sense of luxury while actually costing very little. Luxury boutiques have realized that even the **mass affluent** and **luxorexics** (qq.v.) can morph into **supersavers** when their bargain-hunting instincts become engaged, and so sneak strategically placed reductions into their ranges, while credit card and mobile phone companies are waking up to the exigencies of **rate tarts** (see **stoozing**) who will ruthlessly switch providers until they get the best deal.

See also **Billies**

disease marketing

meaning: treating ailments or 'medical' conditions as consumer identities

Aggressive marketing of health-related products has been controversial, especially in the USA (the only advanced economy, apart from New Zealand, to permit **direct-to-consumer** advertising of drugs), which has around 5 per cent of world population but 50 per cent of spending on medication. There's concern, since US life expectancy and infant mortality rates don't reflect the high spending and consumption levels, but it isn't a one-way process whereby an innocent public is duped by **big pharma** (as the pharmaceutical giants and their regulators are known) and its marketing tools. Consumers themselves have morphed into what media theorists call an **active audience**, a self-aware, increasingly **self-diagnosing** even **self-medicating** constituency exerting pressure on the medical profession and manufacturers to meet increasingly personalized demand.

Where the USA goes, Britain and Australasia follow, so I was intrigued when a UK advertising executive referred to something called **disease marketing** as being beneficial to consumers and society. In fact this ominous-sounding label, like many such buzzwords, implies much more than a simple definition suggests.

A cultural shift has been taking place. People have now incorporated sickness into their lifestyles and expect to manage their own conditions, but, unlike the medical profession, often don't distinguish personal traits like hair-loss or erectile dysfunction from behaviour-related issues such as obesity or mild anxiety, or long-term and chronic problems like diabetes or heart disease. All these are now seen as part of one's identity, just like hair colour, skin type, religious or political views, taste, hobbies, etc.: personal factors to be coped with and catered for.

Customers today don't see just surgery and pharmacology as potentially life-enhancing (rather than just curative); they expect foodstuffs, cosmetics, accessories and even holidays to be customized to match their health profiles. To its critics, disease marketing means using illnesses to sell **ailment-specific** or simply **good-for-you** foods or cosmetics, but to proponents it's a **targeted-but-holistic** approach responding to genuine changes in consumer perceptions.

For producers, the pluses of a **disease-pitch** are opportunities to tap into a highly motivated **must-reach demographic**, potential for **cross-merchandising** (buyers of one health product will be drawn to others), and the chance to exploit **bragging rights** (in this case the flaunting of medical endorsements and official stamps of approval).

Disease marketing, by the way, shouldn't be confused with not-for-profit **social marketing**, intended to promote public health, good behaviour, etc., or with **viral marketing**, which claims to sell any sort of product or service by triggering a 'contagious' word-of-mouth or message-forwarding frenzy.

See also **phood**

earball

meaning: (a) to pay attention by listening; (b) an audio-spot or audio device

Very recently, the British satirical magazine *Private Eye* printed a remarkable sample of corporate gobbledy-gook, purportedly coming from the consultancy Intsys UK. The jargon-filled item read in part: 'Touch base as you think about red tape outside of the box and seize B2B e-tailers and re-envisioneer innovative part-nerships that evolve dot.com initiatives delivering synergistic earballs to incentivize.' I was suspicious: even in the twenty-first century nobody writes like this except as a spoof, and sure enough there was no trace of the original on the Internet. But one bizword in particular caught my eye. The bizarre term **earball** really exists and suddenly seems to be cropping up everywhere. It took some linguistic detective work to uncover the first examples of the word as part of Californian hipster slang of the mid-1960s, although it probably originated much earlier in the lingo of jazz musicians, inspired by the better-known **eyeball**, meaning to glance or stare at. (Eyeballs, by the way, are also units for measuring a viewing public, just as **bellybuttons** are for the apparel and furniture industries.) Still used by just a few hi-fi buffs in the USA, 'earball' took on new life when PCs acquired an audio facility and data ceased to be visual-only. Marketers and designers could be overheard saying 'You'd better earball this', or 'It deserves an earball as well as an eyeball', or 'We'd better set up some earballs' (meaning organize some **informatizing** using music and/or spoken word) and in these senses the expression seems to have spread beyond the USA during 2002. The same term can also refer to a miniature remote earpiece, literally a steel and plastic ball worn inside the ear. For added confusion, one US company is marketing a different sort of earball as a promotional item. These are golf balls with ears printed on them in order, we are told, to hear their executive owners calling desperately from the bunker. From the ridiculous to the sublime: there is yet another and quite different meaning of the word in Scottish and Irish literature. In the Gaelic languages *earball* means either the tail of an animal or a beautiful flower, and as such features on dozens of poetry websites.

econymy

meaning: the science of creating brand names

The difference between a parlour game, a profession and a science can depend on no more than the name you give the activity. A highfalutin title will of course lend credibility to a practice that has yet to establish itself, and often the appropriate term already exists somewhere in the dictionary or in technical manuals. The English-speaking world boasts thousands of **corporate identity consultants** or **brand-designers**, commanding sometimes huge fees for guiding enterprises in the choice of names, but most serious research in the area, a branch of **onomastics** (the science of proper names, from Greek *onomastos*, 'named' and *-ikos*, 'the study of'), has been carried out by German speakers like Ingrid Piller of Basle University and Wolfgang Nedobity, an Austrian name-designer who works in German, English and the undefined 'common European' in which many names are based. The term suggested to define this sort of naming is **econymy**, inspired by German **Ökonomie**, itself inspired by Greek *oikonomia*, 'management' and *-onymos*, '-name'. Though pleasingly quirky, it seems unlikely to catch on, not least because however you pronounce it, it sounds too close to 'economy'.

The craze for **rebranding** peaked in the early **noughties** with the fad for replacing devalued, discredited (**brand damaged**, q.v.) or too transparent names with often meaningless or opaque Latin-sounding inventions like

Aviva, Diageo, Corus, etc. An attempt to satirize the tendency in 2002 succeeded only too well when entrepreneurs actually adopted many of the spoof brand names (Ovisovis, Amplifico, Integriti among them) from the website set up by the Design Conspiracy agency. I tried their free brand-name generator myself in 2006, entering my own name, 'core values' and 'goal' and it came up with 'Cassida', which they claimed symbolized 'power, knowledge and sunshine'. I liked this so much that I thought of registering it, only to find that someone had beaten me to it. In coming up with **naming solutions** (based in fact on no more than a Latin dictionary and a sense of humour) the website offers to provide a £100 million consultancy service for free. Although the claim is tongue-in-cheek I think it may be setting an interesting precedent as well as sending shudders through the ranks of fee-dependent **econymists** (and **onomasts** like me, come to think of it).

the eighty–twenty myth

meaning: the notion that technical equipment is oversophisticated

This expression, prevalent and very influential in the later 1990s, especially among those software developers who were operating outside the dominant fortress of **SillyValley** (their dismissal of Silicon Valley), asserts that 80 per cent of the customers use only 20 per cent of the applications, leading systems designers and manufacturers to think that they need to slim down or drastically simplify their offerings.

In the words of the American science-fiction author and technology buff Bruce Sterling, today's '**gizmos** have more **functionality** than you will ever understand'. The same concern led to the coining of the word **bloatware** to describe software or hardware that was **Christmas-treed** (that is, festooned) with redundant **bells and whistles**.

The consensus by the end of the 1990s was that **the eighty–twenty myth** was not entirely mythical, but had been interpreted too simplistically: the typical user may only access 20 per cent, but every customer was using a different 20 per cent. Nevertheless the expression is still invoked as a mantra by many designers, while others assert that **over-speccing** is an inevitable part of high-speed technological evolution.

embedded intelligence

meaning: the sensitizing and automating of objects and systems in the real world

According to systems specialist Jeff Stefan, **AI** (artificial Intelligence) is 'a field that failed under the weight of its own unrealistic expectations'. The relentless progress of robotics and cybernetics certainly stalled at times during the 1980s and 1990s, but AI is now getting closer to fulfilling its sci-fi promises. The fashionable buzz-term in the field of **intelligent** or **smart**

objects is **embedded**, in other words fully integrated and ideally invisible – the label also applied to journalists working from within allied forces during the Iraq conflict from 2003. Kitchen appliances that know when and what you want to eat, houses that adjust ambience to mood, gadgets like the Japanese **techno-toilets** that respond to their users' state of health, or the **programmable brick** that teaches children the principles of engineering, have entered consumer folklore, but the all-important **tipping point** in **adaptive technology** occurs when objects or environments that have memories and are able to communicate and interact become capable of independent decision-making.

AccentureTechnology Labs have been tracking progress in four distinct areas: **sensor telemetry** (using wireless communication, in their words, to 'generate insight from products, people and places'), **silent commerce** (tracking and tagging), **post-PC computing** (finding new mobile platforms to create so-called **pervasive networks**) and **intelligent home services** (advances in household technology to benefit the elderly in particular). Unsurprisingly, it's in the less spectacular applications that the biggest advances have been made. Whole cities can now benefit from traffic monitoring systems, each element of which is a sophisticated semi-autonomous unit: cars themselves will soon be carrying their own black boxes (both devices are known technically as **EDRs** – event data recorders). More excitingly perhaps, power consumption, changes in humidity or vibration in industrial units, movements of patients in hospital wards – and potentially of soldiers on the battlefield – can all now be tracked by almost invisible remote **MEMs** (microelectromechanical sensors) known as **smart dust** or **motes**, each as big as a grain of sand but equipped with its own wireless communications technology and power supply. Soon the scattered motes will be able to exceed their own limited capacity by **scavenging** from the **ambient** energy sources (light, heat, movement) around them. In a parallel development not long ago scientists in the UK and Japan have attached light-sensitive slime mould to robots to refine their sense of direction, a first step towards blending biological and mechanical systems in one entity.

execute

meaning: to put into effect (sic)

'I have been responsible for executing exhibitions and trade fairs', was a sentence in a job applicant's CV that crossed my desk recently. The candidate was a fluent speaker of international or global English, the business world's lingua franca, but wasn't what we used to call a 'native-' or 'mother-tongue' speaker (the terms are now considered politically incorrect by many linguists), and I thought this use of **execute** was wrong. I've often seen **implement** used in a similar way, as in 'She implemented a meeting on instructions from her boss', or used intransitively: 'We expect to implement shortly.'

Many correspondents ask me to judge the correctness of language used by colleagues from overseas. Examples cited more than once include **forward**, as in 'to forward the concept of human rights' instead of 'take forward', 'put forward' or 'promote', with their different meanings, or **follow** as in 'I will follow after consultation', instead of the standard 'follow up (with)'. The key question is which usages are actually permitted in global and online English, and which are not – and who nowadays is in a position to decide? 'Could someone **catch me up?**' sounds wrong to me when the meaning is 'can someone update me?' or 'help me to catch up?' I've heard it several times, and on querying it was told that 'It's OK, it's an Americanism' – true, possibly, but a handy get-out in that there are so many 'legitimate' varieties of English.

In multinational environments some errors are so prevalent that they become accepted: 'informations' in the plural, 'actual' meaning current or up-to-date, 'realization' to mean carrying out rather than understanding and 'oversight' meaning supervision, not omission, are some of the most common cases. 'Native speakers' of English of course do it, too (see also **conditionate**), saying, for instance, as in estate-agent jargon, 'We are completing', instead of 'finalizing' or 'concluding' with an object following. And a new version of **offshore English** (the intermediate variety which evolved on oil platforms where many nationalities had to communicate at a basic level) has come into being on the Internet. When I see statements like 'It has to scale with the niches so the system doesn't stress', I'm really not sure if it is English or not.

See also **the needful**

extreme archaeology

meaning: *excavating the past in dangerous environments*

When Channel 4 television ran a series under the title of *Extreme Archaeology* in 2004, it was highlighting a trend in leisure and spectacle which had begun much earlier, with the fad for dangerous sports triggered by young British eccentrics on skiing holidays in the 1980s and the first bungee jumpers' emulations of South Sea islanders' rituals a little later. A small minority's hobbies were commercialized during the 1990s to create an industry in **extreme sports** (among them base jumping, canyoning, human catapulting, sandboarding, wing walking, sphering and wakeboarding) and **extreme tourism** (formerly known as adventure holidays: peering into volcanoes, rafting on the Amazon, etc.) – the key word being not only a description, meaning 'extreme conditions', but a slang term of admiration as in: 'Man, that was *extreme*.' Practitioners of course are **extremers**.

The eccentricity remained, in the form of **extreme gardening**, a US fad of the later 1990s which involved cultivating plants in difficult conditions such as urban wildernesses, and **extreme ironing**, a sport invented

by Phil Shaw from Leicester in the UK. Said to combine 'the thrill of a dangerous sport with the satisfaction of a well-pressed shirt', this, as the name suggests, involves ironing on top of mountains, underwater, on moving vehicles, etc.

Adherents of **extreme archaeology** carry out their explorations in the most hazardous locations, underground cave systems and remote peaks or clifftops being favourites, while in ludicrous contrast trendspotters have used the term **extreme connoisseurs** for 'men in the kitchen reconceptualizing techno-cooking'. Should they perspire too freely, Sure deodorant's slogan promises 'Extreme Protection'.

See also **feed the rat**

feed the rat

meaning: *to satisfy a craving for excitement*

An example of the obscure slang of a tiny minority becoming a catchphrase for a global phenomenon, the phrase **feed the rat** was adopted for the title of a 1988 book by Al Alvarez, subtitled *A Climber's Life on the Edge* and profiling mountain climber Mo Anthoine. The rat, according to Anthoine, is 'you really, the other you' and feeding it is a compulsion and a necessity: it's the gnawing inner craving for excitement that, once day-to-day existence is set aside, impels some people to risk their lives and push themselves to their physical and psychological limits. Anthoine did not invent the expression, which had been in use among climbers, skiers and explorers for some time. With the advent of adventure holidays and fashionably dangerous sports such as bungee-jumping, base jumping, canyoning and the rest at the end of the 1980s, the notion of the rat and the need to appease it was picked up by a wider public and became a mantra for all **adrenalin junkies** and **extremers**. By 2006, using the slogan 'get off on what you're into', a Feed the Rat website was inviting practitioners of dangerous sports from all over the planet to share their experiences online.

Punch 'feed the rat' into your Internet search engine and you will be confronted not only by the extremers but by hundreds of sites that take the phrase literally: rat-fanciers are well represented on the Web, and of all the expert advisers on what to feed the little beasts only one suggests poison.

fifty-quid man

meaning: a lazy consumer of electronic entertainment

When an acquaintance who is into 1980s DIY indie music and its recent revival as **nu-post-punk** accused me of turning into a **fifty-quid man**, I knew he wasn't paying me a compliment. The nickname is one conferred by **diggers**, short for **crate diggers** (a hip-hop slang term for seekers of vinyl records, who are also known, approvingly rather than disparagingly, as **vinyl junkies**), to describe the average 'cash-rich, time-poor' consumer of CDs, who buys his (or her, but the pastime, when practised almost as a self-conscious discipline, is largely a male domain) music by the batch (hence a typical spend each time of '£50', rather than the careful bargain-hunting of the dedicated collector).

Among the teeming tribes of online obsessives, classifying, archiving and posting critical reviews of obscure music, written in a special variety of cyber-slang (see **turbochoad**), burgeons; while in the non-virtual world, streetmarkets and conventions serve the same **active audience**. Even among some mainstream consumers there has been a reaction against the digi-talization of music and its dissemination via down-loads to **podsters** (see **iPod**). The specialist digger is not necessarily a **neo-Luddite** and opposed to all new technology *per se*, but more a sufferer of **nanostalgia** for the tactile vulnerability of outmoded (or as they have it, **betamaxed**) technologies, the mystique of **old skool rare grooves** or the output of almost untraceable garage bands who only released on audiocassette.

flashpackers

meaning: intrepid but comfortably-off travellers

In the opening years of the twenty-first century the UK travel and leisure industries identified several new-but-related breeds of traveller. First there were the **Saga-louts**, elderly tourists who misbehaved – drinking to excess, brawling, offending dress-codes – in foreign resorts just like the younger-generation hooligans (the 'lager-louts') of the 1980s and 1990s, Saga being the holiday company catering for the over-50s. These ageing miscreants were also nicknamed **Club 55–80** by analogy with the Club 18–30 package holidays sold to boisterous youngsters. A little later the term **grey geese** was coined to describe elderly tourists who band together, with or without the help of age-specific tour companies, to migrate to congenial overseas destinations. There really are grey geese of course, and they do migrate, but generally up and down the western seaboard of America, not from Duluth to the Gambia or from Dunstable to the Maldives. Increasingly, **mid-lifers**, **empty-nesters** and **third-agers** have been opting for more dangerous pursuits and more exotic destinations. Since 2004 this group, who are willing to travel light and rough it, but are affluent enough to buy the best kit and retreat to a luxury hotel if they wish, has been nicknamed **flashpackers** (from flash(y) and back-pack(er) — not to be confused with **flash mobs** (see **cuddle party**)). The flashpacker concept was given unwelcome publicity in 2006 when several older tourists died or disappeared while travelling alone in rugged and/or remote locations.

FLOSS

meaning: non-proprietary community software

The English word 'floss' comes from an old Scandinavian description of the texture of velvet; it's also the name of a dentists' newsletter, it's slang short-hand for 'dental-floss [i.e. extremely abbreviated female] underwear', and Floss is the name of a market town in northern Bavaria. More significant than all of these, however, according to promoters of **infonomics** (the study of the **information economy**), is **FLOSS**. The acronym, probably first used by researcher Rishab Gosh, achieved prominence with the publication of a report sponsored by the European Commission in 2002: it stands for **Free/Libre/Open Source Software** (*libre* is simply the French and Spanish translation of 'free'). It refers to the practice not only of granting free-of-charge licences for crucial software applications, but of individuals collaborating online *pro bono* to co-design and co-develop such applications. When users become fully integrated into product and system design it yields benefits like **extreme usability** – jargon for the maximum efficiency that results from checking by a wide range of **stakeholders** at every stage of development.

FLOSS is not only a functioning/functional reality, but the symbol of what is claimed as a **paradigm shift** – a transformation of thinking about how global transactions work. The shift is from a **qpq** (quidproquo – money rewards work/exchanges for goods) economy to what Japanese venture capitalist Joi Ito calls a **sharing economy**. Others have discussed **open-source** sharing in the context of **non-monetary** or **trans-monetary** economic activity, more colloquially **capitalism without capital**. They refer to **commons-based** (that is, undertaken by volunteer private citizens) **peer production** as the **third mode** of global production, the first mode being property-based and the second contractual. The big differences are that collaborative innovation, as Microsoft have long understood, benefits everyone and need not rely on monetary reward. At the same time, development which includes players at the margins (for example, snowboarders) as well as controllers at the centre (such as snowboard manufacturers) has been shown to be far more successful.

See also **copyleft**

footprint

meaning: to gauge environmental impact or spread

'Now you can **footprint** your local authority or community yourself,' claims one of many websites featuring a do-it-yourself modelling facility. Feed in your data and the modeller calculates the levels of consumption and/or extent of damage to the environment for which an organization, a social group or an individual is responsible.

In this sense the new verb is of course adapted from the well-known term **ecological footprint** (**eco-footprint** for short), denoting the amount of natural resource consumed, which was popularized by the ecologists William Rees and Matthias Wackernagel working in British Columbia, Canada in 1996. **Carbon footprint** was used shortly thereafter in the context of emissions control. The related concept of the **global footprint** also refers to the reach of a satellite or broadcast system (in technical jargon **downlink coverage**), so that telecommunications giants are busy footprinting each other to assess their relative levels of global domination. In less specialized contexts journalists often refer to the economic and **geopolitical footprint** of the USA, the only contemporary superpower big enough to have a meaningful one.

As a metaphor, 'footprint' of course plays on the notions of 'tell-tale evidence' and 'tracking a fugitive' as well as evoking the spoor of a primitive Homo *sapiens* trudging through or trampling over a virgin landscape. So prevalent has the term become that it is bandied about in office jargon, often meaning nothing more than the surface area an item of hardware occupies, or an identifiable record in a filing system: 'I'll see if I can locate the project's footprint in our system,' I was told just recently by a secretary.

By coincidence, the UK is introducing a national shoeprint database to aid forensic investigation of crimes, while **fingerprint technology**, long familiar from spy movies and science fiction, is now a real presence in the field of **embedded intelligence** (q.v.).

In one of its applications, footprinting is virtually the same as the **eco-tracking**, attempting to trace the tide of discarded and recycled consumer goods that washes from the richer nations around the planet, which has been promoted by US author Juliet Schor and UK journalist Madeleine Bunting.

forking the tree

meaning: creating new and incompatible versions

At an unpredictable moment a word crosses over from the technical ghetto into workplace conversations. Suddenly the word **fork** in its various forms is everywhere: 'Wikipedia faces a fork; if it tightens up its [formerly] open approach, it risks losing its best contributors,' says The Economist. 'The right to fork is essential to the whole idea of open-source software,' insists a blogger.

In slang usage, 'forking' has a sexual sense, either from the physical arrangement involved, by jokey analogy with the old-fashioned 'spooning' (smooching), or as a play on a ruder F-word, while **knife-and-fork it** (q.v.) is an unrelated colloquialism. In technical and professional circles, **forking the tree**, or **forking** for short, comes from the straightforward image of a growing network with its bifurcations and branches. The act of forking can be a part of a natural and healthy process of refining and innovating by individuals or collectives, but more often than not the expression implies something controversial. Creating new and independent versions of proprietary software, or any other commercially protected system, is generally prevented by legal constraints. In the case of **FLOSS** (q.v.) systems it is not, and rogue innovators may create new features and new packages that diverge from the original. Spawning incompatible **mutant versions** risks offending co-developers, confusing users and making a mockery of ethics and protocol, but **forkers** point out that quantum leaps have often happened this way (though the online Disenchanted Dictionary sums up the attitude of many of them as **fork you!**).

In a more abstract and academic context, but with the same sense of divergent, perhaps troubling futures, **forking paths** are an essential concept in Agency Theory, an investigation of choice and responsibility which straddles philosophy, ethics and psychology.

See also **gateway product**

fractional ownership

meaning: *a share in a luxury item or service*

What consumer analysts call **status anxiety** and **self-treating** are the two main drivers in the sale of luxury goods. The latter forms part of the phenomenon which philosopher Gilles Lipovetsky terms **hyperconsumption**: an unfettered desire for enjoyment rather than prestige. The patterns of consumption – actual consumer **behaviours** – have become more complex (see, for example, **stealth wealth** and **staircasing**) and the distinction between the truly rich and the merely **aspirational** is blurred by strategies like **trading-up/trading-down**,

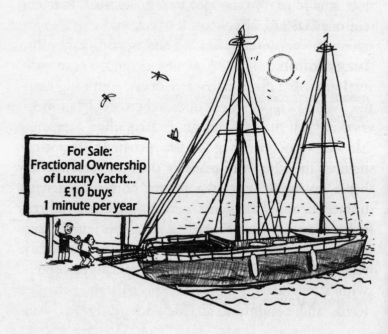

For Sale:
Fractional Ownership
of Luxury Yacht...
£10 buys
1 minute per year

whereby mid-market shoppers prefer a mix of economy items with a few luxury items to the mid-market range they used to gravitate towards; by the appearance of **masstige** (q.v.) product-lines, and by the recent extension of the timeshare concept beyond property into other areas. Now the merely extravagant can mimic the super-rich by acquiring **fractional ownership** of items they cannot hope to possess outright. These range from private jets, luxury yachts and top-of-the-range sports cars, access to which is by subscription, to designer handbags which can be hired by the hour or by the day. I'm not entirely sure how this differs from leasing, though that outmoded word presumably smacks too much of low-budget car fleets and **low-end** commercial property.

fuzzy value

meaning: customer benefits that are impossible to assess or compare

Most of 2005's buzzwords relating to personal finances seemed to carry very negative connotations. Already beset by **fiscal drag** (the failure of government to uprate tax allowances in line with inflation) and prey to the practice of **gapping** (delaying increases in savings rates, even after base rates and mortgage rates have risen), the UK borrower or saver also had to contend with a bewildering range of 'special' rates, charges, terms and conditions attached to mortgages, bank accounts, credit cards, phone contracts, etc., each promising unique benefits, but so complicated that they are virtually impossible to interpret, let alone compare for real value. What the hapless customer is confronted with are known as **fuzzy value propositions**, and the intentional creation of fuzziness has been condemned as **confusion marketing**.

The big debate is over whether, as financial service providers claim, these complications just arise naturally in a highly complex and ultra-competitive marketplace, or whether they are deliberately created to bamboozle the public. In the battle for profitability the sector already employs techniques such as **data-mining** and **personalization**, whereby details of a customer's individual profile are used to predict his or her financial decisions, and the introduction of **relationship managers** (to put your links to the bank on a more intimate footing) and, in the USA, something called a **cash concierge** (a bank representative who 'watches over' the interests of a small group of similar clients). Trying to blur the distinction between provider and customer, or dress up an essential service as a spurious partnership can backfire, as banks have been finding out as clients switch *en masse* to simpler online solutions, and as both government and opposition discovered earlier this year when they made **choice**, rather than **delivery**, their slogan for public services. How much choice do we really need? One UK bank currently offers thirty different – or not so different – savings accounts.

Marketers talk about a hierarchy or **cascade** of benefits which can help guarantee **customer retention**. Perception by the consumer of **satisfaction** is the first priority, realization of **quality** is a step higher up the ladder and recognition of **value** is the ultimate inducement. When values are so fuzzy, however, that a top Cambridge mathematician couldn't work out the small print on UK mortgagers' 5,000 different product offers (as was demonstrated in an investigation, also in 2005), it can't be long before consumers and the watchdogs set up to protect them begin to fight back.

gateway product

meaning: (a) an item designed to lure customers to a product range; (b) a link between two incompatible systems

Some seemingly simple examples of jargon turn out on closer examination to be ambiguous if not downright confusing. The phrase **gateway product**, fashionable since the end of the 1990s, can have one of three meanings – or two or all three simultaneously. In marketing parlance it refers to a straightforward, low-price model designed to introduce consumers to a more sophisticated range, or a product calculated to entice customers to try similar items. Typically, the item will be a simple computer or system aimed at price-sensitive users, or a camera phone leading purchasers towards a digital camera. More notorious were the marihuana-flavoured lollies called Pot Suckers, marketed across the USA in

2004. Six states moved to ban the sweets which carried the slogan 'Every Lick is Like Taking a Hit!' condemning them as gateway products which glamorized and encouraged drug use among young people. Confusingly (and deliberately), one US electronic hardware firm uses the brandname Gateway, so a gateway product may also but not necessarily be a Gateway product.

In datacommunication jargon, gateways are connections which link systems that use different architecture and protocols by repackaging and converting information. Metaphors involving pathways and gates have been prevalent in the English-speaking world of work since the **flowcharting** culture of the late 1970s, the **gatekeeper** for example being a key role in organizational structures and information-flows, and **gateway reviews** (the phrase was borrowed originally from the oil industry) in UK public-sector jargon signify **pre-scrutiny** and **waystage monitoring** of a **project life cycle** by independent experts.

See also **sachet marketing**

glomage

meaning: disposable gifts

Informant Laurie Armstrong from San Francisco recalls a journalist friend using the word **glomage** to describe 'all those promotional goodies, free gifts that PR people give to the media' and 'which would be worth keeping if they didn't have logos plastered all over them'.

Unrelated to the existing slang terms 'glop' (UK student-speak for drinking alcohol) or 'glomp' (an Americanism which means to surprise someone by jumping on their back), except by virtue of the 'gl-' sound (which seems to lend itself in English to notions of excess and lack of restraint, as in glug, globular, gloat, etc.), glomage's origins seem obscure. Is it connected with homage, plumage, Day-Glo? Is it just an arbitrary coinage, or have I missed an allusion? I haven't been able to find any other references to glomage and it's always possible that it is what lexicographers and linguists know as a nonce term – a word created and used only once, or alternatively that, although employed more than once, it forms part of an idiolect – one individual's private language. We tend to think that if a word cannot be found in any dictionary, and if an Internet search turns up no examples at all, then it simply isn't in circulation, but this ignores the vast ocean of spoken language that ebbs and flows through conversations in offices, homes, bars and clubs and may remain forever tantalizingly out of the reach of the 'experts'.

Similar-sounding and equally dismissive is **glurge**, a neologism which has become fairly widespread since its first appearance, probably in postings by Patricia Chapin on the snopes.com website in 1998. This word described sentimental anecdotes or reassuring urban legends – examples can still be found at snopes.com – which are circulated through unofficial networks

by word of mouth or chain e-mails, later being applied
to any piece of cloying, sentimental and/or unintentionally sinister narrative (it is closely related to the
concept of **truthiness**, q.v.) such as television docu-
dramas or Hollywood nouveau-weepies.

American slang abounds with words for those
annoying things that standard English can't describe.
Other terms for different types of junk include **chad**,
for waste paper such as the debris from printers,
copiers and hole-punchers, and **cruft**, for anything
worthless or extraneous, from obsolete data through
office clutter and discarded documents to the stuff
that gets in between the keys of a keyboard. In the
domestic sphere, American housewives have numerous words, like **dust-bunnies**, **dust-kitties**, **ghost
turds** and **fairy-flop**, to describe the balls of fluff
which collect on unswept floors. As far as I know,
their British counterparts, perhaps tellingly, have only
one, **beggar's velvet**, and that is rarely heard these
days.

glossophobia

meaning: a morbid fear of public speaking

Not just one of those spurious conditions expressed
in Greek or Latin which miscellanies love to list but
no one actually uses (see www.phobialist.com for
examples), **glossophobia** is big business. A phobia or
incapacity that attracts a legion of voice coaches, pres-

entation-technique consultants or **pitch doctors** (q.v.), this is not a recognized medical affliction (although there are such things as stress-induced speech disorders) but a pseudo-learned invention based on *glossa*, Greek for the tongue, and the familiar phobia (from Greek *phobos*, fearing). It does not mean a fear of tongues, but a fear of speaking in public. In the past the problem might have been shrugged off as timidity or stage fright and tackled, if at all, by elocution lessons or, more recently, assertiveness training.

The trend towards the **medicalization** of all aspects of our lives has given such personal and professional impairments new prominence and new names. Not to be confused with 'glossolalia' (from Greek *lalein*, to speak), which is ecstatic babbling or 'speaking in tongues' in the biblical sense, glossophobia can also be contrasted with 'logorrhoea' (*logos* is Greek for word, *rhein* to flow or stream), another quasi-medical term which means talkativeness to the point of incoherence, sometimes known as verbal diarrhoea.

Logophilia, which should mean the love of words, is actually used facetiously to describe a love of logos, so that a **logophiliac** is a brand snob or **label-queen**: in the words of *Elle* magazine, 'I am who I wear'.

See also **infobia**, **proctoheliosis**

golden showers

meaning: bathing in urine

The delightful phrase has been in circulation for several decades as a euphemism for sex play – a less evocative synonym is **watersports** – involving **sprinkling** (to use yet another euphemism). Now bathing in someone else's urine for non-sexual motives has caught on among Hollywood celebrities and seems likely to **trickle down** to humbler devotees of **health and wellness** fads.

Urine drinking was practised enthusiastically by some devotees of Tantric ritual and Ayurvedics, and by numerous New Ageists and **naturopaths** from the end of the 1980s, and it took until the first years of the new millennium for the message from orthodox medical experts – that it had no measurable benefits whatsoever and tasted awful – to gain currency. No sooner had drinking the stuff fallen out of favour than Californian therapists began to promote bathing in it, taking their cue from Japanese women who have added human urine to their baths as a beauty treatment and from Hindus who hold that washing in cow urine is spiritually and physically purifying. Not so, insist the medical experts, but enthusiasts (or **urophiles**) are convinced that we are the victims of an ongoing puritan conspiracy to deny the liquid's spectacular effects.

It is too early to say whether this latest form of **urine therapy** will establish itself, but it could bring a new dimension to the **wet room** in your **home spa** or **home**

resort (q.v.). In what was either a spoof, a piece of deliberate irony or a massive blunder, the small US craft brewery Dogfish Head launched a new quality Pilsner beer under the name of Golden Shower in April 2006.

got game

meaning: possessing a knack or talent

North American street or campus slang often crosses over into the workplace and sometimes infiltrates other English-speaking cultures, too. It's when an Americanism is only partially assimilated that it can cause confusion, completely baffling some hearers and risking misunderstanding by others. Correspondent Helen Akif reports that in her estate agency office in south-east London **random** is the in-word, as in 'How random is that?!' or 'That's so totally random'. The word was introduced by the gap-year students they employ, but is now freely used by older colleagues, though presumably not in front of clients. Random is a typical piece of teen slang from the USA, a term of blanket disapproval which can mean 'unstylish', 'mediocre', 'confusing' or just 'bad'.

Other informants in the USA and UK are disturbed by the intrusion of the word **gay**, usually employed without a sexual connotation by younger colleagues to mean (like random) inept or disappointing. Contacts from the Bay Area of the US West Coast tell me 'gay' began to be used pejoratively by would-be-cool-but-actually-conservative twenty- and thirty-somethings at the end of the 1990s. In the USA it seems to signify 'annoying' or 'clumsy': could it then be motivated by jealousy of the dominance of gay taste and supposedly gay attitudes in US popular culture? In the UK it is substituted, like random, for the earlier near-synonyms **lame** or **pants**.

A more exotic usage, heard increasingly among trendy professionals, is **got game**, as in the boast 'we got game!' or the observation 'she got game', sometimes delivered in an attempt at rap or hip-hop intonation. The expression comes from US black street slang of the 1990s, and was soon adopted on campus by other ethnic groups. *He Got Game*, the title of a 1998 movie, translates as something like 'he has got a special talent' (for example, for sport or as a **playa** or **baller** – a seducer), deriving from the notion of 'at the top of one's game'. Sports metaphors are nothing new in the world of business, but few if any are adopted via hip-hop culture. This phrase, however, was picked up by video gamers and the multi-billion-dollar gaming industry, providing the title of a book by John C. Beck and Mitchell Wade which seeks to show how the mentality and strategies of video gaming are **reconceptualizing** the world of business.

gouging

meaning: using unfair or punitive business methods

When a holiday timeshare company pursued hapless pensioners from the Costa del Sol to the UK and

doorstepped them, several accused the firm's directors of **gouging**, that is extorting money by bullying: the phrase evokes the pitiless extraction of a 'pound of flesh'.

This expression often appears in the form of **price-gouging**, which means imposing the very highest price imaginable in the circumstances, usually when the buyer is in no position to argue. This almost invariably happens in the wake of disasters, when petrol, food and other vital commodities are in short supply (as was the case after the Asian tsunami and Hurricane Katrina), and in some US states price-gouging has become the legal term for felonious profiteering in emergency conditions. There is nevertheless no shortage of business specialists and economists who will defend the practice as simply obeying market imperatives, exercising legitimate monopolies or cashing in on windfalls.

A **gouger** still means a petty criminal, especially a thug and/or con-artist who uses intimidation, in Irish slang, and this (once also heard in Boston in the USA, where eye-gouging was a mugging technique) is probably the origin of the business usage.

granularity

meaning: (of a system) complexity and flexibility; (of a concept or scheme) subtlety and depth

Granularity is a case study of how a little-used, standard English word becomes a fairly obscure piece of technical jargon, then a **techie** buzzword, finally mutating into a fashionable centrepiece of business conversations. 'Granularity' had already been employed in astronomy, physics and even linguistics, but in its latest incarnation seems to have derived from the use of **granule** as one of several terms (**particle**, **package** and **module** were others) to describe a discrete component in the hierarchy of a complex system. It was a key issue in **componentization** in the 1990s and thus became familiar to software designers. In 2003 there was an online debate on whether the term was pretentious or simply indispensable when used by IT specialists, some of whom still preferred **fine-grained**, or its opposite, **coarse-grained**. By the mid-**noughties**, though, the word had escaped from its IT ghetto and was heard in advertising agency presentations and boardroom discussions, typically in such formulations as, 'We must aim for more granularity', or more often, 'The scheme as presented is lacking in granularity.' Sometimes 'a **granular** approach' was recommended by non-specialists, mentally associating the word not with software packages but with 'graininess' – the depth of resolution or lack of it in an image.

Continuing a trend in visual or optical metaphors (**closeup**, **focus**, **refocusing** and **scope** as noun and verb are others), the term **high-definition** has also been extended semantically for ideas, for example, as has the ambiguous **resolution**. Ironically, users of

high-end photo-technology now tend to refer to fuzzy pictures as **noisy** rather than grainy.

halo model

meaning: a super-product which enhances an entire brand

'What on earth is **halo modelling**?' asked a friend who had come across it in a motoring magazine. The **halo effect**, a well-known term in data gathering since the 1920s, describes the phenomenon whereby respondents who give a favourable answer to one question tend to let their positive opinion spill over into quite different areas of the survey. So halo marketing doesn't just mean the marketing of *Halo 2*, possibly the most successful electronic game ever, but a technique whereby a key product or campaign can, even if not profitable, generate prestige and even moral authority way beyond its own category. Positive fallout, in other words (negative fallout is known as **collateral**). The same concept has been used in the marketing of higher education in the USA. Getting a college president with both a high public profile and personal charisma is said to 'halo the whole institution'.

'Halo model' first surfaced at the end of the 1980s in the slang of US car dealers, for whom a **halo car** (formerly known as an **image car** or **beacon model**) was a model that would lure customers into the showroom even if they could never afford it. The expression is now used industry-wide to define what

journalist Frank Aukofer calls 'toys with nosebleed price-tags' like the £250K McLaren Mercedes SLR or quirky one-offs such as the Chevy SSR. The halo model isn't simply the most advanced, or always the most expensive, but the one with the indefinable something that inspires an **affective response** – an emotional commitment – to the brand. Like the mythical Alfa Romeo Brera: this prototype sports car was first shown in 2002 and commentators have been saying ever since that this one model, so stylish, potentially affordable and all-round desirable, could conceivably rescue the reputation of the ailing Fiat empire. Bits of the Brera have surfaced on the Alfa GT and GTV, but by 2006 the **über-model**, although in production, had yet to appear on the street.

A halo implies not just the radiating of light, but an aura of saintliness, so Honda announced in late 2005 the concept of **halo motoring**: new buyers were given a temporary subscription to a clean-air scheme and 'never have to feel guilty about car emissions again'.

hazy information

meaning: untrustworthy or imprecise data

Anyone, such as this writer, who depends on the Internet to check facts, stay abreast of trends and explore unfamiliar fields of knowledge will know the frustration of encountering inadequate or clearly flawed information, or of seeing virtually the same texts endlessly repeated, as in a hall of mirrors, all across the World Wide Web. Specialists in digital media and the **knowledge economy** talk of the **homogenization of information**, where news and ideas are endlessly refracted across thousands of sites without any authoritative intervention. They refer to the Internet as a **utopian space** but one crammed with **non-substantive** data. Most of us tend to use the Web to browse casually, access momentarily and **aggregate**, or in more prosaic terms to stack data and endlessly defer serious critical assessment of it (recalling the French philosopher Jacques Derrida – he of deconstruction – and his theory of *différance*, whereby the ultimate meaning of a text is pursued through an infinite number of alternative readings, but is never arrived at).

Those same specialists have stressed the need to

create **vertical infohubs** so that users can more easily access the **deep web**. Formerly known as the **invisible web**, the deep web (a phrase which appeared around the year 2000, probably coined by BrightPlanet Corporation, data systems specialists) consists of the Internet's most specialized as well as most valuable and trustworthy information sources: virtual catalogues and libraries, scientific databases, government data repositories, public records and directories among others, as well as non-textual files such as graphics and software. These are not **user-created** but transferred from print media, and are not susceptible to **open editing** (in more brutal language, interference by amateurs). In contrast to the **surface web**, which is **crawled**, **trawled** or **spidered** by search engines, most of the deep web is only accessible by **user-query.**

The problem of **hazy information** (one of the specialists' more straightforward designations) has been highlighted by the controversy surrounding **wikis**. These are the open-access online reference sources (the term comes from the original Wikipedia, itself named from wiki-wiki, Hawaiian for 'quick [access]') which anyone can contribute to and anyone can edit. At best they rival any longer-established encyclopedia in book form, but they have been plagued by errors and spoof entries.

Compare **fuzzy value**

hedgies

meaning: affluent forty-something professionals

A term heard at dinner parties, where it is bandied about with feigned amusement (and covert pride) by those it refers to, and promoted by journalists such as the Sunday Times's Cosmo Landesman, who advances it as a replacement for the long-obsolescent **yuppie**, **hedgie** is the latest label for the **movers and shakers** of the business world. Predictably, the word has been used in banking circles for years as a nickname for the managers of hedge funds – elite funds using aggressive high-risk investment strategies – who are also known as **the two and twenty crowd** from the fact that their fees are typically made up of a 2 per cent management fee plus 20 per cent of profit, far better than for less glamorous forms of investment. As a new social category, hedgie denotes someone probably, but not absolutely necessarily, working in the upper reaches of the financial sector, perhaps literally managing hedge funds. But the defining characteristics are said to be maturity, at least in chronological terms (they tend to be nudging 40 or already forty-something), discretion, a mild, family-oriented conservatism and a great deal of money deployed carefully – all of which differentiates them from the conspicuous consumption and braggadocio of the yuppie.

To the consternation of some (one commentator sourly characterized hedgies as making money by licensed 'ducking and diving'), hedge funds will probably soon be allowed to go public and float on the stock exchange, in which case their managers will achieve higher visibility – higher possibly than they desire.

Beware: talking about hedgies could cause confusion. The same word is a nickname employed by hedgehog lovers, both those who keep a little *Erinaceus europaeus* as a pet and those who collect them in the form of ceramic models. Oh, and hedgy with a 'y', I should remind you, is a real English word meaning, according to the dictionary, 'abounding in hedges'.

Compare **the mass affluent**, **sellionaires**

heft

meaning: power or influence

Some words become fashionable because they encapsulate some aspect of the *Zeitgeist* or simply because they describe something previously indescribable. Others just seem to catch on and resonate for no discernible reason. Yet other expressions can enjoy exposure in the print media because they are favoured by a particular writer; if they are non-standard or idiosyncratic they form part of the variety of language known to linguists as **journalese**. Journalists have always favoured colourful language, for obvious reasons, and in headlines and captions at least are often constrained to use the most abbreviated alter-

natives on offer. This has created a sort of stylistic
dialect or jargon in which one-syllable words like
'dub', 'probe' and 'cut' replace their longer counterparts 'entitle', 'investigate' and 'reduce'.

There are words which are popular with a range of
journalists though rare in the wider world: examples
I have come across recently include **ramp** or **ramp up**,
meaning to promote or inflate: it's a word that has been
in circulation for decades but which seems to be enjoying a vogue. The rhyming **vamp** (**up**), to renovate and
improve, or to fabricate (an excuse, for example),
is also a favourite of business writers in all English-
speaking areas. A more intriguing expression is **gun
around**, a colloquial phrase (probably based on the
idea of 'gunning a motor' rather than spraying gunfire,
although in console games there's a lot of the latter
going on) which means something like 'cast around
in a proactive and aggressive manner'. Perhaps it's a
coincidence, but, having never encountered the usage
before, I've seen around a dozen instances in the last
twelve months. Now that anyone can propagate their
ideas and their linguistic idiosyncracies across the Web,
the idea of journalese style has morphed into something much broader and more diffuse.

Consider the noun and occasional verb **heft**: short,
sharp, pithy, decisive-sounding, redolent of macho tool-
wielders, perhaps. It has an added allure in that it's
pretty obscure. Not in the business pages, though, where
it is flavour of the moment, witness: 'Microsoft Using

Its Heft To Drive Customers Towards Its Offer' (a *Guardian* headline) or '. . . the combination of gaming players realize that it needs more heft . . .' (*International Herald Tribune*). Most British dictionaries describe the word as a dialect term, whereas US versions see it as standard. It certainly originated as a dialect form of 'heave', better known in the form of the adjective 'hefty'. As a verb, heft, according to the dictionary, signifies to balance and weigh; in American business jargon it has come to mean to pressure, force or add weight, as in 'hefting your capabilities' or 'hefting into the market'.

Another short sharp Anglo-Saxonism beloved of North American business journalists is **roil** (to agitate or provoke), often appearing in the phrase 'roiling the market(s)', where a company or an event is stirring things up. 'Roil' conjures up a similar sense of disruption (something business gurus are currently urging us to embrace) to that evoked by the perennially trendy (if that's not a contradiction) and equally Anglo-Saxon noun and verb **churn** (which can mean rapid-fire reinvestment or market turbulence).

herding cats

meaning: (trying to) get rogue individuals to work together as a group

Like many bizwords this expression probably originated among Silicon Valley software developers – first as a cry of despair: 'Trying to get these consultants to collaborate is like **herding cats!**' What was an obscure piece of in-group slang seems to be gaining respectability: a recently published manual had the title *Herding Cats*, subtitled *A Primer for Programmers Who Lead Programmers*. The same phrase has appeared in marketing magazines: 'Herding Cats Across the Supply Chain', and on US Foreign Service websites; 'Herding Cats – Multipartner Mediating in a Complex World'. In the UK, the term has been picked up in training circles, where it perfectly describes the problem of team-building for business games with participants from widely different backgrounds.

Animal images have always featured in the jargon of the business jungle or workplace menagerie. It began long ago with stockmarket players nicknamed **bulls**, **bears** and **stags**; later **dogs** came to signify worthless shares. Since the 1980s **dog-food** has meant a low-price product for mass consumption – nowadays often more trendily used in the phrase: 'We must eat our own dog-food' (we owe it to the market/ourselves to sample our own products), and even functioning as a verb: 'We should really dog-food that new system before releasing it to end-users.'

Sometimes the animals are predators and demand respect: the **wolf nearest the sledge** describes the most threatening competitor, the **800lb gorilla** is (to mix metaphors) the heaviest hitter in the field. But mostly the animal reference is disparaging: I still cringe when I remember a British CEO telling me: 'I deal with the

strategy, I let the **monkeys** downstairs do the number-crunching.' Nowadays a poorly performing colleague may also be dismissed as a **wombat** – a 'waste of money, bandwidth and time' – while some marketing specialists have taken to referring cynically to gullible consumers as **sheeple**. Which brings us back to herding and the herd instinct, now incidentally replaced in sophisticated demographics-speak by the more volatile **swarm factor** (see also **swarm intelligence**).

Animals have their upside, too. How about the very latest boardroom stress-busting technique from the USA, **pet therapy**, aka **animal friend-bonding** or, less respectfully, **bunny-hugging**. You may end up, if not actually herding cats, then at least workshopping with the furry little individualists.

home resort

meaning: an advanced domestic leisure facility

One of the most significant consumer trends of the last decade is the annexing by private individuals of facilities previously only available outside the home. Home cinemas have mutated into private **intertainment** complexes with added karaoke, gaming, audio and video recording studios; exercise rooms have turned into high-tech gyms and far more sophisticated versions of the **home spa** may now incorporate medical facilities as well as pool, jacuzzi, wet room, rivers and fountains, saunas (or **hammams**, the trendier version of the Turkish bath adopted from Arab cultures), etc. Experts can provide consultancy not only in **clutter control** and **space management**, but can also cater for spirituality by designing shrines and meditation spaces (**feng shui** by now being old hat). With mobile partitioning and climate control both programmed to react to seasonal needs, the distinction between indoor and outdoor has long since disappeared, allowing living space and backyard to merge, perhaps in the form of your own Zen rock garden.

The tendency began with **cocooning**, which was essentially a flight from stress into domestic security (more radically known, especially in Australasia, as **caving** – staying home at all costs), then **hiving** (described as setting up 'a **command central** for a more engaged and connected lifestyle'), or **home**

havens (environments often using **embedded intelligence** – q.v. – creating 'peace and harmony through
order and beauty'), trends now gathered by Dutch
forecasters trendwatching.com under the heading of
insperience. Consumers can henceforth **domesticize**
or recreate almost all desired experiences within their
own **ambit** or **domain**. This trend is in opposition to
the outgoing pursuit of more and more exotic leisure
activities and destinations, as practised by a younger
generation of **extremers**, and it remains to be seen
if one will win out over the other. Post-9/11 global
instability and post-tsunami and hurricane nerves
suggest, though, that the **home resort** may be prefer-
able to the tropical tourist enclave, however luxurious, if the latter is surrounded by authentic-but-hostile
local cultures and subject to **geophysical events**.

infobia

*meaning: the fear of not having enough information, or of
having too much*

The **always-on** digital media and Internet age has
brought with it new anxieties and a host of semi-
serious names for quasi-clinical conditions. One of the
most prevalent of these is the fear of being overwhelmed
with too much data. The malaise isn't that new; in the
1980s it was known as **information overload**. A little
later we heard of **attention fatigue syndrome** (by analogy with **compassion fatigue**), and of course **atten-**

tion deficit disorder, a real and worrying condition affecting growing children, but used facetiously of harassed adult professionals. In 2005 commentators identified **data-glut** and **knowledge pollution**. **Infobia** – the latest name for it – is likely to be suffered by a neurotic, wired population of what my fellow jargon-watcher and self-confessed **informavore**, Gareth Branwyn of *Wired* magazine, calls the **jitterati** (after 'literati' by way of the more recent **digerati**; **dot. commers** and designers infesting the trendy Shoreditch district of East London are known as the **Shoreditcherati**). Many of us also suffer from what I've dubbed **textual harassment**, associated with a non-stop blizzard of e-mails and with the menace of txt msgng. One of 2001's phrases of the year was **attention economics**, an expression singled out for derision by the London author and critic John Lanchester.

It refers to the problem that the volume of information being exchanged is increasing exponentially, whereas our **attention bandwidth** is said to be more or less static. I'm not so sure: the human animal is much more versatile than pessimists think – and perhaps we are even capable of mutating. I used to think of myself as a **technophobe**, but I'm writing this on an electronic notebook which is **wifi'd** into the Internet; although I've so far resisted the iPod, there's a digital dictaphone and a cellphone next to me, the landline keeps bleeping, the hi-fi and television are on and I think I'm coping quite well, even enjoying the **(multi-) sensory overkill**. Of course there's a buzzword for this, too, this time identified by the excellent Word Spy feature at www.logophilia.com. What I am exhibiting is known as **polyattentiveness**. If there's one thing worse than being permanently online, it's when you suspect you are not **copied-in**, in other words are being **left out of the loop**. Infobia is actually a dual condition in the same way as so-called **option paralysis**, whereby you are unable to make choices or decisions as you perceive you have either too much or too little knowledge. In their April 2006 briefing Dutch consultancy trendwatching.com told its subscribers to forget about information overload and coined the new expression **infolust**, an overwhelming desire for information. 'Get ready', they breathlessly advised, 'for a click-and-know, point-and-know, text-and-know, hear-and-know, smell-and-know, touch-and-know and snap-and-know world.'

the Internet of things

meaning: environments that can be read by mobile technology

As technologies advance and lifestyles adapt to them, there can be a short hiatus before language catches up with innovation: in other words, there may be a period, usually only a matter of weeks or months, in which a feature or a capability is without a name. A case in point at the time of writing is the range of ways in which consumers can use their mobile phones and other hand-held devices to read their real-world surroundings. The phenomenon is expanding exponentially and hasn't yet acquired a buzzword that quite encapsulates all its ramifications which include **SMS-ing** (text messaging) in general (to read menus, make reservations, post reviews), **scanning** or **barcoding** (for product ingredients or specifications, comparative prices, etc.), **mobile searches** (of ticket agency databases or local directories, for instance), **upcoding** (exchanging personalized messages with producers or service providers, which now can involve creating one's own codes and tags) and **online interrogation** (spotchecking brands for ethical status, safety or financial probity).

I was casting around for an umbrella name for all of this when Reinier Evers of trendwatching.com came to my rescue with **the Internet of things**, a phrase he had come across a number of times in connection with what are also known as **annotated objects** and

annotated spaces – products, displays, hoardings, interiors, etc. which have been rendered **customer-centric** and machine-readable or **smart** (see **embedded intelligence**) by the adding of digitized (or digitalized, if you prefer) codes, no longer only in the form of adhesive barcodes but also by way of touch- and sound-recognition devices.

iPod

meaning: *a discontented young adult*

The acronym, borrowed by think tank Reform for a report published in mid-2005, stands for 'insecure, pressurised, over-taxed and debt-ridden', although UK journalist Giles Hattersley has proposed a more jaundiced alternative: 'infantile posse of overindulged drunks'. The social reality that this nickname seeks to sum up is the realization that, for the first time since the Second World War, members of a younger generation, despite being spoilt for choice in terms of the music downloaded to their Apple MP3 device of the same name, may not be in for an easier ride than their parents. For these 18–34-year-olds the prohibitive cost of property, the lingering burden of university tuition fees, easy credit opportunities, a culture of institutionalized hedonism and in many cases unrealistic career aspirations leave them resentful and frustrated. Indications are that the future could be even worse.

The **welfare bargain**, the provision of free care in

return for tax payments, will soon no longer operate (the same think tank, Reform, called for a system of **co-payment** – in other words, an end to free welfare), the **graduate premium**, the amount that a graduate can hope to earn in excess of a non-graduate, has been eroded, and many young people continue to indulge in **career drift** (as opposed to carefully planned career-switching) as they listlessly move between underpaid if sometimes glamorous-sounding jobs. Pension prospects are grim across the board.

Reform's use of the name is of course ironic: generally Apple's consumer icon has symbolized, even more than its predecessor the Walkman, not just mobility and mastery but ubiquity; its wearers, called **poddies** or **podsters** in the early days, span the generations. The product's name has inspired many imitations, among them are iBod, a fake suntanning spray; iPad, a miniature starter home; iRemote, a remote control device or **zapper**. In an attempt to corner a younger market sector, editor Sarah Sands proclaimed the *Sunday Telegraph* the print-media equivalent of the iPod; shortly afterwards she was fired. A UK readership has also been subjected to would-be design guru Stephen Bayley's baffling observation that the Penguin paperback was 'the i-Pod of its day', and *iPod, Therefore I Am*, Dylan Jones's excruciating 2005 paean in book form to the device which he calls 'a . . . uniquely egalitarian . . . hotline to God'.

It may be no coincidence that psychologists and

philosophers talk about a number of 'i' tendencies as representative of contemporary culture: not just 'I' as in the **me generation**, but independence, individualism, the interpenetration of multimedia and, much more rarely, **inner-directedness**.

As for **pod**, the word and the objects it describes have been trendy since their use in science fiction of the 1950s and 1960s (alien 'pod people'), more recently in a host of design and lifestyle innovations (see **blobitecture** and **sleep hygiene**) and in the term **podcasting** (posting audiofiles for **asynchronous** access, that is, downloading and listening to whenever you like) which has the distinction of being nothing to do with pods or iPods and not really a form of broadcasting either.

J-Lo

meaning: a pleasing upturn in an equity value

Not surprisingly in a world where even women are expected to be macho, the terminology of the stock market is resolutely unfeminine – and when financial slang does refer to the female it's nearly always with an old-fashioned leer. Wall Street traders apparently still call a sure-fire investment or a stock with an outstanding performance a **Bo Derek**, from the notion of a perfect 10 – the title of the 1979 movie which made Ms Derek's reputation. Back in 1999 the same nickname was conferred on bonds set to mature in 2010.

More up to date is the expression **J-Lo**, as in 'I think we're seeing a J-Lo in United Textiles'. This mock-technical term is used by US share analysts tracking an upward-curving 'bottom' in the value of a key stock – the reference of course is to the megastar Jennifer Lopez and the media's celebration of her outstanding asset. Shares undergoing a J-Lo should not be confused with **rump shares**. These (according to the excellent glossary of commercial terms at www.investopedia.com) belong to the minority group of stockholders who are holding out against a proposed merger or takeover.

The financial sector's interest in bottoms goes back at least twenty years to when **bottoming out** was the jargon *du jour*, even providing the title for a song by rocker Lou Reed. That was followed in the later 1980s by descriptions of the economy **bumping along the bottom**, while investors specializing in dirt-cheap or dodgy shares were said to be **bottom-fishing**.

Another recent bizword with both feminine and sexist overtones is **lipstick indicator**, first published in the *New York Post* of March 2003 but apparently coined by Estée Lauder, eponymous head of the cosmetics empire. The phrase has been much used in the aftermath of 9/11; it refers to the proven fact that sales of lipstick, along with other small luxury items, rise significantly in times of anxiety. The concept is very similar to the much older **skirt-length indicator** which holds that hemlines rise and fall according to confidence in the economy. Judging by recent incarnations of Britney Spears and Christina Aguilera, then, we are in for an unprecedented bull market. Britney and Christina have yet to join J-Lo as items of financial slang, and for the time being the Jennifer-word is confined to North American usage. Having heard it in New York, a friend of mine who trades in the Square Mile is promoting **Kylie** as a more suitable version for bottom-obsessed Brits and Australasians.

jumping the shark

meaning: *the point at which a good idea turns bad*

When a colleague from the USA opines that 'Maybe we just jumped the shark', English-speaking listeners will recognize another of those colourful Americanisms, but they probably won't know whether to rejoice or to panic. In fact the phrase has been circulating in North America for years, but has yet to cross over into global English usage.

Unlike many similar, the origins of this expression are traceable, to a certain Sean J. Connolly who apparently coined it in Ann Arbor, Michigan, in 1985. Twelve years after that a website (www.jumptheshark.com) celebrating the concept was created by his college room-mate, to be followed in 2003 by a paperback of the same title. By 2006 the phrase itself had been trademarked. The original reference was to an episode of the US sitcom *Happy Days*, set in the 1950s but broadcast from the 1970s, in which the scriptwriters were so desperate to maintain novelty that they had the 'cool hero', biker Fonzie, not only move out of character and go waterskiing but jump over a shark while doing so. For Sean Connolly and other fans this marked the pivotal point at which the cult programme peaked, from then on struggling through many other implausibilities and ignominies (it actually survived for another 100 episodes). So **jumping the shark** signals a **tipping point**, subsuming the notions of 'losing the plot', 'going too far' and 'passing the peak', and marks the triggering of a terminal decline.

First referring only to instances from television and cinema (visitors to the website can nominate their own **shark-jumps:** there are still ninety-five web pages debating *Happy Days* alone), the term was extended on the website and in conversation to take in rock bands and musicians, then public, professional or personal behaviour of all kinds. Cynics can enjoy competing to track the demise of a brand or company back to a key moment that may have passed unnoticed at the time, or marked what then seemed to be a great idea. Among aficionados the first inkling of a disastrous change in direction, or an idea too far, is known as **spotting a fin**. In 2005 some humorists began using the alternative form **jump the couch** to describe an ominous and embarrassing misjudgement, as when Hollywood star Tom Cruise jumped onto Oprah Winfrey's television talk-show sofa to proclaim his love for his fiancée. In the business context jumping the shark (the phrase was invoked, for example, in early 2006 in speculations that the mighty Google might have overreached itself) has to be distinguished from sudden occurrences of **brand damage** (q.v.). Once decline is inevitable office slang has its own more brutal terms: a doomed organization is said to be **circling the drain**, before finally and irrevocably **toileting**.

ketchup-bottle effect

meaning: stasis followed by a sudden surge

When in 2005 UK public sector healthcare specialists warned of a **ketchup-bottle effect** it wasn't immediately obvious what they meant. In fact, they were referring to a lengthy build-up of new legislation and policy changes, all involving investment, which were due to come into effect all at once, creating a massive bill and an overwhelming workload. The term has been around for some time – Swedish-speakers know it as the **ketchup effect** – but is probably heard most often in the mouths of economists and finance professionals. Of course it refers to what in technical terms is something called 'thixotropic flow', the best-known example of which is the tendency for ketchup to remain stubbornly immobile in the bottle before spilling out suddenly and uncontrollably. In the working environment it can either describe a long period of inertia followed by a burst of exaggerated activity, or the unplanned release of pent-up forces.

A distantly related but more obscure expression comes also from the jargon of UK financial professionals. The **tontine effect** (from a type of annuity policy with **benefit of survivorship**, invented by Lorenzo Tonti in 1653) is the phenomenon whereby, in the words of *Daily Telegraph* Personal Finance Editor Ian Cowie, 'the last policyholders left standing [when a scheme is wound up] may scoop assets left behind by those who quit early and paid exit penalties'.

kicking dead whales down the beach

meaning: performing a deeply unpleasant, seemingly endless, but often essential task

This vivid term from the transatlantic vocabulary of the put-upon **microserf**, can now be heard echoing round boardrooms in the UK, too; 'Selling them the open-source operating system, making it EU-compliant, then getting them to set it up online, it was like **kicking dead whales down the beach**!' Strictly speaking this doesn't refer to a completely impossible, futile task or a solitary one: those can be likened to pushing rocks uphill or **trying to nail jelly to a tree**. Moving the marine cadaver is a communal effort which has to be made, but which leaves everyone soiled and exhausted. As first used, the whale phrase seems to have been a cry of despair, uttered when faced with an outrageous demand that seems quite reasonable to one's superiors, along the lines of 'Yes, our team could re-set all the user-identities on the system by hand if you really insist, but I have to tell you, it will be like kicking dead whales down the beach'.

The image conjured up is a clue to the ultimate origins of the expression: rotting whale carcasses beached on white sand seemingly first loomed in the imaginations of technicians and junior white-collars labouring in labs and offices up and down the US West Coast and wishing they were catching waves instead. The phrase

DEAD WHALES
BEING KICKED

probably surfaced (pun intended) to accompany the successive transformations of corporate life beginning with the mainframe-to-desktop move back in the 1980s. Analog to digital, bricks and mortar to online, all meant crushing workloads and hideous deadlines for Silicon Valley's **toiling midgets**, as they used to call themselves.

I haven't been able to find any other whale metaphors in the latest lexicon of buzzwords, but from the same subculture of long-suffering subordinates comes a fish-based example: **having a salmon day** is when you feel that you've been swimming upstream all day, only to be comprehensively screwed at the end of it.

Compare **herding cats**

knife-and-fork it

meaning: to deal with a problem or system bit by bit

A public sector manager holding forth to a group of subordinates in a problem-solving session declared at one point: 'We'll have to **knife-and-fork it**.' First problem: what exactly did he mean? And were the colleagues who nodded respectfully really enlightened? The phrase may be related to something in IT parlance called a **knife-and-fork model**, but judging from recent exchanges on the Internet, no one is quite sure what that means either. Many bizwords consist of metaphors, but coining them or using them has its risks. Take **boiling the ocean**, for example, or **squeaky wheel gets the grease!** Hardly transparent, the first means working to excess for minimal results, the second that the noisiest employee is likely to get preference. With no trace of irony North Americans exhort each other to **skate to where the puck is going**, sometimes helpfully adding **not where it's been**. Even when the listener understands, it's questionable whether these figures of speech are any improvement on simple standard language. Whenever I hear **low-hanging fruit** a red mist descends: why can't they say something like 'achievable targets' – or use the existing phrase 'easy pickings'? We've all heard **thinking outside the box** (q.v.) so many times that I'm sure we're focused on the illusory, totally unhelpful box, not the way we should be thinking. Is it more annoying to be urged to **eat your own dog-food**, or to **eat some reality sandwiches**? Wouldn't 'sample your own products' or 'be realistic' do just as well?

Of course jargon also exists to foster team spirit, to liven up otherwise dull discussions. But lame metaphors and grating catchphrases can fall flat. The worst offenders don't stop at one cliché but stretch the imagery until it comes apart, like the boss who along with his 'squeaky wheel' mantra urges his team to **drive more traffic to the site**, refers to his sales people as **road warriors** and to getting market presence as **gaining traction**. For him (it's nearly always a 'he'), a project that is put on ice is **parked**, and if you **roll out** a new concept there's a risk it will **get wound round the axle**.

Metaphors and messages easily get mixed when, for instance, the company's **ideas hamster** has a **light-bulb moment** while trying to **push the peanut forward**. The almost surreal mix of portentousness and banality that some executives indulge in has never been more effectively satirized than in the 1970s UK sitcom *The Fall and Rise of Reginald Perrin*. Reggie's boss CJ was the master of the **executive mantra**, as in: 'I didn't get where I am today by pouring cold water over a wet blanket.'

As for knife-and-fork it, friends claim to have come across it with the meaning given above, so maybe I'll start slipping it into the conversation – ironically, of course.

localizing

meaning: adapting a product or service to a particular socio-cultural environment

Of all the business jargon, buzzwords, catchphrases and clichés traded during 2005, one expression in particular was nominated by my informants as bizword of the year. In itself not especially exotic, the word **localizing** is an example of a standard English term which has a special resonance when borrowed for professional purposes. If you look it up in the dictionary the meaning is given as 'limiting something to a small area', as in 'localizing an outbreak of disease', or 'localized weather conditions', but in business-speak localizing means **internationalizing** or **personalizing** your **generics** by **customizing** them. Until recently this usually referred to a purely linguistic process such as translating your instruction manual into Panjabi or making sure that the 'Skum-bad' brand of Norwegian bath-oil is renamed 'Foaming Pine' for the North American market (a process also referred to in many US companies as **languagiz-ing**). This aspect of what is known grandly as **content management** can nowadays be automated, in the form of software packages which instantly **shepherd** relevant documentation, then apply both **CAT** (computer-aided translation) and **content filtering** (checking data for controversial or easily misunderstood language).

What makes the concept of localizing so topical, though, is a new focus which goes beyond translation to try and engage with more subtle cultural differences. Theorists in intercultural studies have highlighted the need to tailor information and adapt behaviour, not only to what they call **large-culture formations** – nations, regions, religions – but also to so-called **small cultures**, a phrase which may refer to a **hyperlocated** (community-level) geographical **hotspot** like a market-place or key heritage site, or to a place in which a mix (they call it a **mélange**) of different national and cultural identities come together, perhaps just temporarily. An example of the latter would be an international aid project based in Africa but employing Japanese and European consultants as well as African specialists. If you want to design, for example, a training package that will work with all these participants, you will need to build in an appreciation of all their ethnic, linguistic, cultural and professional sensitivities as well as of their different learning styles, attitudes to authority, sense of time, openness to change, etc.

As one of the word's proposers put it, every other

business concept is secondary today: symbolically and practically the 'go global, think local' cliché is finally coming of age.

luxorexic

meaning: an obsessive 'self-pamperer'

The *Sunday Times* Style Magazine has pursued a relentless policy of discovering, on an almost weekly basis, new lifestyle fads and new social categories – **1661s** and **hedgies** (qq.v.) among them. Behavioural specialists assert that we have become more **self-focused**, a term which I would translate as demanding and selfish, and perhaps the most extreme manifestation of this is the so-called **luxorexic** (a word rather tastelessly formed from 'anorexic' and 'luxury' or 'luxuriate'), a living embodiment of the phenomena identified by marketers with a great flourish as **self-treating** (as opposed to treating others) and **selective extravagance.**

The luxorexic's defining features are that he (it is often a he, apparently) or she is not only greedy, egotistical (in the current jargon, possessing a strong **sense of entitlement**), hedonistic and self-indulgent, but is also obsessive and compulsive to the point of addiction. This makes for an ultra-discerning and high-spending consumer regardless of level of actual wealth – hence an extremely enticing target for marketers and servicers. Journalist Simon Mills, who promoted the term, cites several examples of celebrities who exemplify the trend: fashion designer Karl Lagerfeld with his 70 iPods, athlete Linford Christie, who keeps his trainers in customized perspex and mahogany boxes, and hip-hop entrepreneur Damon Dash who discards his trainers after one wearing. In common with royalty, the super-rich and superstars, these super-fastidious individuals will make unprecedented demands on service providers, expecting made-to-measure environments and bespoke accessories and dictating details of their surroundings down to the shade and texture of materials used.

The luxorexic is a version of the **extreme connoisseur**, an expression used by trendspotters mainly in connection with male gourmets who 'turn their kitchen into an amphitheatre' and stage gladiatorial cook-outs amid walk-in winecoolers and cheeserooms. These would-be **alpha consumers** revel in **kitchen envy** and by their own online admissions will only drink wine at a finely calibrated temperature within defined milliseconds of opening.

managed attendance

meaning: the discouraging of absenteeism

When Willie Walsh took the helm of British Airways in 2005, he quickly became famous for his love of jargon and corporate-speak, one notable example being his public endorsement of **managed attendance** – a piece of HR (human resource) management terminology which means, in the language of a pilots' union spokesperson, 'stopping staff **throwing a sickie**'. The obvious concern for the unions was that the bland abstractions of **human logistics** might be masking a new regime of coercion and enforcement. For me this recalled the euphemisms for dismissal and redundancy which, as one becomes notorious and is quietly shelved and another is coined to take its place, just keep on coming.

You may by now be familiar with **managed separation**, **managed closure**, **assisted departure** and the hardy perennial **shakeout**, possibly also with **involuntary severance**, but how about **change of reporting relationship**, reported in 2005, and **worklessness**, the term preferred to unemployment by educationalists in 2006? Brusquer synonyms are **correction** and **retrenchment**, while office slang refers more brutally to **human sacrifice**, **culls** and **muppet shuffles** (q.v.).

The public sector is just as fond of euphemism: a UK government Cabinet Office spokesperson referring to shredding sensitive and irreplaceable documents in 2004 came up with the memorable **aggressive records management**. Not all is negative, though, in the world as defined by jargon: increasingly, companies such as management consultants McKinsey are pursuing a **re-recruitment** strategy: enticing back employees who have left them in the past on the basis that they are 'likely to be trained and already familiar with **corporate DNA'** (q.v.) (in older-fashioned English a case of 'rather the devil you know . . .'). At the same time the policy known as **disaggregation** or **breaking down the silos** means that more and more power is being devolved onto the lower strata of organizations where those traditionally most vulnerable to **decruitment** and managed attendance toil away.

mashup

meaning: combining data from various web-sources

Mash up, in verb or noun form, comes from the jargon of hip-hop DJs where it referred to sampling and mixing, that is, combining pre-existing musical sequences to create a new sound. In youth slang **mashup** can also mean drunk, drugged and/or exhausted as a result of intoxication, or destroyed. The phrase is an example, like **burning** (which has become the industry standard term for recording onto CDs), of how a piece of slang can almost instantaneously transform into a popular technical term, although mixing and sampling themselves are examples that didn't cross over.

More recently mashup has been adopted by the Internet community to denote the process of blending data from various online sources into a unique combination, and the websites which result from this. Mashup (the process) and mashups (the sites) typically overlay maps, statistics, images and sometimes sounds from unrelated mainstream services. What they create may serve the community, showing, for example, crime rates for a local area, but may equally use tweaking, remix and customization techniques to produce subversive or pornographic material.

Mashup takes a **mix-and-match** or **pick-and-mix** approach, two familiar concepts (from fashion and candy retailing respectively) which cultural theorists say are central to modern popular culture. Their significance in terms of online innovation is that, like **blogs**, they are putting the full potential of website design and reach, previously restricted to big dot.com players, into the hands of private individuals, who can now 'programme the web' just as previously they created their own desktop programmes and documents. The long-established IT players, rather than trying to combat a guerrilla-style innovation, are embracing it, designing tools to make mashing up easier (one styles itself a **web concierge**, offering itself as an intermediary to bring scattered services together) and fashioning their own 'inauthentic' versions.

See also **performativity**

the mass affluent

meaning: the really rather rich

Analysts of wealth and those who service the wealthy have coined the term **the mass affluent** for what is for them the most important subset of the rich. These are the new rich — not necessarily *nouveau riche* but new in their behaviour as consumers and in their greatly increased numbers over the last twenty years, relative to the mass of the population and to the **super-rich** (whose numbers have grown but are still tiny).

By some reckonings 'the mass affluent' describes the 4 per cent of the UK population who have liquid assets of more than £144,000. In the USA, where the term originated, there have been several definitions: single individuals with a salary of over $75,000; households with a disposable income of over $100,000 or those with $100,000 to $1 million available to invest. The significance of this buzz-phrase and the group it denotes is that they have replaced or blurred the distinction between traditional categories such as 'middle' or 'upper class' and that they represent new patterns of spending and consumption. Members of this segment are characterized as politically conservative, socially liberal, **tech-savvy**, 'educated, idiosyncratic and flush with **discretionary income**'. According to surveys, they prize above all a sense of being in control, followed by happiness and integrity; they indulge in **spend peaking**, which means that they are willing to splash out on occasion on items previously seen as exclusive to the super-rich. **Fractional ownership** (q.v.) of yachts and resort apartments, and even travel by private plane go along with a full-time insistence on the most expensive accessories, cosmetics, etc.

Above the mass affluent in the financial pecking

order are **HNWs** or high net worth individuals, in Britain comprising the 0.7 per cent of the total who have average liquid assets of £665,000; **ultra-HNWs**: only 135,000 people, with average liquid assets of £6.4 million; and finally the **super-rich** themselves: the 1,000 richest citizens, with an average of £70 million to spend, over and above their property assets.

Compare **luxorexic**, **masstige**

masstige

meaning: *(a) massmarket products or services with up-market connotations; (b) a style which combines exclusive, expensive components with mass-produced and cheap ones*

Market analysts are warning that producers and suppliers face **hypersegmentation**, **hyperindividualization** and what they have dubbed **commoditization chaos** as customers become ever more sophisticated and radically more demanding. The new consumer's preferences can no longer be predicted simply according to age, class or prior spending habits: he or she insists on instant provision of top-quality personalized products and services as well as complete **transparency**: not only how an item's price is justified but what it contains and how it compares with rivals' offerings. The online newsletter www.trendwatching.com has devoted pages to this phenomenon which they call **nouveau niche**. They have dubbed the new breed of

Internet-empowered, information-hungry consumers **masters of the youniverse**.

One of the first tangible effects has been a move towards products and services that manage to be prestigious and affordable, bestowing high status though widely available. The effect is known as **masstige** (trend-watching.com calls it **massclusivity**), and examples include fashion chain Zara, the Mini-Cooper, customized iPods and 'limited editions' and 'privilege clubs' in general. Masstige can also refer to the way **fashion-forward** individuals – designers, decorators, models – juxtapose luxury items with cheap mass-produced ones to create a unique and exclusive look. When it describes how upmarket brands like BMW or Cartier lure buyers by offering **low-end** models, it can also be known more prosaically as **downward brand extension**.

A recent UK survey described how British shoppers are rejecting supermarket and chain-outlet offerings in favour of what has also been called **nonlinear shopping** or **treasure hunting**: assembling idiosyncratic **portfolios of purchases** from local, regional and online sources to suit their very individual tastes. Mintel, who conducted the survey, called this **self-branding**. Like masstige, self-branding can mean slightly different things to different groups. When the concept was popularized by guru Tom Peters in a 1999 book, it meant marketing yourself as if you were a product or service. It can also mean simply putting your own brand on products formerly sold by subsidiaries or bought in, as practised in recent years by Dell computers or buyers of Sputnik software.

The dozens of career-guidance 'experts' promoting self-branding on the Net might not care to know that the phrase actually predates 1999. It referred originally to burning a motif onto one's skin, a practice, like tattooing, piercing and scarification, favoured not by jobseekers but by **neo-pagans**.

maximalism

meaning: the opposite of minimalism, a new fashion for sumptuous ornamentation and general expansiveness

After nearly two decades of austere pastel tones, sparse furnishings and Zen-like restraint in all things (notions which fitted nicely with an era of **downsizing** and **downshifting**), the reign of **minimalism** is over. According to those in the know, **post-minimalism** has already come and gone (although nobody seems very sure what it consisted of), to be replaced by something much more meaningful, namely **maximalism**. This buzzword is applied, for instance, to interior decorating and window and store displays, describing a new and shameless opulence that features an often garish mix of fabrics, colours and styles. It's indirectly tied in with globalization, too, as Western shops and offices embrace ornate decors once favoured only in the Middle and Far East. It also suggests something more abstract: a new classless confidence and un-British extroversion, a determination to express oneself and resist the confines of control, convention or taste. The term is a favourite of consumer-behaviour experts and futurologists, who borrowed it from the design avant-garde, among them the London-based artist Duggie Fields and architect Nigel Coates, who both feature the word on their websites. (Don't confuse maximalism with **maximization**, another piece of corporate pomposity currently enjoying a vogue as in, 'we must energize around maximization of our growth potential', or the older **Maxwellian**, which meant gargantuan greed and dishonesty on a monstrous scale as exemplified by the disgraced tycoon Robert Maxwell.)

Other bizwords inspired by an **in-yer-face** philosophy include **bloatation**, referring to the spectacular overstaffing, lavish entertaining and reckless expansion typical of dot.coms just prior to meltdown. The term survives as a generalized criticism of puffed-upness, whether personal or financial, as does **excessivity**, which likewise has yet to make it into the dictionary. In fact the words maximalist and minimalist were first recorded in pre-revolutionary Russia, where they were the nicknames of two opposing factions of the Social Revolutionaries, forerunners of the Bolsheviks. There's nothing remotely Bolshevik about the latest version of maximalism; the Tsars, though, might have admired the determined self-indulgence it implies. Designers probably picked up the word from literary criticism. It was applied at the end of the 1980s to big, baggy novels like Thomas Pynchon's *Gravity's Rainbow* and Umberto

Eco's *Foucault's Pendulum* which seemed to cram in every possible style and philosophy, a phenomenon which has morphed into the 'totalizing' postmodernism of Jonathan Frantzen, David Foster Wallace or Kurt Anderson. In the words of critic Andrew O'Hagan, 'Today's big novel is the type of book which aims at bigness with the notion that all other big books are folded inside. The example is not *War and Peace* but the World Wide Web.'

metrosexual

meaning: a stylish, narcissistic male consumer

My quest for 2003's Buzzword of the Year involved trawling websites, scanning PR puffs and press releases and talking to business contacts. The result was a hotchpotch of the banal and predictable, the surprising and the fairly ludicrous. There were those abstract nouns: **agility** (currently popular with designers), our old friend **authenticity** (apparently word of the year in the footwear industry), and, still hanging in, **transparency**. Acronyms and abbreviations abounded: among the most prominent had been techno-communication channels **B2G** (business-to-government) and **P2P** (peer-to-peer). End-of-year blues in the City of London were reflected in **BAD**, or bonus anxiety disorder (a second year of less-than-£500K handouts, the poor dears). In organizational strategy, **lean manufacturing** was the name of the game, we were told, and there was a resurgence of **brightsizing**, the phenomenon whereby a company lays off the people with least seniority, thus losing their brightest hopes. Some call it **dumbsizing**. **Client relationship management** was flavour of the moment with its associated concepts of **collaborative advice** and **shared wisdom management**. On a flight late in 2003 I was sitting next to an IBM executive who offered **customer intimacy** as his personal favourite (he was grinning broadly when he said it).

In sales and marketing it was wishful thinking as usual in the form of **conversion marketing**, **high-probability selling** and Accenture's **uCommerce**; the trendy little 'u' was for 'ubiquitous' and it meant apparently selling what you want wherever you want! The latest thing in training circles was **blended learning**,

combining **e-learning** with old-fashioned **face-time** sessions. Other terms-of-the-year ranged from the prosaic – the storage industry's **provisional storage virtualization** – to the weird: one Church group's answer to post-modernism was **modpostalism**, whatever that means.

Best-known Buzzword of the Year must have been **metrosexual**, yet another attempt to define a new consumer category. The metrosexual is an 'urban male heterosexual with gay tastes', a piece of jargon related to ironic slang terms like **stray** (a straight man who acts gay), **stromo** (a homosexual who appears straight) and the intermediate category known as **JGE** ('just gay enough'). Perhaps surprisingly, metrosexual lasted the course and was still heard in conversation, sometimes without even its ironic overtones, three years later. Like other iconic expressions it inspired spin-offs: 2004's

contrasexual (originally a Jungian psychological term for someone whose sexuality is conflicted) denoted a person who made no attempt at all to present themselves as attractive, while in 2005 **übersexual** cropped up, meaning a predatory, unashamed seducer.

Keywords aren't always pretentious. On that same flight in 2003 I asked a US automotive engineer for his Buzzword of the Year. 'Everyone knows there are only two buzzwords in the automotive industry,' he replied, '**India**, and **China**' – a view he is unlikely to have revised.

muppet shuffle

meaning: the redeployment of problem staff

We're all familiar with the corporate euphemisms used when difficult strategic decisions are being taken. New atrocities are reported to me every week, like the following example from a correspondent who prefers to remain anonymous: 'If we can't get **buy-in** from all **stakeholders** and **bring the individual contributors along**, there's going to have to be some serious **decruitment**.' She swears it's authentic, commenting that the wonderful word **agreeance** can be substituted for buy-in, while decruitment is also known as **resource optimization**, and translates the whole thing thus: 'If we can't get our more senior people to pay lip service to – and our powerless menials to shut up and swallow – our unpalatable plans, then

heads will have to roll.'

In the USA, I'm told, the latest weasel words are **transitioned**, for employees on their way out, and **uninstalled** or **alumnized** (in other words invited to join the corporate alumni or ex-workers), for those who are already off the payroll. In private conversation a crueller language prevails: organizations with an ageing workforce are said to be suffering from a **geezer glut**, and in line for a **culling of the herd**: no comforting euphemisms there.

UK correspondent Paul Beatton reports a revealing piece of insider jargon from a recent training session. Reference was made to something called a **muppet shuffle**: the under-performing or troublesome employees, the 'muppets',

were to be 'shuffled', that is, moved out into other unsuspecting departments, or given new roles which would effectively neutralize them.

London office slang has thrown up a host of similarly non-PC expressions. Apart from muppets, menial employees may be dismissed as **penny-boys** (originally an Irish expression), **jubs** (a City term of unknown origin), **monkeys** or **chimps**. Problem colleagues fall into a number of specific categories such as **puckered-ups** or **smoochers** (sycophants), **paint-watchers** or **blobs** (the terminally idle), **buckologists** (experts at delegating or passing the buck) and **madmes** (the office jokers who get on everyone's nerves, from their characteristic attention-seeking cry of 'I'm mad, me!'). These last are not to be confused with the **corporate jesters** that some US companies were hiring a few years ago to inject humour into the workplace: history is silent on the fate of those hapless individuals.

Apart from euphemism there's also a kind of pseudo-technical language tinged with irony. Human resource specialists talk about **bureaupathology**, the dysfunctional aspects of large organizations, **mediocracy**, where the mediocre set the agenda, and **adhocracy** where all decision-making is improvised. Poorly performing managers are said to be suffering from **delusions of adequacy**.

See also **proctoheliosis**

nanopublishing

meaning: minimalist, highly targeted online publishing

The **blogosphere**, the Internet culture based on weblogs, has brought with it a raft of new terminology. Among its key features are stripped-down interactive real-time sites resembling weblogs – sometimes they are weblogs, sometimes commercial or political pitches deliberately disguised as blogs or **vlogs** (the new video versions). Setting these up is known as **nanopublishing**, a term coined in 2003 by Jeff Jarvis of Buzzmachine.com using the modish prefix (meaning one-billionth, from the Latin for dwarf) already familiar from nanosecond and nanotechnology.

Nanopublishing works by targeting **hyperlocal** or **hyperlocated** audiences (that is, neighbourhoods or local communities) or **micro-niches** (shared interest groups from scuba-divers to cancer sufferers) at next-to-no cost. Online journals can simultaneously provide instant news, gossip, and technical updates and a **P2P** (peer-to-peer) conversation whereby enthusiasts can develop ideas together.

The novel jargon has a symbolic resonance beyond its literal meanings. It's central to the hottest debate taking place among **bloggers** and **loggers**: how far can the community politics of the Net allow itself to be compromised by commercialism? For some time a number of blogs have been openly or discreetly sponsored; others carry advertisements. Entrepreneurs have started imitating the blog format and idiom, while a few **cyberprofiteers** have **paid-to-play** bloggers planting 'personal' messages – **adverposts** – praising their products. Affiliate or reciprocal links can extend the reach of a blog, while search engine ratings can be manipulated by skilfully stringing together willing – or unwitting – partners in what is dubbed **link-farming** or **link incest**.

Nanopublishing is touted as an example of user-driven so-called **thin** media, but this fashionable label carries an ambiguous message: **thin solutions** aim to focus all the technology of a multi-site or international IT system at the centre and leave the peripherals as simple as possible, so a **thin client** is a remote slave terminal without its own hard drive.

Is nanopublishing actually corrupting what was a genuinely democratic medium? Are thin solutions disempowering the local in favour of the corporate centre? Or are they both just inevitable stages in cyber-evolution? Either way they've triggered in me a case of **nanostalgia**, the cherishing of warm memories for **instant history** – things that were around only seconds ago, like fat computers and lavish, multifaceted commercial websites.

See also **blook**, **splog**

the needful

meaning: the action required or the necessary amount

A couple of months ago I started to notice an oddity appearing in professional e-mails ('**The needful** is to overwrite the files . . .') and online discussions ('Make sure you remember to provide the needful'). US contacts assured me that the expression often crops up in verbal exchanges over there, as in 'We'll have to rely on our agents to do the needful'. Utah-based systems administrator Matthew P. Barnson noticed it, too, in his own words, 'lurking in my e-mail inbox . . . giggling at me behind the veil of gentility . . . provoking me unintentionally with both its ubiquitousness and its fundamental inaccuracy'. Barnson used his weblog to denounce the term and trigger a debate on its usage.

He's right: according to American English dictionaries 'needful' only exists as an adjective, while in British English 'the needful' is used in religious or deliberately pompous language to mean either someone needy or something lacking.

To a linguist, what's interesting is not the correctness debate but the fact that this may be the first sign of a new influence on global English and a rich new source of bizwords. Examples of the fad for 'the needful' come from North America (Stephen King used the biblical phrase *Needful Things* as the title of a novel that became a movie in 1993), but I think it's inspired by so-called 'Indian English'. So-called because it's a catch-all label for what is really South Asian English, a variety that takes in Bangladeshi, Sri Lankan and Pakistani, sometimes Malaysian too. With a swathe of key services outsourced to the subcontinent and with the massive number of IT and finance specialists originating from

these countries, the English spoken there (by an estimated 100 million people) is already challenging
Anglo-American domination.

As well as vestiges of colonial British accent and
grammar, South Asian English has its own special
vocabulary, as I've found myself when negotiating with
call centres. Along with 'I will be sure to do the needful, Mr Thorne', I was bemused by 'We may be able
to offer you an **upgradation**', and 'We'll arrange to
prepone settlement' (as opposed to postpone). But
bemusement may not be the right response: this brand
of global business-speak may eventually displace my
own version.

omega male

*meaning: the diametrical opposite of the alpha female and
the alpha male*

The concept of **alpha** members of the group, taken from
biology and anthropology, was soon adopted by the
corporate sphere and every office or work-group boasted
its **alpha male** and **female**: self-actualizing, proactive
leaders. Almost every laboratory or computer suite meanwhile has its **alpha-geek** (known alternatively as an
über-nerd, from the facetious use of the German
prefix über-, borrowed from the philosopher Nietzsche's
Übermensch or superman).

Where there is alpha, omega follows and on US
campuses in the 1990s fraternity jocks began referring

to those they deemed losers as **omega males**. Women have embraced the designation: author Wendy Northcutt has compiled *The Darwin Awards*, three volumes of colourful anecdotes about the survival of the fittest and the threat to the gene pool from human stupidity. Under the Omega Male heading she relates stories of men 'confronting their inner idiots' by staging displays of suicidal bravado. *Omega Male* was the title of a 2006 release by the obscure-but-cultish band the Yo-Yos, while in the case of STIFKAs – a series of adjustable toy figurines in the Action Man/Terminator/Bionicle tradition – Alpha Males are the superheroes and Omega Males the supervillains.

A little more seriously, in therapy and media jargon 'omega male' describes a hapless, relatively unsuccessful male partner of an alpha female, as in the phenomenon of absentee **babyfathers** in the Afro-Caribbean community, or white and Asian would-be yuppies struggling to compete with a high-powered significant other. This latter scenario, and the phrase itself ('British men have become weak gelatinous omega males, unwilling to even admit, let alone express their manliness in case they are made to sleep on the couch for having a backbone'), were given prominence by articles published by the novelist Nirpal Dhaliwal (married to high-flying journalist Liz Jones) in which he admitted infidelity and flaunted his financial dependency.

open the kimono

meaning: to reveal secrets or disclose one's negotiating position

'It's time to **open the kimono**,' a US CEO tells the press, finally agreeing to open his corporation's books to scrutiny. 'Intel and HP Open the Kimono' headlines a news item announcing that the software giants have made public details of their new system architecture in advance of its release. When demanding to see the goods, some favour the challenge to **open your kimono!** – a version of London city traders' cheerily vulgar **lift up your skirt!** or **drop your pants!** In 2004 there was an interesting exchange of views about the kimono phrase at an anti-jargon website (www.buzzkiller.net). First opinions were that the expression had originated in Silicon Valley in the mid-1990s, but an Australian had heard it at IT giant NEC in the early 1980s, while a US correspondent dated it to the late 1960s, guessing that the usage originated among managers with Second World War or Korea experience. Wherever it came from, the phrase seems certain to derive from the notion of secrecy and inscrutability as typically Japanese – or oriental – qualities. Is it racist or xenophobic to say so? In February 2005 the UK's liberal daily the *Guardian* warned that any reference to the cliché 'inscrutable' applied to orientals is now unacceptable. If 'open the kimono' implies secrecy, it's politically incorrect; if it evokes a

geisha or bar-girl surrendering herself it's sexist – and yet no one in the USA or Australasia, where the term is common, seems to have objected to it. But wait, techno-consultancy Ronin International promises clients an **open-kimono philosophy** and defines this as 'dealings that are open and honest . . . no hidden agendas and no dissembling'. Ronin state confidently that the concept dates back to feudal Japan, where it signified that your counterpart would 'hide nothing within his clothing that could conceivably be used as a weapon'. If this is true (and it sounds to me more like a fanciful modern reconstruction), then the kimono-wearer becomes male and the sexism disappears. Finally, for trivia buffs only, there *is* such a thing as an 'open kimono'. It's called a *uchikake* and is worn only for wedding ceremonies with another garment underneath – so there's no hint of indecency either.

the orphan problem

meaning: an absentee parent company

In recycling jargon, **the orphan problem** refers to the situation in which the original manufacturer, who should be made responsible for recycling redundant hardware, is no longer in existence to take care of the **e-waste** or **technotrash** in question. Most people are now aware of the difficulty of dismantling (more trendily known as **teardown**, q.v.) and disposing of computer hardware, but almost all advanced economies also have their **fridge mountains**, along with piles of washing machines, television sets, toasters, etc. Orphanage is an issue in disposing of automobiles, too. The latest legislation, an EU directive called **ELV** or **End-of-Life Vehicle(s)**, makes manufacturers responsible for taking back and disposing of their cars, but all those Austins, Wolseleys, Jowetts and Panhards remain the responsibility of what are nowadays called **vehicle dismantlers** (formerly scrap merchants) who operate from **licensed automotive treatment facilities** (formerly scrapyards).

The US exports between 50 and 80 per cent of its waste, much of it, including toxic and hazardous elements, being **cached** in India or China where recycling (aka dumping) and **depolluting** is largely unregulated and undocumented. While the EU has implemented the **WEEE** (for 'waste electrical and electronic equipment'), another directive which makes producers responsible for **take-back**, the US has nothing similar and refused to sign up to the 1992 Basle agreement on responsible waste disposal.

In the financial sphere, where the same expression is encountered, the orphan problem is that the companies responsible for mis-selling, fraud, diversion of pension funds, etc. have been liquidated or have merged or morphed into other entities, shedding their original names and responsibilities along the way. Litigation and investigation by regulators or the ombudsman is generally **time-barred** (that is, a moratorium or 'statute of limitation' applies), so miscreants can escape if their misdeeds were committed long enough ago.

In Africa, of course, where the phrase is constantly invoked, the orphan problem is literally that. When used by aid agencies, other NGOs and the international media it describes the demographic and social effects of the enormous number of children orphaned by AIDS.

outwith

meaning: an old term still in use

My curiosity was piqued when I came across the unusual word **outwith** in my own workplace, in a recent internal memo which declared that '. . . the Centre's finances will be dealt with outwith the faculty budget'. I had seen the term before and knew what it meant, but was uncertain about its status in the wider world. Casual conversations indicated that a majority of colleagues were ignorant of its existence; an Internet search revealed that there has been considerable debate, going back to 2002, about this very term. Although there's agreement on its meaning (outside, or beyond the scope or jurisdiction of, typically, a contract), it has been condemned as pretentious, pompous or simply archaic by many professionals, and rejected as dialect by some self-styled language experts.

The usage seems indeed to have begun as a regionalism, in Lowland Scotland and the north of England, where it occurs in texts from the fourteenth to sixteenth centuries. It is definitely still in use, by the Department of Social Security and Pensions for instance, and in the legal and property professions in England (but not inside the BBC, where it has been explicitly forbidden by internal memo). The word is in regular use by many more professionals and ordinary citizens in Scotland (although online correspondent Vicky from Fife says it 'makes her teeth itch') and occurs occasionally in formal usage in African and Indian English, but it isn't recognized in Australia, Canada or the USA.

To a generation for whom 'moreover' and 'herewith', not to mention 'notwithstanding' and 'heretofore', are part of a foreign language, there is no doubt that 'outwith' is and is likely to remain an exotic oddity.

Other terms which have been debated recently are 'remit' (noun and verb), 'idem', 'sans' (meaning without), 'forfend' (a joke this one, since it would only reasonably be used as a tease), and, surprisingly perhaps, 'entitled' as opposed to 'titled' in the sense of named. The word 'eschew', which occurs in one of the featured quotes in the introduction to this book, caused some problems in communication training sessions I have run: non-native speakers of English were universally baffled by it, but so were some of the natives present, too.

The outwith debate nicely points up the tension between the (in most cases laudable) drive for plain English and an end to deliberate obfuscation, and the opposite view: the idea that we should cherish our language's vast reserves of curiosities and subtleties and the nuances of meaning that they uniquely encode. I'm in favour of preserving, if not promiscuously using for bombastic effect, what used to be criticized as 'inkhorn terms' because they were typically used by scholars (who dipped their quills into inkhorns before drafting their manuscripts).

paraplanner

meaning: an all-purpose assistant; a number-cruncher

When a financial consultant told me that he was passing work down to his **paraplanner**, I had to get him to explain that the person concerned did all his research, data-checking and calculations for him, as well as liaising with some of his less prestigious clients. 'Paraplanner' aims to describe a new mix of functions once spanning multiple roles from dogsbody via Technical Assistant to PA. At the same time it's a fairly fancy-sounding title. We've all heard the jokes about the window-cleaner who had his job-title upgraded to **Optical Illumination Enhancer**, or the sales rep reborn as **Client Solutions Advocate**. I recently came across a somewhat bemused receptionist whose job had been redesignated as **Hub Facilitator**.

The phenomenon is so well established in the USA, where one major bank's management trainees are allowed to call themselves Vice-Presidents, that it has spawned its own bizwords. It is variously known as **title-creep, title-morph** or **uptitling**. Usually change of title means swapping humble for grandiose – the simplest way being just to add the word 'Chief', as in Chief Technical Officer or **CTO** (reinterpreted during lean times as 'career terminally over'): the creep occurs when the Public Relations Officer morphs into an **Information Manager**, then **Media Outreach Coordinator**, finally becoming **Deputy Director for External Affairs**. An alternative route is to go wacky, resulting in novel descriptions like **Marketing Weasel**, **Knowledge Sorceress**, **Code Guru** or **Chief Morale Officer**, all of which really were piloted in the USA, probably inspired by Bill Gates's recasting himself as **Chief Software Architect**. The IT sector was the main offender – or innovator, if you prefer – also indulging in **Database God**, and even **Chief Techie Geek**. Post dot.com meltdown this trend seems to have fizzled out along with many of the companies who tried it. Uptitling as a strategic device, however, is not a joke: a recent UK survey by Reed International revealed that 50 per cent of workers would register greater job satisfaction with a nicer title, even if it made no difference to their duties or salary.

'Paraplanner' may have been coined by analogy with 'paramedic', although some authorities claim that the 'para-' in that word is actually from parachute (doctors and nurses were parachuted into emergency zones) rather than the Greek prefix *para-* meaning alongside or supporting. Either way it's better than being called a **gofer** or a **back office bean-counter**.

performativity

meaning: the decade's most pretentious word?

'The latest wireless technology guarantees optimal **performativity**,' claims a hardware producer, while a management consultancy advises that 'factoring non-executives into the goal-setting process will enhance performativity'. This buzzword and its adjective form **performative** have become emblems of trendiness and dynamism in the last couple of years, but in fact the words, applied to things as diverse as MP3s, web-based innovations such as **mashups** (q.v.) or teams of people making things happen, are highly ambiguous if not based on a misunderstanding.

Performativity came to the business world, via economics and technology, from the jargon of literary critical theory, a source rivalled only by therapy-speak of some of the most infuriatingly opaque or ambivalent terminology around. In business jargon the idea invoked is linked with **performance** (as in **performance enhancement**, **performance-related**, etc.), but performativity began life as a key term from the Speech Act Theory propounded by the Oxford philosopher J. L. Austin in a 1955 series of lectures at Harvard. It originally referred to utterances (acts of speaking) like 'I declare . . .', 'I bet . . .' or 'I warn . . . ', which are examples of language not merely describing, but that is an action in itself; it makes something happen. The classic example is the declaration: 'I hereby pronounce you man and wife', which enacts a marriage contract and binds three individuals within a social convention. It's this enforcing of convention which caused proponents of feminist and fashionable **queer theory** to use performativity to highlight the empowering and disempowering qualities of 'discourse' (language in its widest sense).

It's odd that many terms from critical theory which are immensely important inside academia are not actually defined anywhere. They are too technical for inclusion in standard dictionaries and too new to qualify for glossaries of jargon – although many have been around since they were borrowed from linguistics and taken into other disciplines in the 1970s and 1980s. I defy anyone – including me – to provide an adequate explanation of the term **enunciation**, for example, as used by critical and linguistic theory proponents: all that is certain is that it is part of that forbidding body of discourse – leftist political writing in the 1970s, politically correct verbiage of the 1980s and 1990s – that a colleague of mine held had been only partially translated from its language of origin (in this case French, *énoncé*). **Overdetermined** and **articulation** are two other examples that cause problems for outsiders. The first means having several different origins or causes; the second is not the articulation of speaking clearly, but of the articulated lorry or bone articulation; it means having an essential but tangential connection with something.

As for performativity, it's a good example of an imposing-looking word whose unfamiliarity lends it mystique and prestige, commodities which are eminently saleable.

phood

meaning: foodstuffs treated so as to provide more than nutrition

The anonymous coiners of teenage slang and **SMS** (text messaging) codes and other reprobates such as hackers will frequently re-spell words to assert their ownership of them, so that dudes becomes 'dudez' and real, 'reeel'. Since the 1990s there has been a phad, sorry, fad, for adapting some of the more innocent F-words to give phat (a slang term of approval among skateboarders, hip-hoppers, etc.), phun, phreak and of course **phishing**, when this refers to illicitly obtaining electronic information. A recent example, **phood**, besides being the name of a Swiss 'alternative rock' band, is used in more respectable circles, perhaps with a nod also to the 'ph' of pharmaceuticals, to denote food that is chemically enhanced. A step beyond health foods and probiotics, these products incorporate chemicals, not to improve flavour or induce cravings, but to engineer physical and psychological improvements. They include **clever milk**, **intelligent bread** (which may also combat depression), cereals that reduce the risk of heart attack or cancer, and items increasing fertility and boosting the immune system.

The re-spelling of 'food' is of course only visible when written down, so alternative designations are **functional food** (since it has, in nutritionist jargon, 'added functions'), **technofood**, **analog(ue) food** (which can mean substitute or ersatz, as in 'meat analog', but in California may just be a nickname for organic, non-GM meals) or **nutraceuticals**, the term most popular in marketing circles. The UK is the biggest market in Europe for these innovations, which blur the line between nutrition and medication and test the limits of regulation.

The fad for stretching the definition of food extends (pun intended) to *haute couture* items made from nettles and to Aussiebum's vitamin-enriched underwear, marketed in 2006. In the UK, edible T-shirts have been added to the range of respectable sports apparel, while edible panties, thongs, etc. have been part of the sex-toy and joke-shop repertoire since the 1960s.

See also **disease marketing**, **retro-recipes**

the pig in the python

meaning: the baby-boom generation and its effect on consumer retailing, product development, etc.

The term, used typically by market analysts and prod-uct-planners, refers of course to the demographic blip caused by the high birth rate between 1945 and 1965.

The **pig** is the bulge in population moving slowly along the **python**'s alimentary canal – the horizontal time-line on the graph. The **boomers'** potential spending power makes them an irresistible market, but their unpredictability and refusal to age gracefully have been a long-term headache for retailers, whose jaundiced take is reflected in a series of earlier buzzwords. In the early 1990s when acronyms still ruled it was all about the effects of recession; in the USA less affluent home-owners from this same generation were labelled as a credit risk under the heading of **nebbies** – 'negative-equity **baby-boomers'**; a couple of years later the feck-less children of the 1960s – supposedly as reluctant to put money aside as to take up flossing – were being dismissed as future **dumpies** ('destitute, unprepared mature people') by health-care specialists. An earlier wave of elderly consumers had tried to assert them-selves as a force to be reckoned with under the banner of **grey power**, but in private the marketing people still referred to those old-timers, with their essentially conser-vative tastes and habits and their modest savings, as a **junk population**. Today's marketing-speak is more likely to recognize their free-spending forty- and fifty-some-thing successors as a **splurge generation**. In analysing the post-1945-ers the biggest challenge is predicting their response to innovations – have they finally learned to floss? Will they ever start seriously clubbing? – and in particular to new technology. Once again the pundits got it wrong, deciding in the mid-1990s that the soon-to-be-elderly would be left behind by the digital age. By the turn of the millennium, with 15 per cent of personal online business coming from the over-55s, **e-tailers** started to refer more respectfully to them as the **silver surfers**. However you characterize them (us?), in the words of statistician Brent Michaels, 'No one knows how long the python is, but the pig isn't getting any smaller.' As is often the case with colourful jargon phrases, the component words may have more than surface significance: the pig is renowned as a greedy, troublesome, self-willed animal, but we can be pretty sure that the python will digest its over-size meal in the end.

See also **flashpackers**, **iPod**

pillow fighting

meaning: the latest physical combat game

Pillow fighting wasn't a euphemism, though it would make a good one (for feigned conflict, pulling punches?), but literally true: young urban professionals and older **baby-boomers** were gleefully thrashing one another with pillows in a mass outdoor ritual in the Justin Herman Plaza in San Francisco on a recent St Valentine's Day. Pillow fights have long been part of the sophomoric fun repertoire, along with slumber parties, sleepovers, toga parties and, once upon a time, panty raids, but this particular pillow fight was organized on **flash mob** principles, bringing together strangers through

Internet and mobile phone 'word-of-mouth' for events which combine communal practical jokes and bonding experiences. Like **inflatable sumo wrestling**, a joky fad of the 1990s, but much less elaborate, pillow-fighting allows participants to release tension, engage in harmless combat and cross the social boundaries of privacy and intimacy without any real risk.

Like **cuddle parties** (q.v.), though more anarchic and playful, pillow fighting is an example of a phenomenon dubbed **planned spontaneity** by trendspotters. This seeming oxymoron is a fashionable umbrella term for a range of activities as varied as **guerrilla music gigs** (held at short notice in a public place or private home), **mini-breaks** and **micro-vacations**, **speed-dating**, and making professional presentations or sales pitches. What all these have in common is that they trade on the dynamic of things done on impulse, but actually impose a guiding discipline. Budget airfares and last-minute booking agencies encourage semi-impromptu decisions on leisure; meanwhile communications skills specialists such as **life coaches** or **pitch doctors** (q.v.) take account of improvisational techniques from drama; these set up a framework within which actors are free to ad lib – or at least pretend to – or seize the moment.

pitch doctor

meaning: someone to help refine the message

Making a pitch or **pitching** is a crucial component in the process of winning a client account in the fields of advertising, PR, marketing and management consultancy, and in the film and television industries. It consists usually of a stand-up presentation of ideas to a critical audience. The term is older than it seems: the slang 'pitch it high' or 'strong', in the sense of telling a convincing story, was recorded in the UK in 1836, and forty years later 'pitch' alone was in use with the meaning of sales talk.

Just as few of us these days are naive enough to put together our CVS or résumés (**biodata**, if you prefer) without expert help, and almost no politicians write their own speeches, so few agencies or consultants will pitch, bid or tender without the intervention of the **pitch doctor**, an objective outsider who can critically evaluate their performance and improve it, or in some cases tell them to go back and start again.

Pitch doctor is obviously related to the **spin doctor** nickname which originated with Bill Clinton's presidential campaign and was made notorious in the UK by New Labour's attempts to manipulate the media. It's also a pun on **witch doctor**, a term that was already in use in corporations, where it usually denotes not a publicist but a strategist or financial expert who can (or is expected to) conjure up seemingly magical solutions.

Other shamanistic job titles include **rainmaker**, the role, usually unofficial, of a high-powered employee who can by 'magic' or charm attract clients or generate business, just as the native American sorcerer reputedly brought rainclouds to the desert. The nickname has been heard since at least the mid-1980s (featuring as the title of Martin Baker's business column in the *Sunday Telegraph*). **Doing a raindance** is a little different: this phrase, which dates from the 1970s, implies that a complex and/or spectacular procedure to be carried out will *not* produce results and is either just for show or a complete waste of time.

And then there's the **knowledge wizard** (someone possessing key technical know-how), one of the fanciful attempts at coining 'New Age' job designations to go with the new business models and practices of the dot.com era. An older usage, **voodoo economics** (excessively clever or opaque financial finessing) seems likely to outlast it.

The pitch doctor nickname, by the way, is not exclusively bestowed on presentation-tweakers: he or she might also be a landscape gardener who cares for cricket pitches, while it's also the trademark name of a digital audio voice moderator for use in sound studios.

Compare **paraplanner**

planogramming

meaning: deploying items for sale for maximum effect

The buying public has known for some time that placing items on display in retail outlets is an art, if not a science, and far from improvised or random: as the processes have become more sophisticated, so an impressive jargon has evolved to describe them. **Space management** or **visual merchandising** these days employs a range of techniques including **arraying**, **clustering** and, crucially, so-called **shelf optimization** which is, like everything else, computerized. Automated analysis of sales patterns is an implacable process and a poor performance on the shelf as gauged by software applications can spell the end for small suppliers whose poor performing lines will be **delisted**.

The number and position of **facings**, the items confronting the customer directly, and the **props** (originally short for properties) used to enhance displays were once upon a time sketched out on a paper blueprint known as a **planogram** or **POG** (initials suggested by imperfect analogy with **POS** or point-of-sale) but this is now done by specialist software. Generating the schematic is logically enough known as **planogramming**, a coinage on the lines of **organigramming** (graphically visualizing organization structure), **flowcharting** (mapping a moving process) and **bulletizing** (highlighting and listing key points).

Moving punters physically around the retail floor-space, more properly referred to as **customer traffic management** or **routing**, will steer them towards strategically positioned **impulse items**, **demand/destination products** (the ones the customer came in to buy) and **price points** (where they can get a snapshot impression of the store's pricing profile), and may now incorporate concepts such as **enticement** and engaging in a **journey of consumption** towards the so-called **cash wrap**, the place where they pay and pick up.

See also **stickiness**

poop and scoop

meaning: to drive down a share price by spreading malicious rumours

'It was a classic **poop and scoop** operation,' whispered my informant, worried that he might be tainted by the illegality of the practice being described. What he was lifting the lid on was a concerted attempt to talk down the value of a Wall Street stock in order to buy it cheap and make a quick killing. City analysts in the UK use **bash and dash** to define the same tactic. The rubbishing of reputations is done by means of carefully orchestrated gossip or, much more effective, an Internet campaign of smears and innuendo. The company or equity in question may be copper-bottomed, but once the buzz has taken hold a downturn is almost inevitable.

A very similar massaging of stock value involves borrowing shares that seem to be overvalued in order to sell and then buy back at a cheaper price. When it's a straightforward gamble it's called **short selling** and is perfectly legal, but when it's accompanied by fraudulent suggestions that a firm is going under or about to be investigated, **bulls** turn into **bears**, **scamsters** clean up and the relevant buzz-phrase is **short and distort**.

Ever since someone referred to **the name of the game**, business slang has been fond of rhymes. Originating in the USA, 'poop and scoop' ('pooping' on the reputation, then scooping the rewards) is probably inspired by the earlier **pump and dump**, which describes the opposite strategy of artificially inflating a share price, again by rumour and disinformation, then selling up before the market catches on. This is also known in London as **ramp and de-camp**.

Insider trading and share-price manipulation depend on fellow conspirators, but these are not always trustworthy. So never rely on a **tip-from-a-dip**, where dip may be short for **dipster**, a North American version of 'tipster', or for the less-than-complimentary **dipstick**.

When everything goes **pear-shaped**, **the wheels come off the wagon** and the market is **tanking** (heading for a crash), rhymes are abandoned. Players who are left holding **air-pocket stock** (its price about to plummet uncontrollably) are going to **take a bath** or, more brutally, **get whacked**. In desperation the only answer may be to **pull a Leeson**, also known as a **Rio**

trade, a move so all-out risky that if it doesn't succeed a flight to Brazil is the only option.

poster child

meaning: the visible symbol/public face of a cause or issue

In North America one of the most over-used pieces of recent jargon is **poster child**, as in 'Jeffrey Bezos [founder of Amazon.com] is the poster child of e-commerce'. Now the phrase can be heard in conversation in the UK and Australasia ('Find us a young attractive broker – we need a poster child for "anyone can make it in this business!"'), also showing up as a novelty in the print media (a recent headline: 'Dolly the Sheep: The Poster Child of Cloning'). Poster child originally meant exactly what it says: a child featured on a poster. This comes from the practice, developed in the USA since the 1930s and now ubiquitous, of giving a human face to a fund-raising campaign or a charity by linking it with a real, named individual, usually a victim of disability, disease or abuse. Playing on the emotions of potential donors in this way, although no doubt laudable, has led to overkill. In the USA and Canada every local fund-raising effort now has a winsome, suffering face to go with it, and, with bogus charities and dubious Internet appeals added into the mix, cynicism has set in, just as the Band Aid and Live Aid extravaganzas of the 1980s and 1990s resulted in **compassion fatigue**, **donor burnout** and the **'I've-already-given' syndrome**. And in the words of writer

Jenn Shreve, 'How we media types love our poster children. They are supposed to be the antidotes to soulless
statistics, but turning a real-life tragedy into a nation-
ally broadcast morality play often serves to cheapen, not
to amplify it.'

Alternative forms of the term are **poster girl** and **poster
boy**, and this is probably where the ironic usage originated. Back in the 1940s and 1950s 'poster boy' was a
slightly mocking description of a male pin-up, especially
one whose physical glamour outweighed his talent.

One organization which has neatly exploited the
personalization/exploitation paradox is the anti-
tobacco lobby in British Columbia, which has produced
its own campaign showing a full-colour photo of a
once-attractive teenage girl whose body is graphically
ravaged by the effects of smoking, with the slogan
'Don't Become a Tobacco Industry Poster Child' (access
it on www.tobaccofacts.org/ozone).

proctoheliosis

meaning: overweening self-importance

If you were solemnly informed that your boss had
gone down with a bad case of **proctoheliosis**, you
might feel a pang of sympathy despite yourself. Your
concern would be misplaced. The condition, alternatively known as **helioproctosis**, is more psychological than physical; it describes someone who thinks
that, or behaves as if, the sun (Greek *helios*) shines out

of their – to put it as gently as possible – fundament (*proktos*, Greek for rectum).

This rare modern example of a learned pun – not many professionals have even a smattering of classical languages these days – mocks the delusions of grandeur suffered especially by senior medics, who have been portrayed as playing God since the days of James Robertson Justice's tyrannical Sir Lancelot in the movie *Doctor in the House*. The expression itself is not new; it was a favourite saying of the late Monty Python team member Graham Chapman, himself a qualified physician, in the late 1970s; before that, I'm told, it was frequently heard in nautical slang, too. It's still in use and I came across it on discussion boards debating the future of the BBC, when it was applied to more than one recent leader of the Corporation.

A more recent workplace use of the same root is the notion of labouring under a **proctocracy**, defined as 'rule by assholes'. And a similar if slightly milder critique is reflected in a comment I heard recently: 'He's a legend in his own lunchtime; not so much the CEO, but the **COU**.' The **TLA** ('three-letter acronym') stands for 'centre of (the) universe'.

prosthetic enhancement

meaning: surgical improvement of the human body

We're all familiar with the **nip-and-tuck** culture whereby all age groups indulge in cosmetic surgery (**plastic**

surgery vacations to Colombia and elsewhere, facelifts now complemented by **body-lifts** and even **voice-lifts** in which the vocal cords are manipulated to produce a younger-sounding voice), and the advances in surgical techniques and transplanting which allow the remodelling of damaged surfaces, limb and even face-grafting. Implants have become a commonplace of dental treatment, but we are on the verge of more futuristic applications of **prosthetics** (replacement of natural body parts by artificial, from the Greek *prosthetos*, added).

So-called **emergent technologies** – **bioengineering**, **bionics**, **sensory augmentation**, etc. – are not only being used for corrective purposes for the **differently enabled** (as US healthcare jargon has it) but for aesthetic, if that's the right word, motives. Practitioners of performance art and **body art** have previously undergone plastic surgery and inserted inert objects into their bodies, but the UK's conceptual artist Stelarc is now having a third ear (made of flesh) with inbuilt digital audio functions grafted on to his forearm. The idea of the **cyborg** (short for cyber-organism), an entity which is part human, part machine, has long been a staple of science fiction and has fascinated theoreticians of cultural studies. It is a key component in the predictions of self-styled **extropians** (utopians who wish to leave the planet), **post-humanists** and **cyberfuturists** who envisage a future in which humans and machines will merge leading to a **singularity** or **technorapture** – a defining moment at which humanity will transcend all its current physical limitations. One scientist who has not unwillingly become the **poster child** (q.v.) for such thinking is Professor Kevin Warwick of the University of Reading, who in 1998 had a chip-transmitter implanted in his arm to enable him to communicate automatically with his workplace: he followed this in 2002 with a more complex **electrode microarray** allowing the sensory and motor neurons in the median nerve in his forearm to interact with a computer. US author Ray Kurzweil, a spokesperson for the singularity idea, claims that by 2030 we shall have machines that can exceed human intelligence: 'They will be inserted into our bodies via nanotechnology . . . will go inside our brains through the capillaries.'

Slightly more soberly, the controversial issues involved in enhancement and augmentation have become a central plank of the interdiscipline of **bioethics** which is already debating the 'human' rights of cyborgs and **artilects** (from 'artificial intellect', a new term for non-human superbrains promoted by Professor Hugo de Garis, who envisages a coming conflict between **terrans** who fear them and **cosmists** who endorse them).

quadruple play

meaning: combining electronic services in an ideal package

For several years the Holy Grail of electronic service delivery has been something known in technical and marketing circles as **triple play**. This is a package which combines **IPTV** (Internet protocol television), **VoIP** (voice-over Internet protocol) and data services. The first to offer a version of triple play were cable companies with telephone, broadband and television. They borrowed the expression from baseball, where it describes a spectacular coup in which three players are put out in one single sequence. Now **quadruple play** has become the ideal to strive for: fixed-line and mobile telephony, broadband Internet and television all in one **offer**, probably delivered by a **MVNO**, a mobile virtual network operator, like Virgin, which **piggybacks** on others' networks but sells under its own brand. Virgin's chairman, the irrepressible Sir Richard Branson, favours the punning label **4-play/four-play** and misses no opportunity to try out the *double entendre* on his audiences.

In parallel with these new ways of **bundling** services there is something called **device convergence** which envisages the bringing together of all electronic functions in one handset or **PMG** – personal mobile gateway. Thus the successor to the cellphone/digital camera will add on an MP3 music downloader, a **PIM** (personal information manager – the latest incarnation of the old yuppie filofax), a **GPS** (global positioning system) facility and a games console. The big question is whether consumers will actually pay for this supergadget as opposed to what techies call **distributed functionality** (in plain English, separate services).

redhead

meaning: a spontaneous, impulsive and/or headstrong consumer

Not to be confused with **red-top**, the UK's term for its downmarket tabloid newspapers, or with **red buttons**, therapist-speak for the events and attitudes that trigger an outburst of rage, **redhead** is one of the oddest of the latest crop of labels dreamed up by marketing people in their quest to categorize consumers. No longer referring to the much-mocked ginger-haired minority, this buzzword defines a 'hot-headed', instinctive, risk-taking individual. A typical redhead, we are told, is male, between 15 and 34, enjoys pubs (only theme pubs and cocktail bars, I would have thought), television quiz-shows and soaps, lad-mags and holidays booked at the last minute. Analysts of spending patterns and customer behaviour have coined dozens of these nicknames but it's not always easy to tell one from another; MediaCom, who invented the redhead, also discovered the **adult-escent** (a '26–44-year-old drinker and clubber') who seems to share many of the same characteristics. Rival sets of definitions don't equate; advertising agency BMP has divided consumers into **subtle shoppers** (sophisticated, discerning), **fakers** (label-obsessed wannabes), **stalwarts** (lovers of quiet quality), **no logos** (would-be eco-aware), **radicals** (authentic alternative types) and **cutting-edge eclectics**. It's hard to see where the redheads fit in here. Those eclectics, though, look very similar to another recently discovered tribe, the so-called **cool hunters**, a term that defines both ground-breaking style-setters and the professional trendspotters who steal their ideas.

BMP's subtle shopper also has something in common with the **affluential**, a label recently introduced to the UK and now so familiar that it's often shortened to **aff**. Affs are new low-key versions of the upwardly mobile consumer, shunning vulgar display but using their considerable wealth to fund non-material pleasures like travel, fitness and 'meaningful experiences'. If it wasn't the Spanish word for 'idiot', I'd prefer to be a **bobo**, a 'bourgeois bohemian', a being described as 'half-hippie, half-yuppie', symbolized in the USA by the Apple advertising campaign that uses 'alternative' figures like Jack Kerouac and Gandhi to sell computers.

Finally, though, these attempts at pigeonholing seem increasingly desperate. Some pundits privately admit that today's consumers are so fickle that, beyond generalities like **upscale** and **downscale**, the terminology has little value. (Incidentally, punch 'redhead' into your search engine and discover not a new consumer group but dozens of militant support groups fighting to prove that carrot-tops can be cool.)

Compare **rejuvenile**

re-enchantment

meaning: the (re-)emergence of a sense of magic, awe and spiritual values in the day-to-day lives of consumers

This term implies more than just **the boggle factor**, the special quality that grabs a customer's imagination. It suggests nothing less than a transcendent experience. The grandiose-sounding concept was imported into commerce – particularly product design, retailing and leisure services – from the jargon of New Age religion and psychotherapy in the mid-1990s. There's nothing particularly new about bemoaning the death of family, tradition and organized religion and the collapse of political ideologies. What is novel is the serious claim that the spiritual void can be filled by retailing. Perhaps this is a move to retake the moral high ground by the people who brought us **recreational shopping** and **retail therapy** (aka the **shopaholic**). Tim Greenhalgh, creative director of UK brand designers Fitch and a professional trendspotter, defines **re-enchantment** as 'a return to innocence – the belief that as we move into the new millennium we are entering a period of rebirth and new beginnings – as such there is a growing view that things are possible and there's a naive optimism with regard to the future'. He cites among other phenomena the massive sales of the Harry Potter books, the introduction of crèches for grown-ups and boyfriends in some stores and malls and the constant revisiting of our youth via television (like the former presenters of the children's series *Blue Peter*, John Noakes, Peter Purves and Valerie Singleton, reuniting to create an infotainment show for nostalgic forty-somethings). Does this bizword define a concept whose time has come, or an idea waiting to happen? Apart from Tim Greenhalgh's instances, what does re-enchantment in the real world really add up to? So far the examples are diverse but pretty low-key: shopping multiplexes importing New Age boutiques and market stalls, retail interiors refitted to send customers on a 'mythical' journey, 'transcendent' television ads like the Guinness 'white horses' commercial. Perhaps another good definition of re-enchantment is a negative one: it's precisely that sense of communal wonder that the unlamented Millennium Dome tried and failed to create.

In another context, that of writings on religious experience and New Age mysticism, the word **occulture** has been used alongside re-enchantment to describe the embracing of non-rational, magical or arcane notions. As the late French über-theorist Jacques Derrida observed, technological modernity doesn't neutralize magic, but encourages it to re-emerge.

There is an obvious link between these concepts and the influential notion of **love** as a new keyword for the business world, most forcefully (or embarrassingly, depending on your level of cynicism) set out in the 2002 title *Love is the Killer App: How to Win Business and Influence Friends* by Tim Sanders.

regulatory capture

meaning: *the phenomenon whereby independent regulators turn into toothless stooges of industry or government*

Some examples of specialist jargon cross over into mainstream use almost instantly. Concepts like **guerrilla marketing**, or in its more pompous UK translation, **live ambient point-of-sale**, were no sooner thought of than everyone everywhere seemed to be using them. Not so surprising when they refer to a controversial, in-your-face sales technique, but there's another kind of bizword that may lurk in obscurity for years before going public. **Regulatory capture** was once a little-known technical term, but now seems to be cropping up everywhere. It describes what happens when an independent watchdog ends by serving the interests of the parties he or she is supposed to be policing. What has long been a problem in North America, for instance, where powerful industry forces have succeeded in neutralizing regulators in broadcasting, telecoms, food and drugs, etc., is now a key post-privatization issue in developing countries too. Nowadays the phrase is often shortened to **capture**, as in: 'As environmental lobbyists we must guard against capture by the agrochemical giants,' or: 'I've leaned on the editor of the *Daily Spectre* and I think we have capture.'

Other examples that I've come across recently of old jargon mutating into new buzzword include

forum-shopping and **virement**. Forum-shopping, sometimes known as **jurisdiction abuse** or **jurisdiction-juggling**, was originally a device of high-powered divorce lawyers who would scour the world for the most sympathetic legal system in which to defend their clients against alimony claims. Now the phrase has been extended to cover any attempt to move litigation to a more favourable setting: high-profile recent examples include insurance claims and disputes over intellectual property, pirating and licensing of Internet providers. When, for instance, multinational oil companies start suing each other the cases can pop up in courts all over the planet.

In the original French *virement* simply means a transfer from one bank account to another, but in English it refers to cleverly offsetting losses in one budget-system against profits in another, a practice that often stretches the limits of legality, to put it politely. In fact, all these seemingly different terms have one thing in common: they define ways in which advanced capitalism bends its own rules, **disempowering** the small organization or the individual.

rejuvenile

meaning: a childish adult

The admonitions 'act your age' and 'grow up!' are rarely heard these days, since what constitutes appropriate age-related behaviour is far from clear. 'Get in touch with your inner kid' is for many a more attractive injunction, and according to social scientists and trendspotters doing so has created yet another social category and lifestyle label. Formerly members of this group were dubbed **kidults** or **adultescents**, though both of these expressions are ambiguous as they may refer either to **mid-lifers** acting childish or those in their twenties and early thirties who refuse to leave home (in media slang they are practising **stay-and-delay** or experiencing **launch failure**), or to children affecting grown-up behaviour (the latter have also been nicknamed **tweenagers**). The newer name for thirty- or forty-somethings who read Harry Potter or Philip Pullman books, watch movies of the Narnia books and sing along to the SpongeBob SquarePants theme song, is **rejuvenile**, a blend of 'rejuvenate' and 'juvenile'. In fact the boundaries of children's literature have been crossed by older readers since whimsy and fantasies of a golden childhood became a staple of English-speaking popular culture in the nineteenth century. Awareness of this is now built into book and movie marketing strategies, but the rejuvenile phenomenon doesn't end with simple **crossover**.

Just as **prosthetic enhancement** (q.v.) can radically interfere with the physical effects of ageing, so role-playing and purchasing choices can create an illusion of **perma-youth**. At the extreme end of the spectrum are fetishists who dress as babies, at the other are **baby-boomers** wearing the same brands as their teenage children and affecting to enjoy the same music.

'Going through a second childhood' has acquired new overtones with the advent of **nanostalgia** – a sentimental (and fashionable) desire to celebrate or relive the very recent past. Some behavioural specialists see nothing wrong with what they term **extended adolescence** or **emerging adulthood** if it means prolonging a period of experimentation and exploring the possibilities of a society of plenty. More prosaically, Rejuvenile is also the trademark name of a tonic that inhibits symptoms of the menopause.

See also **re-enchantment**

retrofuturist

meaning: *imagining the future using the sci-fi imagery of the past*

Not exactly a household word, but a key term in the lexicon of product developers, designers, multi-media specialists and architects at the dawn of the twenty-first century, **retrofuturist** defines a curious phenomenon: our ability to visualize the future seems to have stopped around the end of the 1960s. It is still the Sputnik, the Skylon, the comic-book space-explorers with their robot pals who dominate our imaginations. This results in the latest generation of wristwatches looking like accessories from Dan Dare, in the talented UK architect Nicholas Grimshaw unveiling his Eden Project in Cornwall which turns out to be a network of geodesic domes, harking back to Buckminster Fuller's designs of the 1950s and 1960s; in websites using graphics from the 1950s to evoke cyberspace and in **pods** of one sort or another becoming ubiquitous. More tellingly, it means that designers are designing things that don't actually make sense, given new technology, but which bring to life the utopian visions of the past: among these are those Japanese domestic robots that resemble little human servants, wrist-mounted videophones and intelligent synthetic bodysuits that have been touted as the garment of the future since Jules Verne's day.

Retrofuturism should not be confused with the related idea of the **retro-modern**, a word used to describe a trend in interior design which has resulted in a decor of beige and orange hessian walls, pale suede sofas, teak table-lamps and sideboards going global. This look, with accessories in steel, stone and glass, is a re-creation of the Scandinavian-modern trend which swept the UK in the very early 1960s. This again is something different from mere **retro** – designing new products which recall an earlier age and shamelessly press the nostalgia-buttons, examples of which were the Rover 75, the Jaguar 'S'-type and, even more glaringly, the recent offerings from US Ford and Chrysler which hark back to the roadsters and hotrods of the 1950s. When these 1950s gimmicks do work it isn't just on **baby-boomers** suffering from **technostalgia**, as witness the success of the canine robot pet, the hit toy product for the under-12s over several successive

Christmases. We can be forgiven for relying on our cosy retrofuturist images – after all, a *real* future of virtuality, nanotechnology and subatomic cloning is beyond the ability of most of us to picture. But it has yet to be proven that mainstream consumers really want those retro-rehashes, any more than they need the humanoid robots and wrist-videos – and, sadly, it seems that the electronic dog is just for Christmas.

retro-recipes

meaning: *foodstuffs that evoke an earlier era*

Many British consumers, now able to access an enormous range of domestic and foreign – or at least quasi-international – dishes in supermarkets and specialist stores, still retain a yearning for the frankly inferior staples of their childhood, the meals imposed by school and works canteens or indulged in as **comfort food**. With this in mind supermarkets such as Marks and Spencer decided in the mid-**noughties** actively to promote these **nostalgia foods**, reintroducing some discontinued lines and giving more prominence in displays to old favourites. Among the so-called **retro-recipes** were 1970s-style moussaka, macaroni cheese and dishes based on corned beef, Black Forest gateau and Birds Eye Instant Whip. Even plum duff and spotted dick, stars of school dinner stodge, staged a comeback.

The same trend has manifested itself in the USA and

Canada as a craze for preparing authentic retro-recipes taken from the cookbooks of the 1940s and 1950s, sometimes for themed parties where guests sample **bad taste food** like peanut butter (which may optionally be fried), spam (ditto) and meatloaf, accompanied by root

beer or ersatz mint or fruit-flavoured cordials.

Sophisticates can incorporate these often unhealthy items into their diet by indulging in what has been termed **Jekyll and Hyde eating**, in other words mixing bad with good (an almost inevitable practice since expert opinion on substances such as chocolate has been so inconsistent).

Mercifully the retro-trend has not as yet gone so far as to revive horrors such as cheese pie or Watneys Red Barrel beer (a brew so weak that it could have been sold under Prohibition), but in the cultures that brought you the pig-in-a-blanket (a North American speciality consisting of a hot dog wrapped in sweet pastry or cabbage-leaves) and the deep-fried Mars Bar (a delicacy adopted by the English from their Scottish neighbours), nothing can be ruled out.

See also **phood**, **retrofuturist**

road warrior

meaning: a traveller on business

Occasionally an ironic nickname, coined by a member of a small coterie, may catch on and cross over into wider usage; a pejorative epithet may even become a label to be worn with a certain amount of pride. One amusing example is the way that the dismissive terms **nerd** and **geek**, although they have never entirely lost their original senses of clumsy, earnest and physically unprepossessing, acquired more complex and positive overtones when their bearers took over Silicon Valley, acquired stock options and even triggered the phenomenon of **geek-chic** in the turn-of-millennium fashion world.

A less well-known but intriguing expression, **road warrior**, may have arisen, logically, in US armed forces usage, referring to drivers and others who were always away from base, but it became famous – or notorious – as part of the rather risible slang of offices in the later 1970s. This was the era which dramatized the often humdrum world of work with terms like **troubleshooting** and **firefighting**, **hired gun** (consultant), **killer bee** (litigation lawyer) and **800lb gorilla** (the heaviest hitter on the scene), culminating in the 1980s' sublimely grandiose **masters of the universe** (financial traders, and no, they weren't being ironic).

Road Warrior was the subtitle to the 1981 movie *Mad Max 2*, and in more recent years both a wrestler, the late Michael Hegsland, and a boxer, Glen Johnson, have adopted it as a *nom de guerre*. The image conjured up is consistent, whether applied to real soldiers, self-styled sports stars or travelling salesmen: a lone hero (more rarely a heroine), constantly on the move, vigilant and action-ready. In 2003 the *Daily Telegraph*'s Paul Bray listed, with no sign of tongue-in-cheek, the road warrior ('executives, consultants, salespeople or agents . . . spend much of their time off-site . . . work anytime, anywhere'), together with the other sub-species of mobile communications user, as defined by communications hardware suppliers. There's the **corridor cruiser**, who is somewhere on company premises, but rarely at his or her desk (some actually have no fixed workstation and may have to **hot-desk** – settling and/or plugging in temporarily at any vacant access-point). The **homelurker**, also known as the **telecommuter**, is, as the name implies, based at home, probably with a remote office, for at least one working day per week. Last comes the so-called **dataraptor**, a category that includes those once called peripatetic: field service engineers, maintenance and construction workers and market researchers who 'capture' information for transmission or return to head office.

Jargon register Buzzwhack.com also distinguishes between its version of corridor cruisers, workers who spend most of their time offline en route to and from meetings, and **corridor warriors**, those who stay online throughout the process with pocket PCs and cellphones. Meanwhile, definitively beyond the workplace and even beyond telecommuting range, the **weekend warriors** come into their own. This Americanism describes workers or retirees with a mainly sedentary existence who metamorphose at weekends with the aid of vigorous exercise, dangerous sports or pastimes such as paintballing and 'wild man' male-bonding rituals.

rollback

meaning: a return to a previous position or version

Rather pompously I thought, environmental lobbyists were calling on the OPEC nations 'to initiate a **rollback** in oil prices'. Rollback is also a technical term in data management where it means reverting to a previous stage in a transaction, and in US media jargon the same word is shorthand for the reversal of previously liberal policies, especially when they concern the freedom of the press.

Just why is the twenty-first-century world of work so besotted with phrasal verbs and compound nouns based on 'roll'? Perhaps it recalls the conveyor belts, the drums, barrels and bales of early industrial processes; perhaps it's evocative of the relentless onward progress of industrialization itself, and of course **Ro-Ro** (roll-on, roll-off) car ferries were a *cause célèbre* until their withdrawal on safety grounds in the early 1990s.

Whatever deep impulses it taps into, this little word has generated a host of jargon terms. As a verb, **roll back** can mean to retreat, or to curb or reduce, as when a government 'rolls back the power of the trades unions' or when the supermarket chain Asda took as a central plank of their advertising campaign their pledge to 'roll back prices for 2006'. **Roll over** is a favourite in financial circles where it has replaced the more banal **carry forward** as in 'US investors refused to roll over the private banks' debts of 116 billion Icelandic krona', although the same phrase can also of course mean both to surrender without a fight and to crush mercilessly. **Roll down** is the rarest of these usages, but it is heard in a business context denoting the reduction of a debt, often a cluster of credit card bills, by paying off the lowest balance first and proceeding progressively.

Still the most prevalent of the roll buzz-terms are the verb **roll out**, which describes a technique in poker, and the noun **rollout** which literally means an extendable (Americans now say extensible) deck in the back of a truck or van. These of course are little-known secondary senses of a term which has become ultra-fashionable in recent years when it signifies releasing or launching a new, usually by implication impressive, product or service. 'We are going to roll out the new operating system in stages' is typical, as would be 'a post-rollout review'. I think this originated in US military usage, probably in the 1960s, when introducing a new weapon or piece of heavy machinery might literally involve rolling it out of a hangar or from under a canopy. In 1973 *Roll Out* was chosen as the title of a now-forgotten military sitcom, an imitation of the movie and television hit *M.A.S.H.* (I'm not sure what the reference was here; possibly to rolling out of bunks in the morning). In 2005 hip-hop star Ludakris released 'Roll Out (My Business)' whose lyrics seem to conflate the idea of emerging threateningly onto the streets in a newly 'rolled-out' luxury car, and the warning to a rival to 'roll out' of the rapper's way.

What is being rolled out these days is typically the latest generation in a series of hi-tech products (in which case a synonym is the equally trendy **iteration**, a word beloved of bosses like British Airways' CEO Willie Walsh, who is equally fond of **iterative process**). Rollout of software consists of mass installation and is governed, we are told, by the principles of **release management**.

More dramatic than rollout is **breakout**, when a product or process suddenly transits from laboratory to market: 2005 was, according to media reports, the **breakout year** for **triple play** electronic packages (see

quadruple play). In a different context, breakout describes a large group of people splitting into smaller teams, so **breakout spaces** are provided at conferences, etc.

sachet marketing

meaning: using miniature product samples to open up new markets

Selling luxury consumables in tiny quantities or units (**sachet marketing** as it's known), when practised in developed economies, is part of the trend towards minimalism and miniaturization, aimed at sophisticated customers who cherish mobility and travel light. **Sachet** itself is a word, like **capsule** and **pod**, that seems to conjure up a snappy, neatly delineated, hygienic and techno-literate take on consumption and lifestyle. In poorer countries it has long been possible to buy cigarettes in ones or twos. And the same principle is used by manufacturers, usually those based in developed economies, to market their new offerings: first comes the distribution of free samples, then single-servings or miniature packages of detergents, cosmetics, foodstuffs, etc. go on sale at prices locals can afford. This **micro-selling**, or **micro-marketing** as it is also known, is a way of luring customers with **gateway products** (q.v.) that entice them towards a broader range of typically full-priced offerings.

self-storage

meaning: the hoarding of one's possessions, memories, etc.
– and/or oneself

Self-storage is the sign displayed above warehouses,
container-yards and sheds across the UK, an un-
remarkable phrase, but to some progressives a newly
resonant one. Among the least glamorous of industries (at least at first glance), storage nevertheless outsells
Hollywood (it's worth around $25 billion a year in
the USA alone) and may be playing a more significant role in our culture than we realize. The unstop-
pable drive for acquisition and retention by advanced
consumer societies has created a vast and diverse storage industry, ranging from lock-ups to globalized automated containerization systems. 'Putting your things
in storage', the standard meaning of the term as seen
on those signs, is hardly revolutionary, but now dawn-
ing on consumers are the possibilities for new sorts
of self-storage in the form of personalized hoarding
and individual commemoration.

A 2006 profile of socialite and fashion entrepreneur
Tamara Mellon notes that her cast-off clothes and accessories are being **archived** for her 3-year-old daughter
Minty. That buzzword is more interestingly applied to
the **electronic** or **digital archiving** that now allows us
to upload and download personal memories and memorabilia: even pre-digital texts and images can be scanned
into our data storage systems. The storage process has

been more fashionably dubbed **life-cach(e)ing**, **scrap-booking** or **memorabilizing**, and taps into the desire both for total control over and total knowledge of our environment, and for self-celebration – a sort of DIY **microcelebrity** for all. Another version of life-cacheing is the latest incarnation of vanity- or self-publishing: providers like Blurb will supply the necessary software to turn a **blog** into a **blook** (q.v.) or your old diaries into a glossy autobiography.

Yet another aspect of the same phenomenon is **memorialization**: the striving for an afterlife in the real world or the virtual sphere. This can be catered for online by way of **cyberfunerals** (celebrations planned by the pre-deceased, then enacted on a website) and **Internet shrines**, or more tangibly by **space burials** (ashes are transported by missile for scattering into orbit, into deep space or onto the moon's surface). More tangible still, even potentially tactile, is the notion of **new wave taxidermy**. Preserving pets in this way is nothing new (and stuffed animals as decor have returned as part of a retro country-and-western fad), but with fibreglass reproduction, plastification techniques or a hybrid of the two, inspired by the exhibitions of cadavers by Dr Gunther von Hagens, it may soon not be the family portraits on display, but the family members themselves.

sellionaires

meaning: entrepreneurs who have liquidated their assets

Philip Beresford, compiler of the influential *Sunday Times Rich List*, coined the term **sellionaires** in 2005 to describe the new phenomenon whereby young or youngish entrepreneurs, instead of opting to nurture their creations and turn them into family enterprises, sell what they have built up, releasing millions in cash and allowing them to indulge themselves, two decades earlier in most cases than would have been thought seemly a few years ago. What they indulge in varies from intensive leisure to new startups, often both. High-profile examples of the group would include Martha Lane Fox, co-founder of lastminute.com, one of the success stories of the dot.com bubble, who sold up and went travelling before looking at projects that were quirkier than the usual investment prospects, and for which she could provide **seed money** or act as a business backer or **angel**. Sellionaires may be younger than their **hedgie** (q.v.) contemporaries, to whom they may turn to make their fortunes work harder for them; having joined the ranks of **HNWs** (see **the mass affluent**) at a relatively early age they may **de-locate**, becoming **global nomads** with no permanent domicile (Roman Abramovich, the oil magnate and football club owner, is sometimes counted as a UK sellionaire, although he actually retains Russian residency). Wherever they really spend their time, and whatever the nationality on their passports, these *nouveau* plutocrats are likely to use the City of London to provide the **family office** – a dedicated team of legal and financial professionals – who will enable them to safeguard their assets and pass them on to succeeding generations.

sensory sells

meaning: products or services designed to appeal to more than one human sense

In the 1990s a process began whereby familiar, usually hard-edged objects – household implements, electronic gadgets, cars – were given organic or **zoomorphic** shapes, thus **defamiliarizing** them and making them more attractive to sight and touch. While **blobjects**, as they came to be called, may have become a lasting cliché, designers got to work on appealing to the other senses. **Sensory sells**, alternatively known as **sensory branding**, pay attention to the way things sound and smell as well as to their visual and tactile qualities. Examples include the way a car door softly shuts itself, the **olfactory signature** of a hotel lobby and the Proustian tastes of **retro-recipes** (q.v.). Obviously intended to tap into semi-conscious associations and resonances and to reach its target audience at a deeper level, the notion has been broadened out to become a mainstay of **brand differentiation** and **customer engagement**. A training session on sensory branding advertised by the UK Chartered Institute of Marketing in 2006 promised to 'change your approach from 2D to 5D' by 'a more holistic view of the **customer surround**' and communicating 'across all **customer touchpoints**'. Experts in the field promote what they call **sensory audits** and **sensograms** to help assess which tastes, smells, textures and sounds trigger which responses.

By early 2006 the *Independent* newspaper was reporting the new craze for **sensory clubbing**, whereby radical temperature changes, exotic perfumes and variable surface tensions for dance floors and chill-out areas were being used to augment the sound-and-light repertoire of DJs.

See also **blobitecture**

serendipitous

meaning: by happy coincidence

When informants send in examples of bizwords and buzzwords, they are quite often gleefully quoting a boss whose idiolect (as linguists call an individual's private language) they find hilarious or infuriating, or both. I've made a sporadic survey of CEO-isms and although I can't prove anything statistically, I have identified some of their favourite sayings, prominent among them being the imposing word **serendipitous**.

As Sir Tim Berners-Lee, founder of the Internet,

opined in 2006, 'The whole **value-add** of the Web is serendipitous re-use.' (He meant that data put on the Net for one specific audience was then available for others to happen upon.) Kate Ehrlich of IBM opines that 'company collaborations come about serendipitously . . . in conversation around the coffee machine'. This modish adjective is fairly new and possibly an Americanism, while 'serendipity' was coined by Horace Walpole in 1754, from 'Serendip', an old name for Sri Lanka, the setting of a fairy tale in which princes made fortunate discoveries.

Other samples of multisyllabic boss-speak I have been given include **dichotomous** and **specificity** and the old favourites **iteration** (see **rollback**) and **synergize**. There are homemade maxims such as **the successful child has many parents** or **choice is tragic**, exhortations to **break down the silos** (see **silo mentality**), ironic takes on current catchphrases: **been there . . . still there**. Slogans, especially if they are exhortations, are much disliked by subordinates; examples cited were **do the math!**, **get your ducks in a row!** and **the bottom line is the bottom line is the bottom line!** Further examples nominated by more than one informant were **step-change**, **proactive** (one chief executive has managed to turn this into the verb **proact**), **reimagine** (one of business guru Tom Peter's slogans and the title of his 2004 book), **learning curve** (invariably **steep**), and of course **gameplan**. Chief executives like to invent or disseminate new coinages like **impactful** and **actionable**, in the sense of 'we are able to **action** this'. For the sake of snappiness, 'impact upon' is truncated so that 'speed of rollout will **impact** profits'.

We all have our verbal tics and our own *bêtes noires*. In the 1990s I used to rail at the prevalence of **take on board**; nowadays I am irritated by the rampant overuse of **add value** and **high-end**. It's easier to pick up on other people's speech oddities than one's own. I don't think I've ever used 'serendipitous' except ironically, but I'm told that I keep introducing the word **turbulence** into the conversation for some reason.

shoot the puppy

meaning: to dare to do the unthinkable

Desperate measures are needed: 'There's nothing else for it, we're going to have to **shoot the puppy**!' This latest bizword was nominated by correspondent David Murray, who described the context in which the phrase is used: 'Only the true leader has the strength to challenge ideas which are emotionally sensitive . . . and do what nobody else has the heart to do.' So shooting the puppy is all about ultra-macho decision-making, several steps beyond 'grasping the nettle' or 'biting the bullet'. In a corporate climate where **downsizing** has become **capsizing** ('capping' staff numbers until there's no one left to steer the ship) and **rightsizing** has given way to **downclosing**, the idea is often invoked negatively: 'I'm not going to be the one to shoot the puppy; we'd better hire in a consultant to recommend the restructuring.'

Of course the phrase has overtones of irony, satirizing the ruthlessness with which business decisions have to be made, but it started out as a satire on another

institution; the American television game show. Back in the early 1980s US television producer Chuck Barris used to muse about how far the public would be prepared to go if tempted by greed or fame. He fantasized the ultimate television entertainment in which an audience would be presented with a small child holding a puppy and be offered money to shoot the animal live on air. The host would gradually reduce the amount of cash on offer to see who would do it just to appear on television. Barris, incidentally, may have been inspired by an even earlier magazine cover for *National Lampoon*, in which a pistol is held to a puppy's head with the caption, 'Buy this magazine or the dog gets it.' Maybe Barris's black satire doesn't any longer seem so far-fetched, and in a virtual way it has come true. There's now a video game from HappyPuppy.com called *Just Shoot the Thing!* which allows you to take out your frustrations by scanning in your own targets – boss, client, product, etc. – which can then be shot at.

An alternative version of our phrase, **shoot the dog**, was used by singer George Michael as the title of a widely banned anti-Iraq War single attacking George W. Bush and Tony Blair. Michael was probably alluding also to *Wag the Dog* (the movie satirizing war-mongering politicians) and to one of my other favourite clichés, 'Don't shoot the messenger.'

silo mentality

meaning: a compartmentalized view of business operations

In an article promoting Web-based portals as 'the final frontier for Healthcare Organisations' the writer castigates system managers for 'their **silo mentality**'. At a recent conference on international banking an Indian risk-management consultant bemoaned the hopeless complexity that comes from 'using a **locked-in silo approach** as opposed to an enterprise-wide perspective'. Meanwhile a report from the Chartered Management Institute asserts that 'avoiding the creation of **information silos** is the number one **mission-critical priority** for most businesses'.

These silo-based phrases are more than just trendy bizwords, since they do pinpoint a real-world issue, and that's why they have caught on, spreading, as is often the case, from the USA to the rest of the **Anglosphere**, and crossing over from restricted technical usage into general conversation. They are describing the vertically structured organization which has traditionally concentrated on nurturing self-contained departments, **ring-fencing** local finances and building **Chinese walls** or **firewalls** for internal data protection. The result is, as one IT specialist says, **data-rich** but **information-poor** companies, parcelled up into **stand-alone** units, each with its own problems, solutions and information-systems, but mostly unable to talk to each other or to the enterprise as a whole. The image conjured up here is of course of a grain silo used for protective storage, but perhaps also of a missile silo, lurking below the surface and capable of releasing an explosive charge. I haven't yet seen it written down, but the single word silo is now used conversationally as a verb, as in 'we've got to stop **siloing** information and go for more **transparency**'.

The new and alternative approach to managing information is variously described as **holistic**, **stakeholder-based**, **integration-enabling** or simply **horizontal**. Using this sort of terminology can appear pretentious or off-putting to outsiders: the same anti-silo healthcare article proposed solutions that claimed to be **horizontally architected from the ground up** (!) and went on to mention **interactive front-ends, visibility-providing infrastructure, intelligent dynamic middleware, context-aware portlets, bi-directional write-back facilities** and **user-centric frameworks**. But before you scoff, try a simple test. If you try and translate the jargon into standard English, you'll find that there simply isn't another way of expressing these ideas, or if there is, it's clunkingly longwinded.

the silver circle

meaning: second-ranking law firms threatening the top players

There's intense competition among City of London law firms at the best of times, but according to the *Lawyer* magazine's top-100 survey for 2005, a new breed of upstart was snapping at the heels of the established sector leaders. The magazine describes the key players in the increasingly profitable mid-tier as the **silver circle**, as opposed to the **magic circle** that is made up of the top four UK practices and a handful of North American implants. In more gentlemanly days aggressive middle-market contenders, then viewed with snobbish condescension, were known as the **chasing pack**, an image taken from the hunting field. The newer nickname symbolizes a new reality: while magic circle members have been chasing international opportunities, sometimes to the detriment of profits, the silver circle has been cleaning up on the home front.

Within front-runner firms themselves, similar status distinctions have appeared. Success is now measured according to **EPP**, or earnings-per-partner, but those partners are divided into **full equity partners** – the highest earners – and so-called **mezzanine partners** who have to make do (!) with a fixed salary, a bonus and a small share of profits.

The current focus on up-and-coming second-rankers is reflected in another expression, based this time on a confectionery metaphor: for some years the group of city financiers who operate at a level just below the very top have been dubbed the **marzipan layer**. The same term has been applied by London Business School Dean Laura Tyson among others to a layer of skilled professionals inserted into a company just under the existing (and supposedly conservative) senior executives in order to innovate or interface with more progressive outsiders. For the *Financial Times* the marzipan layer denotes non-executive board members who are seen increasingly as playing a vital moderating and mediating role in UK corporate governance.

Like many bizwords, 'silver circle' is an import from the USA, where distinctions of rank and the rituals that accompany them are a national obsession. In return for tax-deductible donations, members of professional associations in North America are inducted into ascending honorary circles, from **bronze** through **silver**, **electrum**, **gold** and **platinum**. For lawyers, rewards may include dinner with leading firms' partners – the crème de la crème, that is, not the marzipan.

sitting next to Nellie

meaning: learning on the job by personal example

Inducting a new recruit, the office manager told her that once the manuals had been read she would do most of her learning by **sitting next to Nellie**. The response was blank incomprehension. Occasionally an old expression surfaces in the conversation, only for its user to realize that no one around them knows what it means. It now sounds very dated in a world more used to concepts like **mentored learning**, **partner learning**, **knowledge-building** and **growing new skill-sets**, but this folksy usage survives in factory, workshop and hospital where 'Nellie' once upon a time conjured up an older, more experienced but probably not very sophisticated co-worker who could show you the ropes: in the USA I believe the equivalent is Joe.

'We'll have to take **Buggins's turn**' is a Britishism of similar vintage, equally mystifying to many youngsters. No one knows where the Dickensian-sounding surname came from, but the phrase is used where a special duty, privilege or promotion is conferred on members of a group one-by-one, regardless of merit.

I've come across other expressions recently which I recognized but which bemused younger acquaintances and some contemporaries, too. When, a year or so ago,

Anne Tergessen wrote an article in *Business Week* entitled 'Don't Let the Taxman Eat Your Lunch', she was using what for the generation of managers working in the 1970s was a well-known cliché. Digby Jones, chairman of the UK CBI (Confederation of British Industry) used it again the other day when he warned London's poorly skilled businesses that 'India wants your lunch and China wants your dinner'. It was commonplace, especially in the car industry, until the mid-80s to hear that the Japanese were 'about to **eat our lunch**', that is, snatch our slice of the market and leave us with an empty plate. I've heard **eat your breakfast** when the implication is that your competitor 'gets up earlier'.

Talking about a probable shakeout in the bloated management consultancy sector, Fiona Radford Parker of Atos Consulting predicts that **commodity** (that is, lower-grade) consultancy will be outsourced and offshored to India, Brazil and China and soon there will be 'maybe just two **soup-to-nuts players**' left in the USA and UK. This food-related metaphor left my colleagues stumped. The full phrase is **from soup to nuts**, meaning 'from A to Z', and dates from around a hundred years ago when these would be the first and last items in a standard five- or six-course meal.

See also **knife-and-fork it**, **whose ox gets gored?**

1661

meaning: a reminder that appearances may be deceptive

The first time I saw the four numbers **1661** written down, in one of those jokey office e-mails, I struggled to find the significance of the date, wondering if it had any connection with references to 1664 in television and cinema commercials by French brewers Kronenbourg (it's their foundation date). There is no connection, unless it's subliminal: 1661 is a misogynist code for a physically ambiguous female, one who looks 16 years old from behind and 61 when seen face-on. However distasteful it may be, the expression exists, even being adopted ironically as the title of a magazine column by UK journalist Christa D'Souza (who, while of a certain age, is not, according to her byline photo, a 1661), and dictionary makers are forced to note it. It is circulating as part of a folk-fad, similar to the jokes about blondes that were heard a few years ago, and about Essex Girls before that.

In the recent version, social types are summed up in acronyms and celebrated by way of chain or viral e-mails as well as in conversation. When I wrote about the slightly older and almost synonymous **BOBFOC** (denoting a woman with a 'body off Baywatch, face off Crimewatch') I was taken to task by the *Spectator* who claimed that such terms were inauthentic and only invented or promoted by lexicographers. It isn't true. BOBFOC probably originated in ribald banter among young males and was disseminated by word of mouth before being picked up by the creatively scurrilous *Viz* comic, which gave it further publicity and added a variant **BOBFOK** ('body of Barbie, face of Ken'). Eventually the expression was adopted by North American speakers, and featured by the UK's high-society *Tatler* magazine. Imported from the USA was **MILF**, a more positive but still disreputable take on the age confusion; it stands for 'mother I'd like to f***'.

Although grotesque, these nicknames only strike a chord because they start from some social reality. In the case of 1661, BOBFOC and MILF it is the culture of makeover, exercise and diet regimes, corrective surgery, the sexualizing of prepubescents and the **baby-boomers**' drive for permanent youthfulness. It's not only misogynists who are forced into a double-take from time to time, and not only women whose appearance is being morphed.

Acronyms continue to flourish in the office: **M&Ms** (the brand name of coated chocolate drops) now refers to conceited or overzealous young recruits who consider themselves automatic 'management material'. **MBAs** are either 'mentally below average' or 'married but available'; **PICNIC** describes a 'problem in chair not in computer'. A troublesome colleague might be dismissed as a **NATO** – 'not a team operator' – or as an **ISA** – 'isn't she awful?'

See also **SPOC**

skiing

meaning: *spending your retirement savings on enjoying yourself*

Having lived through times of austerity in the 1970s, then booms, bubbles and slumps in the 1980s and 1990s, to now see pensions eroded and inheritance tax looming, many **baby-boomers** are opting not to bequeath money to their offspring but to spend it on themselves instead. The trend, known as **skiing**, from 'spending the kids' inheritance', is hotting up thanks to the equity release schemes launched in the UK earlier this year, whereby even those without savings can **draw down** or **free up** – realize part of the value of their homes – and indulge themselves. Providing, that is, that their children aren't part of the **boomerang**

generation who leave the parental home seemingly for good, then move back in and stay put (thus qualifying as **KIPPERS**: 'kids in parental property eroding retirement savings'). The pre-retirement generation, we are told, now contains more and more **LATs** – from 'living apart together' – couples who exist in a stable emotional relationship but keep their finances separate and maintain separate homes. In their early forties are the group defined by Standard Life as 'high-earner, risk-open' individuals or **HEROs**, who are abandoning the corporate rat race to pursue excitement and fulfilment in less orthodox careers. Close behind come what the *Sunday Times* (whose Style Section features two or three of these lifestyle labels a week) refers to as the **big chillers**, in their late thirties and intent on prolonging the relaxed hedonism of their raving/clubbing youth without compromising their secure middle-class jobs. Twenty-somethings divide, we are told, into **extremers** – dangerous sports enthusiasts and would-be **global nomads** – and dithering **yeppies** – 'young experimenting perfection-seekers', who, the Social Issues Research Centre says, are ambitious but confused and won't commit to anything until they know it will bring them lasting happiness, so **browse** jobs, locations and relationships. The puritan in me notes that what all these tribes have in common is the relentless pursuit of self-satisfaction. Whatever happened to idealism and social responsibility?

Whether I decide to ski or not when the time comes,

by the way, may depend on my ethnic origin: according to a survey by the Joseph Rowntree Foundation 52 per cent of Asians and 35 per cent of Afro-Caribbeans favour **budgeting to bequeath** as against only 16 per cent of whites.

See also **flashpackers**

skin partner

meaning: a recruiter of clients for online gaming

In the terminology of online gambling, known more impressively as **remote gaming**, a **skin**, **skin operator** or **skin partner** is an enterprise which, while not having its own platform for gambling activities, attracts potential bettors and passes them on to the platform operator for a cut of the profits. The skin partner may also run so-called **affiliate programmes** whereby already signed-up bettors induce others to open accounts.

The word 'skin' is in linguists' terminology highly *polysemous* and highly *homonymous*, in other words it has multiple senses. This latest piece of gamblers' jargon is actually one of the more mysterious usages. In American slang 'skin' used to mean a dollar, or a card-players' fraud based on collusion (deriving from, respectively, the notion of a pelt as a measure of wealth and the concept of 'fleecing' a victim). It may be the suggestion of complicity or not-quite-honest brokering which inspired this more recent incarnation. Skin partnerships

are not about swindles, but they do belong to a controversial sector of online business, designed to circum-
vent US anti-gaming laws and test the boundaries of
commercial protocol. I'd hazard, without any evidence,
an alternative possible origin for the phrase, in the
notion expressed by 'brothers under the skin', in other
words two superficially different entities with a common
bond or purpose.

Another recent but quite different use of skin is to
describe a graphic masking display or facia which can
be downloaded to enhance and/or change the appearance of a web page.

sleep hygiene

meaning: establishing and maintaining healthy sleep patterns

In 2006 there appeared in London 'Zzed sheds', cubi-
cles located inside Shêd, a private club near the Bank
of England, in which soothing music is played and
into which more affluent city workers (the average
customer was apparently 34 years old and male) could
book for a period of sleep during daylight hours.
Although a novelty in the UK, the concept was not
entirely new; an enterprise called Metro Naps had
been selling sleep, in similar **pods**, to New Yorkers
since 2000, and Tokyo's harassed salarymen have been
checking into **capsule hotels** on an hourly basis since
the end of the 1970s, while with typical bravado the
yuppies of 1980s Wall Street renamed the catnap or

'forty winks' the **power nap** when they inserted it into their accelerated schedule.

Probably coined by analogy with 'dental hygiene', although the analogy barely holds, and to give gravitas to dealing with a condition formerly known as 'insomnia', the phrase **sleep hygiene** is now routinely traded without irony in this context, along with references to something called the **TATT syndrome** – from 'tired all the time' – and to the **sleep economy** and the **sleep market** and even to the journalese slogan 'sleep is the new sex'.

Of course, in the overheated societies of late capitalism, sleep, like leisure, and time itself, becomes both a tantalizingly elusive objective and, as part of the burgeoning **health and wellness** sector, a potentially valuable commodity. Bestsellers like Dr Stanley Coren's *The Sleep Thieves* capitalize on the new lifestyle obsessions; there is a National Sleep Foundation and a British Sleep Association, and **sleep solutions** and **rest management** are on offer from a host of qualified and unqualified private-sector providers. Techniques promoted are many and varied: according to one website, regular didgeridoo playing is a great help. The British Travelodge hotel chain has its own Sleep Manager who is probably tired (sorry!) by now of being told he has landed a dream job.

See also **social jet lag**

the slow movement

meaning: a campaign of resistance against a high-speed society

It was Douglas Coupland, writer and spokesperson for the **Generation X** slackers of the early 1990s, who popularized the notion of an **accelerated culture** and a reaction against it, but the metaphor dates back to the rat race of the 1950s and 1960s. The first fightback took the form of Carlo Petrini's **Slow Food** association which has campaigned since 1986 against the globalizing spread of fast food and promotes ten-course meals eaten over two or more hours. Another key instance of organized resistance occurred in 1999 when four Italian cities banded together and labelled themselves **Città Slow**, publishing environmental guidelines now followed by at least 100 other towns in ten countries. In the UK the *Idler* magazine touted a facetious version of the philosophy, while in Austria more recently the *Verein zur Verzögerung der Zeit* ('Society for the Deceleration of Time') has encouraged urban pedestrians to practise slowing down by walking a mechanical turtle. In the USA a national 'Take Back Your Time' initiative has been organized. All these assaults on **time-poverty** and **over-scheduling** were celebrated by the 2004 book *In Praise of Slowness* by journalist Carl Honoré.

Notwithstanding all this, the cult of speed persists, as witness the UK company Dot Mobile which in 2005 began texting compressed versions of literature classics – books condensed into three or four sentences of text messaging abbreviations – to students revising for exams.

smirting

meaning: flirting while smoking

Among the various new trends in bonding, from speed-dating to **cuddle parties** (q.v.), one stands out in terms of spontaneity and unforcedness. The term describes the new phenomenon resulting from the imposition of smoke-free zones, first in almost all offices, then in places of refreshment and entertainment, added to which is the effect of workplace stress and ennui or **social jet lag** (q.v.). The outcast smokers congregate in lonely groups: forced together, they tend not only to spark up and puff, but to **smirt** – a blend of smoke and flirt. The coinage probably comes from Ireland, the first EU country to impose a total ban on smoking in places of public refreshment in 2004, although it is heard in the USA and UK too.

Once the opening icebreakers ('What do you think of this smoking ban, then?' followed by 'Can you crash me a cig?' seem to be favourites) have been engaged in, it's down to some intensive – to use the current slang – **chirpsing** (flirtatious small talk), **lumbering** (attempted seduction) and possibly **copping off** (successfully making an assignation).

snooze factor

meaning: *the degree of boredom induced by a presentation*

Those forced for professional reasons to attend multiple presentations have developed a facetious system for grading them numerically. The usual system awards points from one to five or one to ten ('This morning was easily **snooze factor** 9') according to how tedious the talk is or how uninspiring the speaker. Other wits posit a more complex sliding scale of dullness moving from **yawn factor** through snooze factor to the ultimate **coma factor**. The particular phrase 'snooze factor', which may originally have been coined by the magazine *Variety* or one of its imitators for movie reviews, is now a standard term of disparagement applied to television programmes and video games, as well as to documents, meetings, etc. in the workplace.

Indications that the boredom threshold has been breached can also be expressed by the adjectives **ho-hum** (mimicking the sound of a yawn or sigh) and, in the UK and Australia, **diddly-dum**, while a meeting may involve 'an inordinate amount of **blah**'. 'A **CRAFT** presentation' in current UK office slang refers not so much to the skills of the presenter but to the reaction of an audience member who 'can't remember a frigging thing', while an alternative take is that of a correspondent from San Francisco who says she suffers from a syndrome called **CRS** – 'can't remember s***t'. I've found myself expressing more generalized frustration or disapproval by imitating the character of Owl in the Disney *Winnie the Pooh* series: 'On a scale of one to ten, it doesn't look good.'

Snooze factor, by the way, need not always have negative connotations. Some manufacturers of beds, sleeping bags and headrests have adopted it, again using a sliding scale, as a measure of degree of comfort.

social jet lag

meaning: a work-related physical malaise

A study recently carried out at Ludwig Maximilians University in Munich concluded that half of all European workers suffer from a permanent form of jet lag because of long hours and lack of daylight. Those seated in front of desktop terminals are the most likely to succumb to the condition. The research divided subjects into two main **chronotypes**, depending on how they set their personal schedules. **Larks** go to bed early, while **night owls** (no marks for linguistic innovation here, but to be fair the terms have to serve in, that is, be easily translatable into, a number of languages apart from English) prefer to stay up late. If one's own diurnal preference isn't matched by one's working hours, the result is a biological clock that is permanently out of sync. The research found that women tend to be larkier than men, and that these biases can change with age.

The findings from other contemporary research may appear at first sight contradictory: shift-workers are found to suffer from the most work-related sickness, while casual and part-time workers suffer lower stress levels than those in full-time jobs. What seems to be significant is how work is scheduled; when in the day – or night – it takes place and how it is handled. The various ways of working – **monotasking**, **multitasking** or what has come to be known as **CPA** or continuous partial attention (doing a little more than one thing rather absently, typical of many of us most of the time) – are all unhealthy to an extent. The concept of chronotypes or the degree of **morningness** or **eveningness** (to use their technical terms) that each person exhibits was highlighted in a study by the University of Surrey in 2004 and has been picked up subsequently by time-and-motion specialists and coaches applying it to sports performance. Yet another survey carried out for the stationery giant Esselte found that labour-saving gadgets, particularly IT-related, actually increased workloads (by 150 million hours per day across Europe apparently) and workplace stress considerably.

A corollary of **social jet lag** is that sufferers turn to stimulants to keep them going, and not only in the workplace, in the form mainly of coffee and cigarettes (see **smirting**), either: according to recent health studies up to five million Britons may be **self-medicating**, predominantly with alcohol but also with cannabis, cocaine and illicitly obtained prescription drugs, against low-level depression.

See also **sleep hygiene**

the solo pound

meaning: spending by single people

By 2021 35 per cent of UK citizens will be living alone, according to a study by the Institute for Public Policy Research and the food enterprise Unilever. Their report stresses the importance of new spending patterns and consumer preferences on the part of these **singletons**, who are not all the relatively successful **aspirationals** personified in book and movie by the fictional Bridget Jones, but in many cases struggle to survive without a family infrastructure and are forced to practice **thrift economics**. The report, entitled *Home Alone*, revealed that **single households** were often the result of a conscious choice to seek independence despite the extra costs; emotional reactions to solo living vary, with women finding it empowering whereas many men experience loneliness. The key findings are hardly astonishing: poorer individuals are less likely to choose this option and, if alone, likely to undergo greater hardship. Singletons spend more than average on alcohol, tobacco, gas and electricity as well as slimming aids, herbal tea and Marmite; predictably they prefer to buy in smaller packages, a message for manufacturers of **fcmgs** (fast-moving consumer goods).

In the days of rampant inflation **the pound in your pocket** was a political catchphrase designed to create panic at the erosion of purchasing power. Since the early 1990s we have been given more positive messages

attached to the notions of the **pink pound** (the unprecedented economic potential of the gay community) and
the **grey pound** (the financial power of **third-agers**,
empty-nesters, **silver surfers** and **grey panthers**).

See also **rejuvenile**

splog

meaning: a profiteering Internet site masquerading as a blog

The great tradition of the Internet is that each technological advance is almost instantly matched by an
associated scam, and so it was in 2005. Cybertrickery
proliferated at such a rate that new buzzwords were
coined in anticipation of crimes that may not yet have
been committed. Cirond Corp warned against
WiPhishing, the setting up by hackers of a wireless
AP (access point) designed to attract enabled laptops
prior to disabling or penetrating them (sometimes in
the form of an **evil twin**, a cloned or disguised
hotspot). AirMagnet highlighted **phlooding**, sabo-
tage, typically in the form of a **DoS** (denial of service to users) **attack** whereby wireless corporate
networks would be overwhelmed by simultaneous
mass logins. Recently, too, the well-established scourge
of **spam** (often in the form of so-called **dictionary
attacks** – automated direct marketing to random
targets) has mutated via **spim**, unsolicited instant
messaging pop-ups, into **spit**, spam received through

Internet telephony or **VoIP** (it stands for voice-over Internet protocol), and **SMS** (text-messaging) **spam** for which nobody seems to have found a catchy acronym.

At the same time **blogging** evolved at high speed from a hobbyist pastime into big business. In retrospect, the original purists' hope of keeping the **blogo-sphere** free from commercialism was always a lost cause, and with an estimated 70,000 blogs created every day, policing them is a daunting prospect. Now we face a new **convergence**, the blending of spamming and blogging in the form of the bogus or junk posting known as the **splog**. Sploggers profit from registering high search engine rankings and by featuring **pay-per-click** commercials for respectable e-commerce providers who are unaware of their activities.

Not all blog-related innovations are negative, though this may depend on your point of view. Some weblogs have established themselves as opinion formers, or opinion forums: independent, partly **user-driven** alternatives to the mainstream print and broadcast media. It was the Iraq conflict which triggered the boom, first in the USA, then in the UK, in regularly updated online journals that debated political as well as social and commercial issues, a vastly more influential medium than old-style **bitch-boards**. The hosts of these sites, many but not all of which have a radical, anti-establishment agenda, have been dubbed the new **commentariat** (a semi-ironic coinage inspired by proletariat and more recent usages such as **professor-iat**, **salariat**).

See also **bitch–fest**

SPOC

meaning: '*single point of contact*'

A quick survey of professionals reveals that of all the varieties of bizword and buzzword the most irritating by far is the acronym. Acronyms – initials or broken syllables used as if they were real words – are especially infuriating when they mutate from nouns into verbs and adjectives, like **SPOC**. What started as a useful term, meaning the place or person to go to for information, is now heard in utterances like, 'Alison will be SPOCing on this project', or 'The tendering process is highly SPOC-dependent'. Some acronyms function as mottos or slogans, like the rueful **BOHICA** (used by menials suffering under tyrannical bosses – it stands for 'bend over, here it comes again'), the irritated e-mail exclamation **NABA** ('not another bloody acronym!'), or **BHAG** which means 'big hairy audacious (substitute 'hairy-arsed' in spoken usage) goal', a rallying cry of motivators. Others in this vein include **JOOTT** (pronounced 'jute') – 'just one of those things' – and **EMG**, for 'empty magnanimous gesture'. A few months back UK dictionary publishers Collins nominated the acronym **MVVD** their jargon term of 2002.

Ever heard of it? I thought not. It stands for 'male vertical volume drinker', apparently not a spoof but a definition of the ideal retail alcohol consumer, a heavy
drinking bar-hopper. Fans claim that acronyms exist to
save time but we all know they are really designed to
mystify and humiliate the uninitiated. If you need help,
try the Internet site www.acronymfinder.com. There you
can key in the initials that are puzzling you and find
out what they stand for, or activate their automatic
buzzphrase and acronym generator which will instantly
spew out a completely new (and completely spurious)
personalized acronym from its vast database (I got **RDC**
– 'responsive digital concept'). MVVD, though, had
them stumped.

Acronyms can be fun but they don't tend to last
despite the over-excited linguists and sociologists who
periodically claim that, for example, net-speak or text
messaging is going to transform the language. In fact
these restricted codes rarely cross over into mainstream
English; **asap** is one of the few exceptions, and when
used as a verb as in 'Can you asap me those figures?'
is easily as annoying as SPOC, isn't it? (**NRN** – no
response necessary.)

staircasing

meaning: acquiring rights in successive stages

Notting Hill Housing Association in London announced
in 2006 that more and more of its tenants were opting

for **staircasing**, a process whereby they can buy a partial stake in the flat or house they are living in, paying rent on the remainder, then up their equity share phase by phase until they own the property outright. Such shared-ownership schemes were a hot topic in the UK's over-heated housing market and what had been an obscure piece of jargon crossed over to become a media buzz-word. Staircasing had been used for years by finance professionals to describe, for example, debt repayments structured in steps; the same expression is employed, especially in New Zealand and Australia, in education to refer to students achieving educational credits level by level at their own pace in a flexible **uplinked quali-fication** system. In a quite different context, in refer-ring to computing bitmap displays, staircasing, also known more colloquially as **jaggies**, describes an effect whereby a slope appears to have a jagged edge.

stealth wealth

meaning: riches concealed from public scrutiny

An expression which probably dates back to the 1970s in US usage (it was used then to refer, for example, to rich professionals driving downmarket cars to deflect jealousy), the phrase **stealth wealth** (in linguistic jargon an example of 'reduplication') has more recently been popularized by style journalists such as Dylan Jones and on the Internet where it is used to describe the potential profits from get-rich-quick schemes. In fact, avoiding displays of affluence, dubbed by social commentators **inconspicuous consumption** or **conspicuous austerity**, has long been the practice of the British aristocracy; since 2000 it has been repackaged as the latest consumer fad (or pose) under the banners of **nu-austerity**, **thrifting** or **thrift economics** (marketers also sometimes refer to **resistant consumers** – those over 65 who refuse to engage with new trends and new technologies – as **no-gos** or **thrifters**).

A similar concept to stealth wealth and thrifting is so-called **mattress money**; savings, usually in cash or in the form of valuables not kept in a bank but concealed in domestic surroundings. Far more than a joke, this kind of hidden asset can have serious economic effects, as when the advent of the euro triggered the spending of billions in old currencies (on property deals in particular) which had been stashed away by savers, and by players in the black economy of southern Europe.

Related is **f.o. money** or **f.o. funds**, where the initials stand for a rude phrase and the meaning is money put aside for an eventual escape from drudgery. Quite unrelated is another verbal reduplication: **trash cash**, which refers to revenue from recycling rubbish.

See also **masstige**

stickiness

meaning: a lure or allure

In an online **co-creation** exercise, whereby producers and customers join forces to brainstorm (sorry, **thought-shower** – q.v.) new methods and new products, the discussion revolved around two main issues: how to market the concept of the **virtual child** (q.v.) globally, and how to enlarge the organization's **footprint** (q.v.) in the Far East. One participant observed that the two objectives could be neatly combined: setting up a website featuring the child would introduce not only this cyber-novelty but the whole brand, and the quirky, interactive site 'would be bound to create **stickiness** in China'. The site would thus act like flypaper, or like the sticky web spun by a spider (and this analogy is probably the origin of the expression).

Stickiness was a key concept for those involved in the dot.com boom, or bubble, of the turn of the millennium. Received wisdom then was that constructing a complex website – one which set up an **online community** or **conversation** and involved lengthy **navigation** of its features – would thereby lure and then retain consumers. It looked as if this idea was going to be discredited as **task-oriented** users became annoyed at distractions and the need to navigate, and the loyal hoped-for communities failed to material-ize. Some experts posited an opposite strategy of **slip-periness**, which would clear away the hurdles and hurry the customer through, but the original and obvious insight, that an exciting, involving **web-presence** would entice customers and have a **halo effect** (see **halo model**) on the host's other activities, has survived intact. Although most of the associated jargon (**customer-capture**, **user-behaviour management**, **driving traffic to the site**), has been ditched, stickiness is sometimes employed as a **metric**, using **SLA** (server log-analysis) to gauge the number of visits to a site or the number of minutes per month spent there.

In the **noughties** the sticky metaphor has been extended beyond websites, so that it's now possible to talk of the stickiness of an idea, a concept or a proposal, meaning the likelihood of its being adopted.

stoozing

meaning: profiting from credit card special offers

Cash-strapped Dana T. (not her real name), an MBA student and one of my network of jargon-collectors, says she was recommended to start **stoozing**, and at first didn't know whether to be grateful or offended. An online search quickly enlightened her: to **stooze** is to take up free credit period offers from card providers, then borrow and bank the proceeds (known as your **stooze-pot**) before switching cards as soon as interest kicks in. **Stoozers'** activities are not strictly illegal, as long as no false declarations are involved, but morally dubious at the very least and banks are right now taking steps to curb the practice.

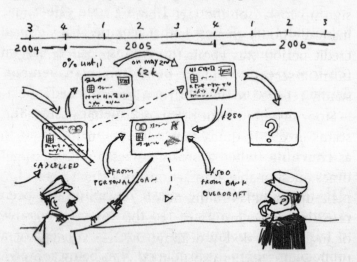

Several acquaintances have asked about the etymology of the word. It originated in the online pseudonym Stooz, used by the otherwise anonymous tipster who first publicized the technique on the UK-based financial website The Motley Fool (www.fool.com) in 2004. Where he or she derives the nickname from is a mystery: my guess is that it's an alteration of a name like Stuart.

Dana declined to stooze and didn't go either for **finessing** cashback offers, also a source of short-term profits from credit cards. As far as I know no one has come up with a slang expression for this 'wheeze' (as its proponents call it).

Stoozing is also known colloquially as **card tarting** (from the camp and slang use of 'tart' to mean anyone

behaving promiscuously), simply **tarting** or sometimes **supertarting**. For a while **rate tarts** could even
sign up for an online **tart alert** which would automatically notify them when their current card's free
credit period was about to expire. In the jargon of
financial service providers, stoozing and tarting is more
staidly referred to as **debt rotation**.

Stoozing reminds me of earlier slang terms for semi-
scams involving quick turnover or turnaround, such
as **churning** (when a broker makes multiple, sometimes questionable, transactions on a client's behalf to
pick up the maximum number of commissions),
nurdling (used in City of London slang for any sort
of high-speed dodgy dealing; the term comes from
tiddlywinks, and is also used in cricket fans' jargon)
and a recent non-financial example from the USA,
swirling, which means enrolling for authorized training or education simultaneously or consecutively in
several different institutions.

sunlighting

*meaning: doing a quite different job on one day of the work-
ing week*

'I just can't imagine going back to a five-day week,'
says Sabine Voss, corporate finance executive from
Monday to Thursday, but boss of her own fabric design
business on Fridays. The bizword that describes this,
sunlighting, also known as **dual jobbing**, defines a

concept whose time has come. Coined of course by analogy with **moonlighting**, the difference is that moonlighting, taking extra jobs outside office hours, and **undertime**, doing something else while supposedly at one's desk, are illicit, whereas sunlighting is negotiated time off to pursue an alternative ambition. The word probably first appeared in the USA in the 1980s, but has come into its own in an environment in which the UK tops the European league for long working hours and the world league for job insecurity. First there was **flexitime**, then **telecommuting** or **distance working**, more drastically **downshifting** or **de-careering** altogether. Now there's no need to give up the day job, just agree with your regular employers that (usually in return for a proportionate pay cut) for one day a week you can follow a quite different career, one that ideally satisfies different needs and develops new talents. The potential benefits to both sides are obvious: no motive for absenteeism (cost to the UK £5 billion per annum) – and hopefully an end, too, to the British scourge of **presenteeism**: putting in long hours because of paranoia or **workaholic** tendencies. Typically, bureaucrats mutate into landscape gardeners, bankers into yoga teachers, engineers into hoteliers, but the new job can be anything you find fulfilling. The shifts of role that are usually involved – from employee to consultant, contractor, employer, sometimes all three – are trendily termed **portfolio working**.

'Time is the new money . . . happiness is the new

success,' trumpeted a recent article in the *Guardian* news-paper, signalling a radical rethink particularly by **alpha females**, high-achievers who were until recently content to be **corporate whores**, as the paper colourfully dubs them, dedicating all their energies to a single job and workplace. The new slogans are 'I'm **reconfiguring**' or 'restoring the **work–life balance**'. This strikes me as healthy if it results in genuine de-stressing, but it's ironic that the twenty-first-century professional is apparently choosing to do it by taking yet another job.

swarm intelligence

meaning: a collective capability

Interested loggers-on to the Internet will often swarm to a new website, and lemmings are imagined to swarm over cliffs, but there are other swarm-related activities which may have far greater significance for technology and culture in the widest sense. The phenomenon whereby unintelligent members of an insect colony can act together to achieve intelligent solutions has fascinated thinkers like Eric Bonabeau, founder of Icosystems, and San Francisco author Kevin Kelly, who was one of the first to apply terms like **swarm logic**, **swarm intelligence** and the **hive mind** to human systems and organizations.

The positive counterpart of the herd instinct, swarm intelligence allows living things (or **vivisystems** in the jargon) to form self-organizing **optimization** networks. Members use trial and error, plus what is now known as **feedback** and **adaptive learning**, to accomplish localized tasks, making decisions and interacting like ants or bees without any awareness of the big picture. Extrapolating this to human organizations suggests a paradigm shift, away from traditional notions of (in Bonabeau's words) **control**, **preprogramming** and **centralization** towards **autonomy**, **emergence and distributedness**. 'Emergence' is itself a key term: it describes the behaviour of a complex whole emerging **bottom-up** from the collective actions of its parts. In the workplace it's hoped that the old hierarchical model of **top-down** decision-making will give way to the socialized enterprise in which individuals will be empowered to react autonomously to each other, just as wireless components in buildings can now correct each other's frequency interferences independently of any controlling power.

Swarm insights and emergence theory obviously key into the well-known view of the earth as a living, self-regulating entity, popularized as the **Gaia hypothesis**, and into the slightly more prosaic idea of the **global brain** which has received attention more recently in business circles. This imagines a global network of empowered consumers instantaneously able to interact, share information and exercise choice, in effect a planet-wide living entity which producers and providers must take account of by such means as **customer co-creation** (involvement by clients and other 'outside' stakeholders in developing new items or systems).

Swarm logic and global intelligence similarly form part of the futuristic visions of self-styled **extropians** and **post-humanists** who posit both global catastrophes and the imminent merging of human beings with machines. The dramatic point at which nanotechnologized post-humans with unthinkably enhanced semi-artificial intelligence do manage to transcend has been called a **singularity** (astrophysics jargon for a unique event such as the big bang) or, more fancifully, the **technorapture** (from the religious idea of cult members having an ecstatic experience *en masse*). One version of transcendence involves leaving the planet altogether, either, if the personality/soul can be uploaded and downloaded, for a virtual destination in cyberspace, or physically to what is sometimes referred to as **Planet B**, a hypothetical new home. Scenarios focus on the possibility of 'greening' a currently inhospitable neighbour like Mars. The same expression is being used by environmentalists with a different slant, inspired by the strategist's warning, 'there is no plan B', in other words there is no fall-back solution or viable alternative. The slogan 'There is No Planet B' first appeared in 2006, popularized if not invented by the British comedian and eco-activist Robert Newman.

See also **embedded intelligence**

sweet spot

meaning: the point at which something becomes viable or profitable, the optimum position

'Solar Computronics Hits The Wireless Market Sweet Spot', runs a trade paper headline. 'We've got to get our pricing in the sweet spot' is the rallying cry for the marketing department's briefing. This once obscure piece of sports jargon increasingly features in US and Pacific Rim biz-speak and in the punning names of dozens of North American companies, from sporting goods outlets through patisseries to honeymoon motels.

Sweet spot figures in the terminology of tennis and golf and in motorcycle tuning, too, but probably originated in baseball. It is the point on the bat (technically called a node or centre of percussion) where vibrations in the wood are neutralized and maximum force can be transferred to the ball. As business jargon the phrase can refer to the threshold at which effort begins to translate into results or more provocatively to a sort of customer **G-spot** – the mythical point where consumer resistance gives way and undreamed-of profits come onstream. Related buzz-terms which are all about successful positioning are **optimization** or **optimalization** while their opposite is conveyed by the modish euphemism **dis-optimal** (in most cases read disastrous). The nearest thing to the opposite of a sweet spot is probably a **pain-point**, a trendy designation of the areas of an organization that are especially vulnerable or troublesome.

Back in the 1970s and 1980s a host of sports expressions crossed over into biz-speak (**ballpark**, **level playing field**, **moving the goalposts**, **heavy-hitter** and the rest). The website www.buzzwhack.com, an excellent source of US buzzwords, comments: 'It's clear that business is dominated by men . . . otherwise there wouldn't be so many testosterone-driven sports terms masquerading as business phrases.' No one knows exactly why a bizword like sweet spot suddenly catches on, nor why some business-as-ballpark Americanisms like this have been adopted by British and Australasian professionals and others haven't. Apart from sweet spot, recent examples of sports slang crossovers are rare. One which hasn't yet reached the UK is the US term **bench**, as in: 'We have bench!', which roughly translates as weight, presence or clout, the image being of a whole team of heavy-hitters or high-scorers on hand to back up the players in the field.

teardown

meaning: dismantling for analysis or cannibalization

One of the trendiest buzzwords of 2006, **teardown** began life as a piece of technical jargon, probably first used by aerospace technicians, then adopted for the IT world. It describes the process whereby a machine is aggressively dismantled: in the case of an obsolescent plane, for instance, some parts are scavenged for re-use. But teardown is also practised by manufacturers who obtain a rival's product, then take it apart to assess its components, or by computer engineers engaged in troubleshooting. This sort of disassembling appeals to both male aggression and the (also typically male) urge to tinker, and practitioners advertise themselves proudly as **teardown artists**. The same process is sometimes termed **reverse engineering**. Both these expressions have come to be used metaphorically and applied to situations in which a plan, a system or a process has to be radically re-examined.

techfluentials

meaning: *new technology's opinion-formers*

The most common technique for forming new words in English, at least those relating to the business world, is no longer to look for a Greek or Latin root, or to borrow from French, but to create what linguists call a 'blend', that is a word made by merging two or more existing terms. One such is **techfluential**, from '(high or new) technology' and 'influential', a buzzword introduced by the Burston-Marsteller consultancy in its April 2005 report on the hi-tech sector. We were already familiar with jargon labels like **opinion-formers** and **early adopters**, and parallel studies by Jupiter Research and Yahoo had given us **influentials** and **social sparks** as alternative designations for these ground-breakers who test, buy and use the latest gadgets and systems. The key characteristic of the **techfluentials** is that they not only innovate and lead by example, but actively promote their choices, communicating their message to a potentially huge constituency.

It is not pundits but **active users** on the Internet who are changing the **national** and **global conversation**. They are not necessarily representative of the millions of **passive users** (those who may respond but only if prompted) or **lurkers** (who never declare themselves at all), but effectively only their views count. In part, then, the techfluentials can be equated with the **blogocracy** – the unofficial **commentariat** made up of the bloggers with the widest reach. But techfluentials also disseminate their opinions and preferences by word of mouth, through traditional publishing outlets (from academic papers to technical manuals) and from their vantage points as **agents of change** within organizations. As Idil Cakim, Burston-Marsteller's Director of Knowledge Development, put it, 'They set the vibe . . . it makes more sense for marketers to **cascade** their messages through this group.'

See also **redhead**, **splog**

teflegate

meaning: to pass the buck effortlessly and/or surreptitiously

A buzzword nominated by correspondent David Loewy, who says he sees examples of it regularly, the verb to **teflegate** is clearly a descendant of the notion of **Teflon manager/management**, itself deriving perhaps from references in the early 1990s to Bill Clinton as the 'Teflon President'. Teflon, the non-stick coating for kitchenware etc., is a trademark of the DuPont corporation and the essence of the phrases is of course that 'nothing sticks to this guy' (or more rarely, 'girl').

David Loewy explains that his term defines 'the way some managers deal with tasks that land on their shoulders'. He goes on to observe that 'frequently **teflegation** is carried out using a **teflegram**, i.e. an e-mail or text message forwarded to the (un)fortunate recipient of the task'. This last may even be tagged with a tell-tale **teflicon**;-). The verb can be intransitive, as in, 'When in doubt, teflegate,' or transitive, as in, 'We're going to have to teflegate this down the chain.' So well established is the concept that sales management-training courses and manuals now have the Teflon manager listed as one of the key representatives of management styles, alongside **micromanager**, **expressive manager**, **hero manager**, **manager-mentor** (these categories courtesy of Steve Martin, author of *Heavy Hitter Selling*).

think outside the box

meaning: *the most irritating buzz-phrase of the decade*

Consistently voted, and confirmed by my informal surveys of colleagues and friends as, the most annoying piece of **noughties** jargon, most people, even those far from the corporate environment, know what **think outside the box** means – trying unconventional approaches rather than orthodoxy – but few are aware of its origins.

There are two theories as to where the expression originated. The most convincing is that it became a catchphrase of management trainers and consultants in the later 1970s, when problem-solving was the methodology *du jour*. 'Experts' liked to use the example of the intelligence test whereby the subject was presented with nine points arranged in a square on a sheet of paper. The object was to join all the points with only four straight lines, drawn without removing pen from paper – something that is impossible unless two lines are extended and intersected outside the square, or 'box'. Soon afterwards the phrase was adopted as an exhortation by some bosses to their underlings, but only really became a universal cliché after 2000.

The simple image of the box was in use from the end of the 1970s in the phrase **black box**, referring to hidden or opaque technologies that enabled remarkable outcomes (not to be confused with a **black bag operation**, a phrase borrowed from the intelligence community to mean the transfer of illicit funds). Nowadays, **it does what it says on the box** (in British usage sometimes **tin** is substituted, even when referring to people: Patrick Barclay in his biography of football manager José Mourinho says several times that the man 'does exactly what it says on the tin'), means that a device performs its obvious function, no more, no less. **Straight from the box** is used to emphasize that a device has **turnkey status**, that is, is ready for immediate use, while **put it/him/her back in its/his/her box** denotes removing a danger or irritation from circulation.

Although this phrase was out ahead in most polls, there were competing annoyances: a survey of Irish office employees in 2005 threw up a hit list of (in order of distaste): **touching base**, **going forward**, **fill your boots**, **shoot the breeze**, think outside the box, **low-hanging fruit**, **helicopter view**, **play hardball**, **blue-sky ideas**, **get your ducks in a row**. Although 'think outside the box' only ranked fifth, 70 per cent of respondents stated that they had been instructed to do it during the last year.

thoughtshower

meaning: to brainstorm

Judging by e-mails from correspondents there was a clear frontrunner as Buzzword of the Year for 2004. 'At a recent **soft-skills-enhancement** training session,' wrote property sales consultant Lucy Childs, 'we were told to get together in a group and **thoughtshower**.' Robert Goodman added that 'I haven't come across any new terms of political correctness for some time, but this one certainly makes up for that. It's completely laughable.'

The word first became notorious in May 2004 when it was reported that the BBC were insisting on its use in internal training courses. **Brainstorm** is henceforth banned, a facilitator explained, 'because it's offensive to those suffering from epilepsy'. Used as a verb since at least the 1970s, 'brainstorm' may have – briefly at the end of the nineteenth century – referred to a mental seizure, but since then has invariably been used metaphorically rather than medically, and never as far as I know to mock or discriminate. **Blamestorming** was a jokey variation dating from the 1990s, describing supposedly cathartic corporate guilt-fests in which colleagues publicly denounced one another.

No one seems to have anything good to say about 'thoughtshower' except for a couple of correspondents who were proud that it was for once British rather than North American in origin. This appears to be true, although the earliest example I can find dates from an international conference on education held in Bruges, Belgium, in February 2001.

Other buzzwords of 2004 which were nominated by several correspondents included **dormantizing**, the term used by the Woolwich to describe how it had closed customers' accounts that were being under-used – without the account-holders' knowledge – and **sunset clauses**, a similar concept whereby conditions sneaked into the small print of contracts state that the contract will lapse automatically unless it is renewed at regular intervals (a concession, incidentally, that Tony Blair wrote, under that name, into his much-contested terrorism legislation at the end of 2005).

'Thoughtshower' and 'dormantize' were both cited as examples of the language-mangling that jargon often indulges in, turning familiar nouns and adjectives into new and outlandish verbs. Another example of this which offended several people was a noun-turned-verb-turned-adjective: **ovenable**, a label invented for frozen-food packaging by retailers like Marks and Spencer. Nokia's new slogan, **connectivity**, on the other hand, was on the whole approved of as having dynamic, innovative overtones.

3BL

meaning: a holistic measure of company performance

Given the growing importance of **ethical consumerism** and **corporate social responsibility** (**CSR**, q.v.), the business world has been searching for ways to quantify the hitherto intangible notions of social and environmental impact and to build them into the balance sheet. The motives for doing this are both to demonstrate to the wider world that the organization has earned the right to operate in society, and to evaluate the financial consequences for its own **stakeholders** (investors, workers, customers). The most attractive solution on offer seems to be what is called the **triple bottom line**, **3BL** or **3bl** for short. This is a new paradigm that aims to move managers beyond thinking only in terms of the familiar financial bottom line (literally, the figures at the end of a financial statement, metaphorically the unarguable essence of a situation) and add in a **social bottom line** and an **environmental bottom line** when assessing performance. Proponents talk about **3BL investment** strategies and **3BL management**, but the crucial aspect is **3BL accounting** or **reporting**, which requires **metrics** or **benchmarks** to make these aspects graspable. In the same way that **KBD**, or key business drivers, and **KPI**, key performance indicators, can now be given mathematical values for the purposes of modelling, so environmental and social **scenarios** (of **ecological loss** or **deficit**, **social risk**, etc.) can be fed into a **matrix** to yield measurable results.

Not everyone accepts the validity of 3BL or other versions of **sustainability accounting**; hard-line free-marketers point out that they distract businesses from their **core competencies**, are likely to unbalance costs and won't necessarily key into private consumers' or nations' self-interest. Some progressives consider that accountability can be better enforced by more targeted and context-specific methods.

TMI

meaning: more information than is required

Informant Patrick Clarke has come up with a new acronym, **MITIN**, pronounced 'my tin', for an innovation he is recommending. The letters stand for 'more information than I need', and he's proposing that that well-known entity **File 13** (aka the waste paper bin) be brought into the electronic age, by way of a website at which all unwanted or redundant information can be dumped. This would be more fun than a delete button, he says, and all the superfluous data would be there on display as a lesson.

Clarke's acronym relates to an existing usage, **TMI** (too much information), the shorthand e-mail putdown used by grumpy programmers, then picked up as (spoken as well as written) US teen slang and heard particularly in late 1990s sitcoms. The dismissal (**too much input** is a variant version) comes when instructions are too detailed or messages too long-winded, or if the information offered is too personal.

Over-informing is the curse of the knowledge economy (see **infobia**) and the same culture of excess has given rise to **TMC** or 'too much choice' and **TMT**, too much technology. In an editorial in the *Wall Street Journal*, Peggy Noonan comments that 'we live in a time in which people routinely violate their own privacy', volunteering their sexual orientation or marital problems at first meeting, for example; and I remember debating the opposing ideas of **emotional literacy** ('getting in touch with your feelings') and **emotional incontinence** (maudlin gushing) at the time of the outpouring of grief at the death of Princess Diana. I've since picked up the habit of countering embarrassing revelations with the ironic catchphrase **TYFS** or 'thank you for sharing (that) (with us)'.

Research at the University of Queensland into information processing (sometimes trendily labelled **cognitive management**) by human subjects found that too much information for most people was more than four variables within the same decision-making task. Five or more factors in play at the same time exceed the brain's processing capacity and the worker in question will 'drop their mental bundle'.

truthiness

meaning: plausibility based on feeling, not fact

Truthiness, posited as a new form of truth, is an interestingly charged term coined by US satirist Stephen Colbert, named word of the year for 2005 by the American Dialect Society, and widely publicized by chatshow host Oprah Winfrey's recantation over her promotion of James Frey's bestselling memoir of addiction, *A Million Little Pieces*, which turned out to be heavily fictionalized. Colbert defined truthiness as 'a good story, one that feels right, but doesn't correspond to reality'. The examples he cited were George W. Bush's appointment of Harriet Miers to the US Supreme Court on the grounds that he 'knew her heart', and the invasion of Iraq, on the grounds that, as Colbert had it, 'it felt right'.

Truthiness is a close relation of the contemporary Americanism **glurge** (heartrending but ambivalent anecdotes – see **glomage**), and harks back to the slogan used forty years ago by the right-wing senator Barry Goldwater's supporters, 'In your heart you know he's right.' (Liberals coined the counter-slogan, 'In your guts, you know he's nuts.') It also recalls the unease some felt and still feel about **faction**, the blend of the documentary and the novelistic, pioneered by Truman Capote and Norman Mailer in the 1960s, sometimes called **drama documentary** or **news fiction**, and the concepts embodied by **factoid**, an unprovable statement (the urban legend that more people have been killed by donkeys than by aircraft crashes is one such) which has gained unquestioning acceptance by virtue of repetition.

It's easy to become confused by these and other legitimate, albeit rarely used, words like **facticity** and **factualness** (the quality of being true), which are synonyms, and **factitious**, which looks similar but is only distantly related and means artificial; and then there's **actuality** which in broadcasting jargon doesn't denote what is actual or true, but is a translation from French *actualités* (news or current events) and means something topical recorded at the time and on the spot.

Truthiness, although not under that name, exists or is employed everywhere, but seems to resonate particularly with a tendency in the USA to appeal to emotion over objectivity in making political or social judgements, so that old-fashioned wishful thinking or wish-fulfilment can supplant reasoned argument. The politicians and bureaucrats who resort to truthiness don't acknowledge the fact and have no word of their own to describe it, but, at least in the UK, there is a related expression in official usage: the **body of fact** is how experts refer to 'what the public thinks it knows' – for example, widely accepted though not necessarily well-informed opinions on organic produce, GM foods or nuclear power.

Truthiness, by the way, is a modern coinage by one individual, but the adjective 'truthy', apparently an unambiguous synonym for the standard 'true' or 'truthful', actually existed in British dialect and is still found in some dictionaries.

turbochoad

meaning: an extremely irritating and/or unfortunate individual

'Pillowy drama-nerd indie or Crampsian swamp-gurgle?' 'Too low-pro, he's lately lax-murdered the odd mixtape freestyle and famously thug lullaby'd "La daa da".' These to most outsiders impenetrable observations are typical of the cyberslang traded among fans and other militant obessives on the Web, written in a sub-dialect of youth and media slang dubbed **blog-lish** by London journalist Lynsey Hanley, who also talks of 'translating from the Geek'. In fact they are nearly impossible to translate unless you are intimate with the **micro-scenes** they revolve around and hip to the allusions, the special blend of semi-technical **muso** jargon and adolescent argot, and the obtuse, hectoring style. Among the key items in these examples are 'Crampsian' (sometimes rendered as 'Crampsesque') which means evocative of the Psychobilly rock played in the 1980s by the cartoon-ghoulish US band The Cramps, and 'thug' (it can be a noun, adjective, or verb), here used approvingly to denote bravura, swagger and an appealing brutality. Sasha Frere-Jones, whose day job is music critic of the august *New Yorker* magazine, lapses expansively into 'unfiltered' blog-lish on his influential website, damning Burt Bacharach as 'dire bougie [from 'bourgeois'] make-out piffle' and a certain purveyor of smooth jazz as 'a **turbochoad** who speaks in marketing pre-cum' (don't ask).

The prefix turbo- (inspired of course by 'turbocharged') dates from the 1990s and was used in teenage slang in expressions such as '(to have a) turbocrush on someone'. **Choad** or **chode** is a rude North American word particularly beloved of Canadians, but used by connoisseurs of slang at least since the mid-1960s across the **Anglosphere** and, since the late 1990s, as a sort of icon of belonging for hackers, slackers, geeks and bloggers engaged in online banter. It literally refers to the male member, but, like many of its synonyms, by extension (sorry!) can denote a fool or villain; as an adjective it means truly awful. The precise etymology is a challenge for linguists: heated online debates have considered subcontinental Indian and Native American origins, but there is no actual supporting evidence for either. What is certain is that 'choad' is a word its users like to relish, to play with and elaborate upon (coming up – sorry again – with **choad-lick**, **choad-wad**, **choadsmoker** and **choadmonger**, for example), and, since so much online chat involves insults, to use a great deal.

unbanked

meaning: *(those) without the benefit of banking facilities*

We first had the snappier substitution of **jobless** for unemployed, then the supposedly more dignified

unwaged was introduced. More recently some in the public sector have preferred the term **workless(ness)** as being an abstraction with no overtones of blame or failure. These are of course not innocent words but terms loaded with associations: if used in place of more hurtful expressions they are euphemisms (from Greek *euphemos*, 'sounding good'); when used for devious purposes some have called them 'weasel-words'. Some new words are coined not to replace an existing term but to fill a void in the language – what linguists refer to as a 'lexical gap'. When in the early **noughties** US credit card companies tried to extend their services even further, to the segment of the population (22 million of them) with little income, no savings or minimal contact with financial institutions, they came up with the neologisms **unbanked** (only ever used before in the sense of not-yet-banked cash/proceeds/profits) and **underbanked** to describe their targets.

In early 2006 the UK adopted the term in campaigns (billed as '**outreach** to the unbanked') promoting so-called **stored-value cards** – debit cards issued by employers, unions, agencies etc – to a **financially underserved customer base** of the young or the marginal (migrants for example) or the simply **bank-averse**, who according to US research account for the majority.

vanillacide

meaning: how radical concepts are destroyed by too much consultation

I first heard this bizword when I shared a microphone recently with a Californian, Steve Manning. The occasion was a BBC radio discussion of the ongoing craze for **re-branding** companies, something Steve, boss of the US naming agency Igor (as in the doctor's assistant in Mel Brooks' *Young Frankenstein*, by the way), is an expert on. **Vanillacide** is an updated version of the old notions of **death-by-committee** or the **death-of-a-thousand-cuts** by which new and creative proposals are diluted and diluted until they become universally acceptable – and wholly unoriginal.

Agencies like Igor are paid big money to pitch new names to companies looking for a change of image. In Steve's own words, 'The best way to get 100 people to sign off on a name is to come up with something that has no meaning and offends no one – the surest pathway to vanillacide.' This example of what used to be called a 'portmanteau word', known to linguists as a 'blend', is formed by bolting together the suffix of 'suicide' (if you think of it as self-destruction) or 'homicide' (if you think it's a crime) and the slang use of 'vanilla' meaning insipid, conformist or harmless which probably began with the gay and feminist movements in the late 1970s.

It's not only progressives like Steve Manning who

fig 1. Carlos makes his presentation to the committee...

fig 2. The committee returns... Vanillacide!!!

perceive a general tendency in global corporate capitalism towards a deadening uniformity. Insider ironists now refer to **blanding** and **blandwidth**. Timid, over-systematized decision-makers are accused scornfully of **blanding out**. Doubts about conformism coincide with growing doubts about the value of using focus groups in order to test out new names, products or services. There is, however, a trick for getting round the play-safe herd instinct displayed by committees or focus groups: it's sometimes referred to as **wild-carding** and consists of giving your client a list containing your favoured suggestions plus at least a couple of ultra-radical, even crazy solutions. In rejecting the most extreme they are likely to 'compromise' on something which is still fairly daring. It might not work for everyone, but the Californian corrective to vanillacide is to junk consensus-seeking and embrace **go-with-the-gut antimethodology**, or, to use another trendy biz-term, **corporate voodoo**.

Viking raids

meaning: Icelandic incursions onto the UK High Street

One of the most spectacular and unexpected eruptions into the UK business world – itself renowned as frenetic, overheated and home to some world-class predators – occurred during 2005 and 2006 in the form of so-called **Viking raids**. The Vikings in question this time were all from the same Norse settlement, Iceland, whence flamboyant entrepreneur Jon Asgeir Johannessen, delayed only briefly by successfully fighting corruption charges at home, used his vehicle Baugur to buy up swathes of the UK High Street, including appropriately the Iceland food supermarket chain, while fellow Icelanders FL went in and out of low-cost airline EasyJet at great profit, Dagsbrun bought the important British magazine printer

Wyndeham and fashion chain MK One went Icelandic for £55 million.

The drama of these sorties from outside the EU brings back memories, not only of the original eighth-century raids by Norse seafarers into the open, well-regulated, lucrative markets of the south, but of the merger-and-acquisition wars of the 1970s and the imagery which accompanied them: **dawn raids**, **white knights** and **poison pills** – and perhaps raises the spectre of **danegeld**, a term used then to describe attempts to bribe a predator into staying away.

What had taken place in Iceland itself (population 300,000) was what the Danish Danske Bank called 'a stunning expansion of debt, leverage and risk-taking with few precedents anywhere in the world'. The Icelandic Central Bank's cautious approach to damping down the geyser-like eruptions of its business sector were derided in London as **baby steps**, the results (to somewhat deflate the metaphor) as an unsustainable **bubble**. By Easter 2006 the *Daily Telegraph*'s Ambrose Evans-Pritchard was reporting a sudden reversal in the so-called **carry trade** – the flow of **hot money** funds from subdued or **soft-spot** economies like Switzerland and Japan to higher risk and higher yield environments, of which Iceland had been a prime example.

virtual child

meaning: a daughter or son who exists only electronically

The notion of adopting an unreal child probably began with the Cabbage Patch dolls of the 1980s, but these were aimed at children themselves. The first electronic beings that required nurturing were the pocket-sized cute (or cringemakingly kitsch, depending upon your point of view) Tamagotchis of the 1990s, primarily marketed to children, but cheerfully embraced by some who were, chronologically speaking, adult. Imaginary children had also been used with adolescents in the 1990s in therapy and educational sessions to help teach parenting skills. A child would be created, named and entrusted to its carer (sometimes in the form of a doll) and its care regime would be monitored by experts.

In 2004 the concept was adapted for the **IM** (instant-messaging) **generation** by Media Republic with their 'virtual love child' called Eccky, developed in the Netherlands and relaunched with much fanfare and an eye on the US market in 2006. Strangers can **partner up** by messaging (flirting with potential **co-parents** if they wish before committing) and fill in a questionnaire which establishes their 'genetic' characteristics, whereupon, after a fee (currently 1.5 euros) has been paid, a virtual baby is delivered. The 'parents' are then responsible for its upbringing, purchasing credits to feed and clothe it, until its majority is reached

– a process which takes months rather than real-time years.

The virtual child is both an **avatar**, a spun-off conceptual entity, and a **chatbot**, a robot programmed to respond convincingly to a whole host of prompts in online conversation. Eccky has a repertoire of 45,000 answers on 3,500 different topics.

The idea does perhaps induce some queasiness, given its distant relationship to adoptions that seem like purchases and to **cyber-impersonators** and **Internet shapeshifters**, adults who pose online as children for fetishistic or more sinister purposes, and vice versa.

Meanwhile the messy business of keeping what are now known politically correctly as **animal companions**, or more fancifully as **furkids** – formerly, and supposedly demeaningly, termed 'pets' – was revolutionized by the introduction of **neopets**. Seventy million people worldwide have apparently become owners of these virtual animals, which resemble miniaturized cartoon mutations of kittens, piglets, chicks, etc.

vocation vacation

meaning: a temporary change of career

The only alternatives to a traditional seaside chill-out used to be a busman's holiday (not very politically correct, presumably 'transport operative' should be substituted) or a working holiday – something like shovelling hay on a farm or fruit-picking. In the twenty-first century the concepts of work and leisure are becoming blurred in much more interesting ways. Professionals, especially the thirty-something generation, are interested in a more **holistic work–life balance**, in **fusion** (a contender for Buzzword of the Year in 2003 across many different sectors), and especially in **cross-shifting**, that is, introducing more varied tempos and different philosophies into one integrated way of life. Cross-shifting means that you don't have to **downshift** once and for all: no need to abandon your high-pressure, quintessentially urban capitalist job. Instead you leaven your lifestyle with some time spent in radically different working modes and on less materialistic, more human-scale pursuits. New

Age, though, is old hat, and the herbalism, healing and shamanic drumming of a few years ago have been replaced for the hyper-cool (who refer to themselves as **New Authentics**) by, for example, exploring the folk culture of the newly fashionable Eastern European **accession states**.

Not surprisingly, it's in the USA that these innovations have first been put together (by **wantrepreneurs**) into a marketable form and given a new label. By taking a **vocation vacation**, harassed **cubicle monkeys** can escape their terminals and offices temporarily to **test-drive** an alternative occupation. Again, it's not surprising that the opt-outs are nearly all in the same direction; banker becomes baker, corporate headhunter becomes wine-maker, IT manager becomes racehorse-trainer. Rural cheesemakers don't seem to be lining up to enlist as financial traders. The vocational taster idea isn't entirely new: for some time the Disney Institute in Orlando, Florida, has offered similar learning vacations on its own campus, but these lack the allure of a total **lifeswap**.

Only time will tell if what might be just dilettantism (most of these vacations only last a matter of days) becomes something more meaningful. I'm left with the uneasy feeling, though, that vocation vacations are less an enriching extension of personal repertoires than the victims of a work-obsessed culture finding yet another excuse to work-obsess.

wall acne

meaning: unsightly electronic connections

Sam Sethi, CEO of Abrocour, tipped me off about the problem of **wall acne**, which is a scourge his company is keen to eradicate. Abrocour supply housing developers with the **black goods** (IT fixtures and fittings) that go into new homes. The new media and broadband package in question is a form of **triple play** (see **quadruple play**) and the custom now is for these to be **pre-installed** and included in the house price.

With today's universal embracing of modernist interiors, at least in show homes, it isn't only **luxorexics** (q.v.) who refuse to tolerate any ugly protuberances and trailing electronic wires. Wall acne, in Sethi's words 'the mess created by wall sockets and CAT5 cabling', is the design equivalent of fashion's **VPL** (visible pantie-line), that terrible pre-thong solecism. The environment must be totally wireless, with devices like television sets no longer disguised as mahogany cocktail cabinets, but set (**alcoved, recessed** or **embedded** is trendier) into walls, along with slimline fishtanks and other **high-end** items du jour. I have even heard a devotee of this sort of quasi-minimalism refer to a **de-decor'd** ambience – but meanwhile in quite different circles **maximalism** (q.v.) holds its own.

who moved my cheese?

meaning: the lament of the disoriented victim

Catchphrases adopted from popular literature are actually quite rare in the business world, although Scott Adams's daily cartoon strip *Dilbert*, about the travails of the eponymous white-collar worker, gave office slang the term **Dilberted**, meaning suffering under oppressive micromanagement. Though the character appeared as long ago as 1989, the name still resonates: as management guru Tom Peters pronounced in 2006, 'I'm on a mission to drive Dilbertian Cynicism and Cubicle Slavery and Terminal Insipidity out of the Workplace.'

Another popular icon, Barney the purple dinosaur, inspired in the late 1990s the expression **Barneyware**, denoting outdated software or hardware. One further example is still spreading across the **Anglosphere** nearly a decade after its appearance, often in the form of an ironic enquiry, such as one I heard the other day in a training simulation exercise, 'Did someone move your cheese?', directed at a hapless or disoriented colleague. The phrase is an adaptation of *Who Moved My Cheese?*, title of the worldwide bestseller published by Spencer Johnson MD in 1998. Unsnappily but explicitly subtitled *An Amazing Way to Deal with Change in Your Work and Your Life*, this was a manual or self-help guide to coping with **change** (then the most prevalent business buzzword around), presented in the form of a childish fable or parable.

The simple, harsh lesson to be learned was that when the working environment changes around them, the unprepared may be stranded. In the book this is illustrated by two mice negotiating a maze in search of cheese which has been moved, one benefiting from insights such as 'change happens' and 'adapt to change quickly', the other left behind. Perhaps not surprisingly, the profundity of the work has been questioned, but its global sales figures are beyond dispute.

whose ox gets gored?

meaning: *who stands to lose (if we adopt this plan)?*

There's a kind of language that's essential to the business world, but which is neither slang nor jargon nor acronym. I'm talking about the picturesque, folksy sayings that English-speaking professionals use to spice up their meetings round the table and the private networking that goes on afterwards.

But whose Ox gets gored?

The Signing of the Magna Carta

One US executive, Robert L. Sharpe, put together a list of the expressions he uses after realizing that the Japanese partners he was negotiating with were left completely baffled by them (access it at RobertLSharpe@ pacificovertures.com). What strikes an Aussie or Brit is how many of Sharpe's terms are unfamiliar to us, too. How about, for example, **received over the transom**, **whistling past the graveyard** or **hold feet to fire**? The first means unsolicited or arriving by an unorthodox route – the transom being the latched glass hatch above an old-fashioned doorway, through which outsize packages or secret parcels could be passed.

More predictably, 'whistling past the graveyard' is putting a brave face on a disastrous situation or trying desperately to cheer up one's colleagues. 'Hold feet to fire' conjures up a medieval torture and means exerting maximum pressure to get what you want. **Whose ox gets gored?** is also a favourite of Sharpe's. It's reminiscent of an old Chinese proverb or Zen saying, but no one seems to know where it came from originally.

Confusion works both ways. When an Aussie heaves a sigh of relief and announces that 'We're **home and hosed**', he means that the deal is concluded and the loose ends tied up (the original image is of a winning racehorse, safely back in its stable). I was at a meeting the other day where a fellow Brit complained that a petulant client was **throwing his toys out of the pram**: the North Americans present looked blank. The even bigger problems that these colourful phrases pose for non-English speakers may be offset by bringing in an interpreter, but not always. On one famous occasion, China's top translator was lost for words when the US trade team declared: 'The bottom line is the bottom line is the bottom line!' When another negotiator, a Brit this time, told his US colleagues in an aside **don't get your knickers in a twist**, they rightly recognized their own **don't get your panties in a bunch**. Fortunately, someone at the top-level telecom meeting persuaded their hosts' interpreter not to translate this particular piece of dialogue into Arabic.

wipe one's face

meaning: to break even on a deal

'We just about managed to wipe our face on that one,' says racing driver and television broadcaster Jason Plato after trying to re-sell a secondhand Peugeot at a UK car auction. He failed to make the profit he was after, but covered his costs.

The slang of London City brokers shares a good deal of its vocabulary with the slang of used-car dealers and bookies, but the precise origin of **wipe one's face** are obscure. It may well be related to other expressions using the cleaning/water metaphor – to 'clean up', to be 'cleaned out' or 'taken to the cleaners', for instance, date back to gamblers' slang of the early twentieth century and may be much older. The hoary old expression **take a bath** is still employed across the business world to describe suffering a major financial loss, while in the jargon of accountants and bookkeepers the **big bath** is the name of the tactic whereby year-end figures are massaged to make a poor position look even worse. This is usually done by CEOs whose motive is either to scapegoat their predecessor or artificially to boost next year's earnings in order to qualify for a bonus.

Connoisseurs of old-fashioned slang may remember another expression, still used by a few macho CEOs in the USA, which uses almost the same metaphor, but to **clean someone's clock** (clockface,

that is) means to beat them up or defeat them comprehensively.

zombie funds

meaning: moribund investment policies

Jittery UK savers became even more terrified as it emerged
in mid-2005 that ten million of them had £190 million
tied up in **zombie funds**. Less alarmingly known as
silent funds or **closed funds**, these are long-term with-
profit schemes (twenty-five-year endowments, for example) which have been closed to new business. Many of
them are underperforming badly, but are not required
to declare results. Financial journalists revelled in horror-
movie metaphor when reporting the situation: 'the with-
profits graveyard' and 'somnambulist fund managers and
regulators' were typical examples, while the original
image is that of the animated corpse or walking dead
(from Congolese *zumbi*) of Caribbean voodoo legend.

As former skinhead ranter, now journalist, Steven Wells
noted in the *Guardian* newspaper in January 2006, 2005
had been the USA's **year of the zombie**. **Flash mobs**
dressed as zombies invaded city centres; video games,
rock bands and toy manufacturers adopted the image
and more than sixty zombie-related movies were released,
including *Punk Rock Zombie Kung Fu Catfight* and more tellingly,
the ultra-controversial made-for-television *Homecoming*,
in which American soldiers killed in Iraq rise from their
graves to oust a warmongering President.

Lest talk of zombies, vampires and werewolves causes you to reach for your revolver, don't think you can rely on its **silver bullets**. To start off 2006, www.edge.org asked its contributors to name their 'most dangerous ideas'. Mihalyi Csikszentmihalyi, director of the Quality of Life Research Centre at Claremont Graduate University in California, chose the free market, which he described as the political economy's silver bullet, an idea that must take precedence over all others and will create universal peace and prosperity. ('Like all silver bullets,' he said, 'it is an intellectual and political scam, that might benefit some, but ultimately requires the majority to pay for the destruction it causes.' When allowed to reign unchallenged it erodes health, the environment and public safety.)

Free markets tolerate zombie funds and they also create **dead money**, in the case of the US economy a great deal of it. Dead money is available cash that languishes unclaimed and impossible to reinvest, usually in the form of compensation payments to shareholders after successful litigation. Tens of thousands of those eligible for reimbursement fail to file a claim, leaving hundreds of millions of dollars in limbo.

Glossary of Terms Highlighted in the Text

The words are defined as they are used in the book, not as they might be in a standard dictionary

above the parapet: exposed to danger or criticism

abs: an abbreviation for 'abbreviations'

accelerated culture: a bewildering rate of social change

acceptation: a trendy version of 'acceptance'

accessorizing: buying and deploying decorative items

ackers: a slang term for money

acs: an abbreviation for 'acronyms'

action: to put into effect

actionable: potentially do-able

active audience: knowledgeable and responsive consumers

active users: those who interact with media rather than passively consume

actuality: a recording of topical material made on the spot for television or radio

adaptive enterprise: an organization which embraces change

adaptive learning: transforming oneself through experience gained

adaptive technology: electronic devices which react to and learn from their environment

ad-busting: sabotaging or subverting advertisements

add value: to enhance development or potential earnings

adhocracy: improvised decision-making

ad-jamming: sabotaging or subverting advertisements

adrenalin junkies: aficionados of dangerous sports

adultescent: an adult who behaves like an adolescent

advance purchasing: ordering more than you need at the moment

adverposts: advertisements disguised as internet postings by private individuals

aff: an affluent but discreet consumer

affective response: an emotional reaction

affiliate programmes: a system whereby existing clients persuade new clients to sign up

affluential: an affluent and self-aware consumer (who may influence others in their consumer choices)

agents of change: individuals who are able to influence or trigger innovation

aggressive records management: a euphemism for destroying incriminating documents

agility: a flexible and creative approach

agreeance: a trendy version of 'agreement'

AI: artificial intelligence

ailment-specific: designed for sufferers of a particular disorder or condition

air-pocket stock: shares whose price is about to collapse

aisle-rage: a bout of fury by a supermarket shopper

à la car: in one's automobile

alcoved: set into the physical surroundings

alpha: dominant and/or more highly gifted

alpha consumers: discerning, sophisticated purchasers of goods and services

alpha females: dominant female members of a group or groups

alpha-geeks: the most gifted or successful technical specialists

alpha male: a dominant male member of a group

alumnized: a euphemism for dismissed or made redundant

always on: permanently or constantly electronically connected

ambient: physically surrounding

ambit: physical and electronic environment

analog[ue] food: chemically enhanced foodstuffs

angel: a financial backer, usually in the form of a private individual

anger contagion: bad temper or rage which is communicated from person to person

anger management: training or therapy to control one's rage

Anglosphere: the English-speaking areas of the globe

animal companions: a 'politically correct' term for pets

animal friend-bonding: getting close to domesticated animals to alleviate one's stress

annotated objects: physical objects which can scan or be scanned electronically

annotated spaces: physical environments which are electronically sensitive

AP: an access-point for wireless communication

apathize: to become or to render apathetic

apathist: an apathetic person

apps: an abbreviation for 'applications', and sometimes for 'appointments' or 'appraisals'

archived: classified and stored

area denial: devastation of a landscape by military action

Argos bling: cheap, flashy jewellery as worn by chavs

arraying: arranging items in a visual display

articulation: the connection(s) between different disciplines, subjects or ideas

artilects: 'artificial intellects' or electronic 'brains'

asap: an abbreviation for 'as soon as possible'

aspirational: (someone who is) ambitious for more material success

assisted departure: a euphemism for dismissal or redundancy

asynchronous: at a time of one's free choosing (rather than at the time of transmission)

attention bandwidth: capacity for reception and processing of information

attention deficit disorder: an inability to concentrate or process information efficiently

attention economics: the managing of information by a person, group or society

attention fatigue syndrome: a feeling or fear of being overwhelmed by information

authenticity: the quality of being (perceived to be) genuine, natural, true and/or original

autonomy: independence of action

avatar: a virtual entity or 'personality'

aye-aye [Popeye!]: an expression of assent or agreement

baby-boomers: those members of the population born between 1945 and 1965

babyfathers: males who abandon their partner and offspring

baby steps: tentative and/or ineffectual actions

back office bean-counter: a lowly bookkeeper or accounts clerk

BAD: 'bonus anxiety disorder', the fear of not receiving a large enough year-end bonus payment

bad taste food: unsophisticated and/or unappetizing food products or dishes

baller: a seducer

ballpark: the limits within which a negotiation, transaction or calculation is carried out

bamboo ceiling: a barrier to professional advancement by people of oriental origin

bank-averse: hostile to or intimidated by the banking system

bar: slang for £1 or £1 million

barcoding: incorporating machine-readable labels on products and using these to check consumer information

Barneyware: obsolete software or hardware

bash and dash: to undermine confidence in a quoted stock so as to make a quick profit on it

Batna: a 'best alternative to a negotiated agreement'

beacon model: a desirable item which attracts customers to a wider range of products

bears: pessimistic investors

Becks: a nickname for young Jewish females

been there . . . still there: a wry reflection that inertia has set in or that innovation is not possible

beer spa: a resort or facility where clients undergo beer-based therapies

beggar's velvet: fluff collecting on an unswept floor

behaviours: characteristic ways of consuming

be-ins: spontaneous or staged gatherings in public spaces as practised by hippies

bells and whistles: product or service embellishments

bellybuttons: units of measurement of customers in the garment and furniture industries

bench: (potential) strength, power, influence

benchmarks: agreed criteria

benefit of survivorship: the right to receive payment for as long as the recipient is still alive

Benny Hill: rhyming slang for a till or cashbox

betamaxed: superseded or outmoded

betamax technology: technical equipment or processes using an obsolete format

beta-releasing: deliberately employing a dated format or technology

Betties: a slang term for young females

BF: a 'bitch-fit' or bout of anger and/or spite

BHAG: a 'big hairy audacious (or hairy-arsed) goal', very ambitious objective

bi-directional write-back facilities: the capability of communicating with both designers and users within a system

big bath: the alteration of year-end figures to suggest a poorer financial situation

big chillers: hedonistic middle-class 'thirty-somethings'

big pharma: the combined power of US pharmaceutical companies and their government associates

bike rage: a bout of fury occasioned by or during cycling

Billy Bunters: rhyming slang for 'punters' or customers

bingo bling: cheap, flashy jewellery as worn by chavs

biodata: personal employment history

bioengineering: the combining and manipulating of biological and technical processes

bioethics: the discussion of moral and legal issues arising from innovations in biology, medicine and technology

biomorphic architecture: building and design using shapes inspired by animals, plants and other natural forms

bionics: the combining of synthetic and natural substances or systems

BITC: Business in the Community, a UK charity encouraging corporate social responsibility

bitch-boards: online message-boards on which complaints and criticisms can be posted

bitch-fit: a bout of anger and/or spite

bitchin': excellent, impressive, exciting

bitch 'n' swap party: a social gathering at which participants gossip and exchange clothing or accessories

bitch-slap: a sudden and spiteful attack

black bag operation: a covert and/or illicit manoeuvre such as a transfer of funds

BlackBerry rage: a bout of fury occasioned by use of a handheld communication device such as a BlackBerry

black box: opaque, mysterious, hidden

black goods: high-tech electronic equipment and installations

blah: empty or boring verbiage

blamestorming: (a session involving) mutual and/or collective criticism

blanding: behaving in an uninspired, conformist manner

blanding out: opting for timid, uninspired decision-making

blandwidth: a working environment characterized by timidity and uniformity

blang: a more recent and trendy version of 'bling'

BLC: 'bag-lady chic', deliberate or unintentional scruffiness

bleaders: readers of blogs

blended learning: teaching and learning approaches which integrate e-mail and Internet

bling: cheap flashy jewellery and the culture of display characteristic of hip-hop and chavs

blingage: a more recent version of the slang term 'bling'

bloatation: stockmarket flotation accompanied by excessive spending and display

blobbiness: curvilinear and/or globular form

blobists: proponents or devotees of rounded, globular or organic design forms

blobjects: curvilinear or globular objects

blobmeisters: proponents of 'blobi-tecture'

blobs: idle, inert employees

blog: a weblog

blogagery: graphics and images used to enhance weblogs

bloggers: weblog hosts and those who communicate with them

blogging: hosting and communicating with weblogs

blog-lish: the slangy codes favoured by Internet aficionados

blogocracy: the most influential bloggers

blogosphere: the ambit and activities of bloggers

blogroll: a list of other selected blogs featured on a particular weblog

blood in the elevator: the signs of a struggle for professional supremacy

blood on the floor: signs that a serious workplace conflict has taken place

blood on the stairs: the signs of a struggle for professional supremacy

blood on the walls: signs that a savage workplace conflict has occurred

blue-sky ideas: (hopefully inspirational) insights gained through free association or unstructured thinking

BOBFOC: (a person with) a 'body off *Baywatch*, face off *Crimewatch*'

BOBFOK: (a person with) the 'body of Barbie, face of Ken'

bobo: a 'bourgeois bohemian', an affluent middle-class consumer who affects 'unorthodox' tastes

Bo Derek: an outstandingly attractive stock or investment

body-lifts: cosmetic procedures to reshape or firm up the human body

body of fact: a consensus of public perceptions on important issues

bogans: an Australian underclass group, sharing some characteristics of UK chavs

boggle factor: a quality imparting a sense of wonder

BOGOF: an abbreviation of 'buy one, get one free'

BOHICA: an abbreviation of 'bend over, here it comes again'

bollers: slang for money

boiling the ocean: carrying out a very onerous task for little result

bolt-ons: fixtures or features added to an existing device or system

boomerang generation: young(-ish) people returning to live in the family home, having once left it

boomers: members of the 'baby-boom' generation born between 1945 and 1965

bootlegging: making illicit copies, infringing copyright or plagiarizing

bottom fishing: trading in very cheap or suspect shares

bottoming out: reaching a lowest point before potentially climbing again

bottom line: the final and conclusive figures on a financial statement; the essence of a position or situation

bottom line is the bottom line is the bottom line: an insistence on a financial figure or strategic stance

bottom-up: from subordinate members of a system rather than from those directing the system

boyz: slang for money

BPR: Business Process Re-engineering; focusing on processes rather than structures

bragging: claiming attributes such as superior safety compliance or ethical superiority

bragging rights: permission to make, or grounds for, claims of superiority or excellence

brainstorm: to share ideas in an unstructured and spontaneous discussion

brand-designers: specialists who help to create corporate identities and image

brand differentiation: setting one brand apart from its competitors

brand reputation: the public or sector image and renown of a brand

brass: slang for money

breaking down the silos: getting rid of internal barriers to information flow

breakout: the (perhaps dramatic) emergence of a product or system onto the market

breakout spaces: places where those meeting in a large group can reconvene in smaller groups

breakout year: the year in which a product or service emerges onto the market

Brian: a slang nickname typically applied to a footballer or football commentator

brightsizing: reducing the workforce, thereby losing the brightest employees

Brillo pads!: an exclamation of enthusiasm

bring the individual contributors along: to convince those involved to agree and/or endorse

broccoli: slang for money

bronze circle: the lowest in an ascending order of honorary memberships

browse: to review and consider (options) in a leisurely manner

B2G: an abbreviation of '(from) business to government'

bubble: a dramatic and shortlived boom

buckologists: employees who offload responsibility onto others

budgeting to bequeath: making personal economies in order to leave assets to one's descendants

Buffalo Bill: rhyming slang for a till or cashbox

Bugerup: an Australasian group dedicated to subverting and altering public advertisements

Buggins's turn: the assignment of responsibility by rotation rather than according to merit

bulletizing: listing and highlighting key points

bulls: optimistic investors

bumping along the bottom: undergoing a (prolonged) period of depression

bunce: slang for profit or money

bundling: combining (separate components) into a package

bunny-hugging: bonding with or caring for tame animals

bureaupathology: the dysfunctional aspects of organizations

burning: recording onto compact disc

Business in the Community: a UK charity encouraging corporate social responsibility

buy-in: agreement and/or endorsement

cached: stored and/or secreted

calendarize: to note on a schedule or agenda

capitalism without capital: transactions based on mutual interests rather than directly on money

capsizing: setting limits on staff levels (thereby risking damage to the organization)

capsule: a small container (of progressive design)

capsule hotels: facilities in which guests sleep in small 'drawers' or 'pods'

capture: excessive influence from authority, with resultant loss of independence

carbon footprint: the amount of fuel consumed and consequent volume of emissions

card tarting: switching credit card provider in search of best rates

career drift: unplanned or haphazard career progression

carry forward: to transfer to a later period

carry-overs: stock left over from a previous period

carry trade: the reinvestment of cash or currencies in more attractive economies

cascade: a hierarchy or descending order

cash concierge: a bank employee delegated to watch over the finances of an individual or small group

cash wrap: the location in a retail outlet where the customer pays and receives purchases

CAT: computer-aided translation

catalogue-man: a male who dresses unimaginatively

catch me up: to bring me up to date

caving: leading a reclusive existence at home

centralization: the dominance of a system by central authority or direction

chad: waste paper generated by computers and office equipment

change: the transformation of the working environment

change of reporting relationship: a euphemism for dismissal, redundancy or demotion

chasing pack: a group of competitors challenging the supremacy of market leaders

chatbot: a virtual entity designed to simulate the conversation of a real person

chav: a member of an aggressively uncultured, economically unprivileged social group

chavalier: a car belonging to (and perhaps customized by) a chav

chav chariots: a car belonging to (and perhaps customized by) a chav

chav-chic: clothing styles and accessories of the sort favoured by chavs

chavesses: female chavs

chavettes: female chavs

checkout-rage: a bout of fury experienced while waiting to pay for purchases in a retail outlet

chewing-gum-in-hair: an annoying impediment or frustration

Chief Morale Officer: (a novel job title for) an employee designated to raise organizational spirits

Chief Techie Geek: (a novel job title for) a senior technical specialist

chimerical forms: designed shapes and structures that do not occur in nature

chimps: lowly employees performing menial functions

China syndrome: the economic power of China and perceptions of it

Chinese walls: invisible internal barriers between organizational interests

chirpsing: flirting

choad: an obnoxious individual

choad-lick: an obnoxious individual

choadmonger: an obnoxious individual

choadsmoker: an obnoxious individual

choad-wad: an obnoxious individual

chode: an obnoxious individual

choice: the opportunity to select from competing offers

choice is tragic: a slogan implying that over-differentiation may be bad for business

Christmas-treed: embellished with a spectacular array of additional features

chronotypes: individuals characterized according to their pattern of daily activities

churning: retrading a set of investments at high speed or causing market turbulence

circling the drain: at a stage just prior to failure or liquidation

Città Slow: an urbanization dedicated to reducing the pace of socioeconomic activity

civilians: non-specialist customers

clean someone's clock: to defeat, thwart or destroy

clever milk: milk fortified with health-enhancing chemicals such as Omega 3 acids

clever old dogs: established organizations who are able to adapt to change

client: an individual undergoing personalized training or coaching

client-relationship management: concentration on the personal interactions between provider and customer

Client Solutions Advocate: (a novel job title for) a sales representative

closed funds: financial schemes which no longer admit new investment

closeup: detailed scrutiny

Club 58–80: boisterous elderly tourists

clustering: grouping items in a retail display

clutter control: arranging domestic spaces for maximum freedom of movement

coaching: personalized training and/or guidance

coarse-grained: lacking fine detail or finesse

cocooning: ensuring and remaining within a safe home environment

co-creation: collaborating in the development of products or services

Code Guru: (a novel job title for) a leading expert in software development

cognitive management: processing of information received (by the human brain)

cognito: named, acknowledged or known

collaborative advice: proposals based on the sharing of ideas by partners, stakeholders, etc.

collateral: incidental damage

coma factor: the degree of tedium (ascribed typically to a talk or text)

comfort food: foodstuffs that console or satisfy psychologically

command-and-control: centralized imposition of decisions

command central: a single facility which directs activities across a wider area

commentariat: a group of influential social commentators

commoditization chaos: confusion arising from a proliferation of customer demands (and resultant product differentiation)

commodity consultancy: management consultancy focusing on simple processing and production

Commodore: slang for the sum of £15 ('Three Times a Lady')

commons-based peer production: the development of products, services and ideas by collaboration between individuals of equal status

community banking: financial services organized by and for groups of private individuals

compassion fatigue: a lassitude caused by caring for the needs of others

complement magnet: a boss who is adept at attracting contacts and collaborators

componentization: the developing of the separate parts of complex systems

computer rage: a bout of fury occasioned by a desktop, laptop or handheld electronic device

confusion marketing: intentionally presenting customers with offers that are hard to understand

connectivity: optimum potential for electronic communication

conspicuous austerity: a deliberate and perceptible avoidance of displays of affluence

consumanism: ethical consumption

consumer-centric: treating the consumer as the primary focus

content filtering: checking language in order to remove problematical usages

content management: the monitoring and manipulation of language used in commercial and professional contexts

context-aware portlets: nodes in a system which can react to or cater for specific circumstances

contingent commission: a euphemism for a bribe or kickback

contragoogling: using Internet search engines to obtain information on customers

contrasexual: an individual who is indifferent to or incapable of enhancing their own sexual attractiveness

control: direction of organizational activities by a small group of empowered individuals

convergence: the coming-together of disparate technologies

conversion marketing: selling by persuading consumers to switch preferences and loyalties

cool hunters: seekers after the latest fashions and trends

co-parents: individuals who collaborate in the creation of a 'virtual child'

co-payment: the funding of welfare by a combination of the state and private individuals

copied-in: consulted and/or informed

copping off: successfully making a romantic assignation

cordon sanitaire: an exclusion or buffer zone, protective boundary or limitation

core competencies: essential capabilities

corporate entropy: the in-built tendency of an organization to become dysfunctional

corporate identity consultants: specialists who help define the way in which an organization is perceived

corporate jesters: employees designated to amuse colleagues

corporate social responsibility: an organization's awareness of and compliance with moral and social imperatives

corporate voodoo: mysterious, unusual and/or spectacular business practices

corporate whores: women willing to subject themselves to (demeaning) workplace demands in return for money

correction: a euphemism for radical reduction of the workforce

corridor cruiser: a worker who moves around within company premises, sometimes out of range of electronic connections

corridor warriors: workers who rove the workplace while remaining constantly connected electronically

COU: an abbreviation of '(the) centre of the universe'

CPA: an abbreviation of 'continuous partial attention', occupying oneself with more than one thing at a time crackberry: a compulsive user of a handheld electronic communication device

crackers: private individuals who illicitly access confidential online information, typically by penetrating protective systems

CRAFT: an abbreviation of 'can't remember a freaking/frigging/f***ing thing'

crash and burn: to fail suddenly and visibly

crate diggers: collectors of vinyl music recordings

crawled: scanned electronically in a systematic way

CRI: an abbreviation of 'corporate responsibility index', a measure of organizations' social behaviour

cross-merchandising: using proximity or association to draw consumers of one item towards others

crossover: the adoption of a genre, style or item by a group for whom it was not originally intended

cross-shifting: incorporating disparate influences into one's lifestyle or work practices

Croydon facelift: a hairstyle in which the hair is scraped back from the face, as favoured by chavs

CRS: an abbreviation of 'can't remember s**t'

cruft: worthless material or workplace debris

CTO: an abbreviation of Chief Technical Officer or of 'career terminally over'

cubicle monkeys: low-level employees confined within small workspaces

cuddle-puddle: a heap of exhausted revellers

cuddletech: a design approach which favours rounded, comfortable and/or comforting objects

culling of the herd: a drastic reduction in workforce numbers

culls: drastic reductions of personnel

customer-capture: the enticement and retention of potential consumers

customer-centric: treating the client or consumer as one's primary focus

customer co-creation: development of goods or services through collaboration between provider and consumer

customer engagement: a consumer's relationship with a brand or product that is based upon more than mere utility or price

customer intimacy: close and positive personal relations between provider and consumer

customer retention: keeping one's customers' interest and loyalty

customer surround: the environment within which consumers view and buy

customer touchpoints: locations where customers may handle items or be influenced to make selections

customer traffic management: controlling the movement of potential buyers in a retail outlet

customer traffic routing: influencing the movement of buyers through a retail outlet

customer trauma: distress or harm suffered by a client

customizing: adapting to a specific use or uses

cutting edge: (at the) forefront of current technology or practice

cutting-edge eclectics: trend-conscious consumers who reflect disparate influences

cyberfunerals: an Internet announcement of a death and celebration of the deceased

cyberfuturists: those who envisage a future governed by information technology

cyber-impersonators: individuals who adopt false identities when online

cyberprofiteers: those using Internet-based practices (in many cases deviously or illicitly) to make money

cyberstalking: using the Internet to trace, pursue and/or harass another person

cyber-venting: using the Internet to express criticisms and make complaints

CXO: an (approximate) abbreviation of Chief Executive Officer

danegeld: funds paid to keep an adversary at bay

dash: a word used in Africa to mean a bribe

dashboard dining: eating while inside an automobile

Database God: (a novel job title for) a very important IT specialist

data glut: an excess of information

data-mining: using electronic technology to retrieve hard-to-access information such as personal details

dataraptor: a worker who retrieves information in the field for forwarding or storage

data-rich: retaining (but not necessarily managing) high volumes of (perhaps unprocessed) information

dawn raids: sudden and unexpected hostile moves by speculators, business rivals, etc.

dead money: unclaimed and unusable cash, such as unpaid compensation

death by committee: the spoiling of a proposal or plan by collective (hence tentative) decision-making

death-of-a-thousand-cuts: the ruining of a proposal or plan by numerous small amendments

debt rotation: the transfer of debt to obtain more favourable credit terms

de-careering: giving up one's job and/or abandoning one's career

decruitment: laying off employees

decryption tools: techniques for deciphering restricted information

de-décor'd: stripped of excess decoration and/or furnishings

deep web: the part of the Internet consisting of hard-to-access data repositories

defamiliarizing: redesigning or reformulating (a known object) so as to render it novel

defenestration: forcible ejection from one's post

delisted: no longer given shelf-space in a retail outlet

delivery: the most effective provision of service

de-locate: to move from one's original base and/or become peripatetic

delusions of adequacy: an exaggerated notion of one's own competence

demand/destination products: the items a customer has set out to buy

demographics: statistics relating to communities and populations

Deputy Director for External Affairs: a rather grandiose title for someone dealing with public relations

deskfast: breakfast eaten at one's workstation or workplace

détournement: the altering, adapting or using of existing texts for subversive purposes

device convergence: the combining of formerly disparate functions in one piece of equipment

dichotomous: consisting of two distinct or opposed parts or aspects

dictionary attacks: the automatic sending of electronic messages to random recipients (chosen from scanning directories, etc.)

diddly-dum: slang for tedious and/or mediocre

diff: an abbreviation of 'difference'

differently abled: physically and/or intellectually deficient or impaired

difficult: a euphemism for awful and/or unacceptable

digerati: expert users of electronic communications and new technology

diggers: collectors of vinyl music recordings

digital aesthetic: graphic conventions and stylistic preferences arising from electronic design technology

digital archiving: storing information electronically

Dilberted: subjected to oppressive management and work practices

dimensionless territories: undefined or illimitable virtual spaces

dipster: a person providing unofficial investment tips or advice

dipstick: a foolish and/or obnoxious individual

direction: fashion tendency

direct-to-consumer: without the intervention of intermediaries such as regulators

disaggregation: splitting up an organization or its parts into smaller units

discretionary income: cash which may be spent freely

disease-pitch: a selling proposition based on consumer awareness of health issues

disempowering: reducing the power of or removing power from (a person or group)

dish the dirt: to spread malicious gossip, reveal embarrassing secrets

dis-optimal: less than ideal, perhaps disastrous

dissing: treating with contempt or derision, or simply criticizing

distributed functionality: separate services provided or accessed separately

distributedness: a situation in which (usually or previously centralized) responsibility or activity is shared out extensively

divatude: the characteristics of an ultra-discerning shopper or other primadonna

D-list micro-celebrities: slightly famous (but unimpressive) individuals

dog-food: a low-priced product intended for mass consumption

dogs: poor-performing and/or unpopular stocks

doing a raindance: carrying out an impressive or complex, but possibly futile procedure

doing a Ratners: damaging one's reputation through facetiousness or excessive honesty

domain: physical surroundings or setting

domesticize: incorporate into one's home

DONM: an abbreviation of 'date of next meeting'

donor burnout: a feeling that one has given enough, or more than enough, to good causes

don't get your knickers in a twist: a British injunction not to become flustered

don't get your panties in a bunch: an American injunction not to become flustered

doorstepped: solicited from someone in person at their place of residence

dormantizing: suspending or closing an account (that is deemed to be under-used)

DoS attack: illicit interference with electronic facilities so as to deny service

dosh: slang for money

dot.commers: those engaged in online enterprises, particularly Internet entrepreneurs

dot.cons: Internet-based swindles

do the math!: an injunction to check the relevant figures

downclosing: closing down (an activity or enterprise)

downlink coverage: the area of reach of an electronic communication system

downscale: (among) the cheaper or smaller of a range of possibilities

downshifting: reducing one's responsibilities and/or tempo of existence

downsizing: reducing the size, complexity and/or scope (of an organization)

downward brand extension: adding cheaper products to one's range

drama documentary: a broadcast media dramatization of factual events

draw down: to cash in (part of an investment or asset)

drill-down: a detailed search of dense data

drive more traffic to the site: to persuade more customers to show interest or buy

dropping in: covertly adding one's own item(s) to a display

drop your pants!: to reveal one's product, price or position

dual jobbing: having two jobs or performing two different activities

due diligence: the necessary observances and compliance

dumbsizing: reducing the workforce with the result that expertise is lost

dumpies: an (approximate) abbreviation of 'destitute, unprepared mature people'

dumping¹: selling surplus goods into a market at rock-bottom prices

dumping²: disposing of waste material

dumpster-diver: a forager for free (waste) food

dust-bunnies: balls of fluff collecting on an unswept floor

dust-kitties: balls of fluff collecting on an unswept floor

early adopters: the first individuals or organizations to embrace an innovation

easy peasy, lemon squeezy!: an exclamation of triumph or derision

eat our lunch: take our share of the market and/or profits

eat some reality sandwiches: to face up to exigencies

eat your breakfast: take your share of the market and/or profits, especially by timely action

eat your own dog-food: to sample one's own product(s) or service(s), especially where these are inferior

ecological deficit: (quantifiable) damage caused to the environment

ecological footprint/eco-footprint: an amount of resources consumed and/or resultant damage caused

ecological loss: (quantifiable) damage caused to the environment

econymists: specialists in naming (products and businesses)

eco-system: an environment in which interdependent entities and functions coexist

eco-tracking: following waste, pollution and surplus products as they are moved around the globe

EDRs: an abbreviation of 'event data-recorders', in-built electronic monitors

800lb gorilla: the most powerful and/or intimidating person or participant involved in a transaction or project

e-learning: technology-assisted and online learning

electrode microarray: a miniaturized set of electronic sensors

electronic archiving: using digital technology to store and retrieve personal information

electrum circle: one of an ascending order of honorary memberships, coming between silver and gold

ELV: an abbreviation of 'End-of-Life Vehicle', an EU directive on automobile disposal

embedded: integrated into the environment

emergence: innovation which suggests itself in the course of natural development

emergent technologies: innovative processes arising in the course of technical evolution

emerging adulthood: a gradual transition from adolescence

EMG: an abbreviation of 'empty magnanimous gesture'

emotional design: the creation of objects intended to evoke or engage feelings

emotional incontinence: excessive indulgence and/or display of feelings

emotional literacy: a capacity to manage one's feelings and human relationships

employee trauma: stress or harm suffered by workers

empty-nesters: parents whose children have grown up and left home

EMU: an abbreviation of '(European) economic and monetary union'

enter you in: to note a potential appointment with you

enticement: luring and entrancing a potential customer

entreprenerds: earnest young creators of new, especially IT or new-technology-based businesses

enunciation: the expressing or enacting of a sociocultural convention, such as a language rule or a social role

environmental bottom line: a quantification of environmental factors and costs

envision: to envisage

EOD: an abbreviation of 'end of discussion'

EPP: an abbreviation of 'earnings per partner'

ept: competent

erosion: gradual diminution or destruction

ert: active, lively

e-tailers: retailers using online communication channels

ethical proposition: a policy, stance or offer based on fairness and/or social responsibility

ethical responsibility: compliance with moral and social imperatives

EUREKA: an acronym for the Europe-wide network for collaborative research and development (an EU initiative)

eurocentrism: a tendency to favour a European perspective

eveningness: a personal tendency toward increased activity in the later part of the day

eventuated: occurred

evitable: avoidable

e-waste: discarded computing hardware or consumables

excessivity: overabundance or exaggeration

executive mantra: a catchphrase or slogan used by senior professionals

expressive manager: a manager who makes clear his or her feelings and opinions

extended adolescence: a prolonged youthful phase of experimentation

externalities: deprivation experienced by those excluded from aid or reconstruction schemes

extreme connoisseurs: flamboyant, exigent consumers

extreme gardening: gardening practised in uncongenial or harsh surroundings

extreme ironing: ironing carried out in dangerous locations

extreme sports: hazardous sporting activities

extremers: devotees of dangerous sports and hobbies

extreme tourism: travel to risky, unusual and/or remote destinations

extreme usability: meeting the requirements of the widest range of users and contexts

extropians: utopian futurists who envisage migration from planet Earth

eyeball: to view

eyeballs: viewers or viewings

face-time: (time spent in) person-to-person interaction

facings: products or displays arranged to confront a potential customer

facticity: the quality of being true or real

faction: a blend of fact and fiction

factitious: constructed rather than naturally occurring

factoid: an idea or statement which appears to be true, but may not be

factualness: the quality of being true or real

fair trade: commerce conducted according to ethical principles and equity

fairy-flop: fluff collecting on an unswept floor

fakers: consumers aspiring to or projecting an image at odds with their true status

family office: a small group of specialists providing personalized expertise and assistance to a family

fanny-fit: a bout of hysteria or bad temper

fashion-forward: original and/or avant-garde in taste in clothing, accessories, etc.

fashionista: an extremely 'fashion-conscious' individual and/or an influential member of the fashion industry or fashion media

fashion mavens: influential figures in the fashion industry and/or fashion media

fashion victim: an obsessive follower of fashion

fearless maverick: a bold and individualistic manager

featurectomy: the removal of additional or superfluous components

feedback: reflection and resultant adaptation

feng shui: alignment of objects in an environment according to mystical principles

fill your boots: enrich yourself

financially underserved customer base: actual or potential clients with limited access to banking facilities

fine-grained: detailed or nuanced

finessing: cleverly manipulating

fingerprint technology: electronic reading of human fingerprints

Fingerspitzengefühl: an instinctive understanding or appreciation

firefighting: dealing with urgent problems

firewalls: safeguards designed to prevent the spread of a harmful force

first wave: an initial impact

fiscal drag: the failure of tax allowances to keep pace with inflation

flash: a pitch or allocated space used by a market trader

flash crowd: a large number of Internet users simultaneously accessing a specific site

flash flood: a large number of Internet users simultaneously accessing a specific site

flash mobs: groups of strangers instructed to mass at a particular location

flattening the pyramid: reducing the number of layers in a hierarchical structure or system

flexitime: a flexible daily timetable or work schedule

flook: a film based on a blook (itself a book derived from a blog)

flowcharting: mapping processes on a diagram showing interconnecting pathways

fmcgs: fast-moving consumer goods

focus: concentration or attention

focus groups: small groups of people assembled to provide a representative sample of opinion

f.o. funds: money enabling one to escape

follow: a trendy or mistaken version of 'follow up'

f.o. money: money enabling one to escape

footfall: extent of coverage of or impact on a market

fork: (to subject to or experience) a divergence

forkers: creators or proponents of divergent systems

forking paths: alternative routes towards one's objectives

fork you!: a rude exclamation of defiance

format-protection: the safeguarding of intellectual property and copyrighted systems

for-profit: operating with the object of financial gain

forum-shopping: seeking the most favourable geographical setting for legal action

forward (adj.): daring and/or progressive (in one's tastes)

forward (vb): to advance or promote

forward purchasing: buying stocks in excess of current needs/ anticipation of future needs

4-play/four-play: (a service package combining) mobile and fixed-line telephony, Internet and television

fractional ownership: (possession of) a partial stake in an asset

freegan: a forager for free food or other discarded items

free up: to cash in (part of an investment or asset)

fridge mountains: large quantities of discarded refrigerators and freezers

from soup to nuts: from beginning to end, covering all aspects

full equity partners: the most senior members of a firm who enjoy the most generous share options

functional food: foodstuffs enhanced with additives or special treatment

functionality: capacity for multiple uses

furkids: pets

FWIW: an abbreviation of 'for what it's worth'

Gaia hypothesis: the contention that the Earth is a self-regulating entity possessing a form of intelligence or purpose

Gaijin: a foreigner, expatriate

gaining traction: achieving increased share or influence in a market

gameplan: strategy for success

gapping: delaying the passing on of favourable changes in interest rates

gatekeeper: a person strategically placed to control or influence access to a process

gateway reviews: periodic checking by independent monitors of a plan or system

gay: unimpressive, inept

geek: an earnest, unprepossessing (but perhaps technically adept) individual

geek-chic: allure associated with formerly unglamorous technical specialists

geezer glut: an excess or abundance of older workers

gelt: slang for money

Generation X: those born between 1965 and 1980

Generation Y: those born after 1980; adolescents and young adults

generics: products or services designed for non-specialist markets

geocentrism: a view of the world or set of assumptions based on one's place of origin or residence

geo-economics: the study of international and global economic trends

geophysical events: natural disasters

geopolitical footprint: the extent of political influence and military-industrial impact

get whacked: to suffer a dramatic financial loss or setback

get wound round the axle: to be forestalled, frustrated or paralysed by complexity

get your ducks in a row: to organize yourself; behave in a logical, efficient manner

ghost turds: balls of fluff collecting on an unswept floor

give someone the mushroom treatment: to deny someone information while oppressing them

gizmos: devices, gadgets

glass ceiling: an invisible barrier to professional advancement, based typically on gender prejudice

global brain: a capacity to process information, interact and exercise choice on a worldwide scale

global conversation: the exchange of opinions and ideas on a worldwide scale

global footprint: the extent of reach of a communication system or impact of a socio-economic force

global nomads: individuals whose lifestyles involve frequent travel and multiple or no home bases

glurge: a sentimental story which may or may not be based on fact

goalposts move: the parameters and/or rules (of a transaction or plan) change

gofer: a menial assistant, messenger or go-between

going forward: making progress or strategically advancing

gold circle: one of an ascending order of honorary memberships or a hypothetical high ranking in a sector

good-for-you: healthy and/or enhancing well-being

good plan, Batman!: an enthusiastic assent or agreement

goodwill: the intangible but sometimes quantifiable repute of an organization (and respect engendered)

googling: searching or looking up by means of an Internet search engine such as Google

gorilla: slang for the sum of £5,000 or £5 million

gouger: a petty fraudster and/or thuggish aggressor

go-with-the-gut antimethodology: a reliance on instinct rather than rational procedure(s)

GPS: an abbreviation of 'global positioning system'

graduate premium: the additional earnings commanded by graduates as opposed to non-graduates

granular: concentrating on or composed of fine detail

granule: a single part of a complex system

gravitational pull: the inexorable drawing of resources (out of a particular sector)

grey ceiling: a barrier to professional advancement based on ageism

grey geese: elderly tourists or travellers

grey-matter economy: economic activity deriving from human knowledge and exchange of information

grey panthers: assertive and/or exigent elderly consumers

grey pound: spending by older members of the UK population

group-grope: mutual fondling by several people

growing new skill-sets: developing additional personal and professional capacities

gruntled: satisfied, unconcerned

G-spot: a notional site of pleasurable stimulation

guerrilla marketing: attempting to sell by surprising potential customers with physical confrontation or other unorthodox techniques

guerrilla music gigs: impromptu performances in unofficial locations such as private homes or public spaces

gun around: to move about or look around energetically and/or aggressively

hackers: individuals who illicitly access electronic information, especially Internet communications

halo car: a model whose qualities enhance the prestige of others in the range

halo effect: a positive reaction in one context which extends into another related context or contexts

halo marketing: using selected prestige items to enhance associated products or services

halo motoring: guilt-free driving (resulting from compliance with anti-pollution imperatives)

hammams: Arab or Turkish-style baths

happenings: unscripted one-off gatherings or events

hard-edged: sharply-defined, rigid

having a salmon day: undergoing a frustrating, ultimately demeaning experience

Hawaii: slang for £50 or £500

heads-up: a forewarning, notification or encouragement

health and wellness: physical and psychological well-being

heavy hitter: a powerful and/or influential individual

helicopter grazing: briefly visiting a venue (solely) in order to sample food on offer

helicopter view: an overview, wide perspective

helioproctosis: overweening self-esteem, unjustifiable arrogance

hero manager: a manager who boldly accepts personal responsibility and/or exercises individual leadership

HEROs: an abbreviation of 'high-earner [or -earning], risk-open (individuals)'

heteroflexible: a heterosexual who affects or tolerates some homosexual attitudes or tastes

high-definition: detailed, nuanced

high-end: prestigious, luxurious, affluent

high-flying: achieving spectacular success

high-probability selling: selling desirable products or services to willing customers

hired gun: a specialist engaged to carry out a difficult or distasteful task

hissy-fit: a bout of angry impatience

hive mind: a hypothetical collective intelligence exercised by multiple members of a complex system

hiving: creating and remaining within a (complex and) secure domestic environment

HNWs: an abbreviation of 'high net worth (individuals)'

ho-hum: tedious, unimpressive

hold feet to fire: to force (someone) to concede or accede

holistic: from a totalizing perspective

holistic work–life balance: a lifestyle in which professional and non-professional aspects are harmoniously integrated

hollowed out: diminished and/or impoverished

home and hosed: successfully concluded, safe and sound

home havens: peaceful, pleasant and secure domestic environments

homelurker: a worker who is based at home for some or all of their working time

home spa: a domestic environment incorporating sophisticated bathing and hygiene facilities

homogenization of information: the proliferation of near-identical messages and pieces of data

horizontal: favouring sharing on an equal basis, avoiding hierarchies of responsibility, knowledge and/or access

horizontally architected from the ground up: constructed to offer maximum access at all stages

hot-desk: to settle temporarily at an available workstation

hot money: funds available for speedy (re)investment

hotspot: a focus of intense electronic activity or media interest

Hub Facilitator: (a novel job title for) a receptionist, office assistant or administrator

HUD: an abbreviation for 'heads-up display'

huddling: crowding together (to confer and/or express fellow-feeling)

huggability: a comforting tactile quality

human inventories: reviews of personnel, their activities and attributes

human logistics: reviewing and deploying personnel

human sacrifice: (enforcing) dismissal or redundancy

hyperconsumption: uncontrolled acquisition and material indulgence (for hedonistic motives rather than for display)

hyperindividualization: increased differentiation of products and services to cater for very varied consumer preferences

hyperlocal: geographically restricted, based upon small communities

hyperlocated: targeted at or based upon geographically restricted areas and/or small communities

hypersegmentation: increased specialization of products and services to cater for very varied consumer preferences

ideas hamster: an employee charged with generating or proposing innovative concepts

ideation: spontaneous generation or contribution of ideas

IIRC: an abbreviation of 'if I recall correctly'

image car: a model whose qualities enhance the prestige of others in the range

IM generation: the age group who are enthusiasts for instant messaging; texting and mobile phone usage

impact: to have an effect, particularly a noticeable or radical effect, upon

impactful: dynamically effective

implement: to arrange or put into effect

impulse items: products which (it is hoped) customers will purchase without prior intention

incent: to inspire (to action), motivate

incentivize: to inspire (to action), motivate

inconspicuous consumption: discreet purchasing and usage

industrial migration: transferring production and services to other regions

inflatable sumo wrestling: feigned sumo combat wearing blow-up plastic costumes and wigs

influentials: experimental consumers who disseminate product news and encourage emulation

infolust: a compulsive and/or insatiable desire for information

infonomics: the study of economic activity based on exchange of information

information economy: commercialization of and trade in knowledge and data

Information Manager: an employee responsible for communications and/or public relations

information poor: lacking in or deficient in processing usable data

information overload: (a sense of / being overwhelmed by) an excess of data

information silos: separated repositories of data within an organization or system

informatizing: providing (a blend of) information and promotional material

informavore: a voracious consumer of information

inner-directedness: a reflective, self-analytical capacity

insperience: bringing a range of technologies and leisure experiences within an enclosed domestic environment

instant history: events, ideas and objects recalled from the very recent past

institutional memory loss: the inability of an organization to retain an idea of its own history or essential attributes

integration-enabling: encouraging and/or permitting exchange and communication between constituent parts or parties

intelligent dynamic middleware: software enabling effective communication between the initial and terminal stages, or higher and lower functions of a system

intelligent home services: computerized aids to domestic comfort and efficiency

intelligent bread: bread fortified with additives (such as omega-3 acids) or subject to treatment designed to aid brain activity

intelligent objects: appliances or fitments with built-in reactive or interactive capability

interactive front-ends: automated first entry-points and/or introductory stages in a system

interflow: generation and exchange of insights, inspirations and feelings

internationalizing: adapting products and services for overseas consumption

Internet price: the lowest price obtainable online

Internet shrines: web-based personal memorials or devotional sites

Internet shapeshifters: individuals assuming alternative identities while online

intertainment: entertainment facilities, typically enabled by new technology, incorporated into one's home

intractability: a refusal or inability to compromise or progress (in a negotiation)

invisible web: the less accessible parts of the Internet, where key data repositories are located

involuntary severance: redundancy or dismissal

in-yer-face: flagrant, blatant or confrontational

IPTV: an abbreviation of 'Internet protocol television'

ISA: an abbreviation of 'isn't she awful?'

issuance: releasing and/or circulating

ITA: an abbreviation of 'I totally agree'

it does what it says on the box/tin: it functions simply as required or as stated

item du jour: the latest and most fashionable article of clothing or accessory

iteration: (the release in succession of) a new version

iterative process: a procedure (such as a consultation) involving repeated steps or successive stages

'I've already-given' syndrome: a disinclination to go on contributing (to charity for example), having done so previously

jaggies: jagged edges on a computer bitmap display

jargonauts: devotees of jargon

Jekyll and Hyde eating: combining or alternating between healthy and unhealthy foods

JFDI: an abbreviation of 'just f***ing do it!'

JGE: an abbreviation of 'just gay enough'

JHTV: an abbreviation of 'just had to vent (my anger/feelings)'

jitterati: those rendered nervous or insecure by involvement with electronic communications

jobless: unemployed

JOOTT: an abbreviation of 'just one of those things'

journalese: the stylistic conventions favoured by newspaper and magazine writers

journey of consumption: a customer's trajectory through a retail outlet

jubs: menial employees

jump the couch: to commit an embarrassing public act such as a declaration or outburst

junk population: a group (of consumers) of little economic significance or potential

jurisdiction abuse: taking (supposedly unfair) advantage of favourable local conditions for legal action

jurisdiction-juggling: selecting the most favourable among competing settings for legal action

KBD: an abbreviation of 'key business drivers'

ketchup effect: a build-up followed by a sudden release

Kevin: a slang nickname for a lower-class and/or uncultured male

kidults: young people affecting (inappropriate) adult behaviour or adults behaving (inappropriately) like younger people

killer bee: a highly aggressive legal consultant, engaged typically to inflict damage on an adversary

KIPPERS: an abbreviation of 'kids in parental property eroding retirement savings'

kitchen envy: jealousy and competition provoked by comparisons of kitchens and cooking accessories

knockoffs: illicit copies of products such as fashion garments

knowledge-building: gradual, planned acquisition of skills and know-how

knowledge economy: commercialization of and trade in know-how and information

knowledge-mapping: recording and assessing the areas of expertise within an organization

knowledge pollution: the deleterious effects of an excess of information

Knowledge Sorceress: (a novel job title for) a senior female employee seen as a repository of specialized know-how

knowledge wizard: an employee possessing specialized know-how

KPI: an abbreviation of 'key performance indicators'

Kylie: a pleasing upturn, as appearing on a profit curve for instance

label-queen: a fashion consumer who sets great store by designer labels and logos

laddish: reflecting the attitudes and tastes of boisterous young males

lady (Godiva): slang for the sum of £5

lame: disappointing, uninspiring, of poor quality

land grabber: an aggressively acquisitive manager

languagizing: translating texts into local languages (and adapting for local cultures)

large-culture formations: concepts, such as region, nation, ethnic group, that subsume large numbers of people

larks: those who function best in the first part of the day, and go early to bed

LATs: an abbreviation for '(people) living apart together'

launch failure: an inability or unwillingness to achieve independence from one's family

leading edge: the most modern and/or progressive (in current thinking, practice or attainment)

lean manufacturing: production based on using the minimum of (material or human) resources

learning curve: a progression in understanding and/or acquisition of skills

learnings: skills and knowledge acquired

left out of the loop: excluded from communication

level playing field: conditions for a negotiation or transaction in which all parties are treated equally or fairly

leverage: to (use one's assets, influence or ingenuity to) negotiate or achieve

licensed automotive treatment facilities: car breakers' premises

life-cacheing: storing personal memories and memorabilia (with the aid of electronic technology)

life coaches: consultants engaged to help improve one's existence

lifeswap: the exchange of one's lifestyle for someone else's, usually as a temporary experiment

lift up your skirt!: an injunction to reveal one's financial status or negotiating position

lightbulb moment: a flash of inspiration

limited-sovereignty: unable to exercise total rule or legal authority

link-farming: adding and manipulating website links in order to boost a site's ratings

link incest: adding and manipulating website links in order to boost a site's ratings

lip: a trendy way of saying 'lipstick'

lipstick indicator: a means of assessing levels of social anxiety according to sales of small luxury items

live ambient point-of-sale: a personal confrontation between a seller and potential customer

loading: inflating year-end sales figures

load of old Ratners: poor quality merchandise, 'crap'

locked-in silo approach: a compartmentalized or secretive approach to information-sharing

loggers: those logging on to Internet sites

logophilia: a fondness for designer labels or prestigious logos or brands

logophiliac: a devotee of prestigious brands and/or designer labels

look: a designer garment shown in a fashion event or display

look-and-feel: the general appearance and function (associated with a product or service)

loose cannons: volatile, unstable and often unpredictable individuals

love: intimacy and fellow-feeling (in professional relationships)

low-end: inexpensive, unsophisticated, low-status

low-hanging fruit: rewards or assets that are easily attained

lumbering: (successfully) making a romantic assignation

lurkers: anonymous, passive participants in online communications

madmes: would-be or self-styled humorists or eccentrics

magic circle: the small group of highest earning and most prestigious law firms

Mainland: the People's Republic of China

making a pitch: presenting a commercial proposal, usually verbally in person

managed closure: the shutting down of part or all of an enterprise

managed separation: the laying-off of staff

manager-mentor: a supervising colleague who also provides personal tutelage

man at C&A: an unstylish and/or cheaply dressed male

Mandies: slang for working class and/or uncultured young females

M&Ms: (over)ambitious young employees who see themselves as future managers

mano a mano: in direct contact and/or confrontation

Marketing Weasel: an employee responsible for clever selling strategies

marzipan layer: the group who are ranked below the very top in their profession, but ahead of the majority

mash up: retrieving data such as musical sequences or graphics and combining it in new permutations

massclusivity: prestige attaching to products and services which are nevertheless affordable to many

masters of the universe: top-earning and highly influential financial professionals

masters of the youniverse: consumers who exercise command of electronic communications

matrix: a plan or calculation that draws together disparate information into a whole

mattress money: personal savings secreted in a private location

maximization: making the most of (potential), increasing to the maximum

Maxwellian: characteristic of the (outrageous) behaviour of the late Robert Maxwell

mazuma: slang for money

MBAs: individuals who are 'mentally below average' or 'married, but available'

MDL: an abbreviation of 'mutton dressed as lamb'

Media Outreach Coordinator: a rather pretentious title for a public relations or communications professional

medicalization: the incorporation or intrusion of medical concepts

mediocracy: a regime in which the mediocre set standards

me-generation: an age group characterized by selfishness and greed

mélange: a mix(ture)

melanin ceiling: a barrier to professional advancement based on skin colour or ethnic prejudice

mêléeing: (staging) a disorganized mingling of people

memorabilizing: storing personal memorabilia and memories

memorialization: visible or tangible commemoration of the dead

MEMs: an abbreviation of 'micro-electromechanical sensors'

mentee: a person who is being mentored

mentor (vb): to act as a guide and personal adviser (to a subordinate)

mentor (noun): a senior person providing personal guidance to a junior

mentored learning: acquiring know-how and/or skills with the help of a personal supervisor

metrics: measurable criteria or statistics

mezzanine partners: members of a firm (such as a legal partnership) whose terms and conditions are slightly less advantageous than the most senior members

microcelebrity: (a person enjoying) some small renown or brief fame

microfinancing: small-scale funding provided by private individuals, especially to support good causes

microlending: small loans provided by private individuals, typically to encourage local projects

microloans: small-scale loans provided by private philanthropists

micromanager: a manager who monitors and directs the fine details of subordinates' activities

micro-marketing: attracting and selling to customers using small-sized packages

micro-niches: small groups of individuals sharing activities, personal characteristics and/or consumer behaviour

micro-scenes: shared enthusiasms (for music styles for example) restricted to small numbers of individuals

micro-selling: attracting and selling to customers using small-sized packages

microserf: a lowly employee working in the IT or high-tech sector

micro-vacations: very brief holidays

Middle England: a constituency of citizens thought to embody conservative, conformist values and preferences

mid-lifers: those aged between 30 and 60

MILF: an abbreviation for '(a) mother I'd like to f***', an attractive older female

mini-breaks: short holidays

minimalism: a stylistic preference for minimal ornamentation, detail and/or clutter

minipreneurs: small-scale entrepreneurs

mission-creep: the tendency for a project to grow in extent, complexity and difficulty

mission-critical priority: a requirement which is essential to the success of a strategy

mitigate: restrain or restrict one's own actions, temper one's aggression

MITIN: an abbreviation of 'more information than I need/is necessary'

mix-and-match: selecting and combining both disparate and similar components

mobile searches: using a cellphone or similar device to access stored information

modelling: simulating situations or structures (mathematically and/or electronically)

modpostalism: a facetious version of 'postmodernism', based on 'mod(ern)(ism)' and 'going postal' (that is, berserk)

module: a discrete component of a system

monetized: given a monetary value and/or made to yield income or profit

monkey: slang for £500

monkeys: lowly, menial employees

monotasking: performing one activity at a time

moolah: slang for money

moonlighting: (covertly) undertaking additional paid work outside normal hours

moratorium: a time limit, statute of limitation

morningness: a personal tendency towards increased activity in the earlier part of the day

motes: tiny particle-like electronic sensors

movers and shakers: dynamic and influential individuals

moving the goalposts: changing the terms of a negotiation or agreement during its course

Mr Byrite: a cheaply dressed, unstylish male

muggles: a dismissive or derisive word for customers

mugs: a dismissive or derisive word for customers

multi-sensory overkill: the sensation of being overwhelmed by (excess) information via various media

multi-tasking: undertaking several activities simultaneously

muso: a ('progressive') music fan and/or expert

must-have: highly desirable

must-reach demographic: a segment of the population that represents a highly attractive market

mutant versions: new and transformed incarnations or spin-offs

MVNO: an abbreviation of 'mobile virtual network operator'

NABA: an abbreviation of 'not another bloody acronym!'

name of the game: the activity in question, the crucial element

naming solutions: appropriate (new) product or brand names

nanocelebrities: very slightly and/or only briefly (and probably undeservedly) famous individuals

nanostalgia: sentimental recollection of the very recent past

national conversation: the prevalent and/or public debates and discussions going on in a particular society at a particular time

NATO: an abbreviation of 'not a team operator'

natural architecture: building and design using organic forms and substances found in nature

naturopaths: enthusiasts for herbal medicine and therapies based on 'natural' processes

navigation: negotiating a path through or across (an online site for example)

nebbies: an abbreviation of 'negative-equity baby-boomers'

neo-Luddite: a modern opponent or saboteur of industrial or technological processes

neo-pagans: modern proponents of non-Christian spiritual beliefs and ritual practices

neopets: virtual electronic 'animal' companions

nerd: an earnest, unattractive individual

neurolinguistic programming: a set of techniques used in personal development, therapy and training, based on quasi-scientific and/or New Age principles

New Authentics: dedicated followers – and leaders – of fashions and lifestyle trends

new math: changed geo-economic realities, such as trade balances

news fiction: a blend of factual and fictionalized reportage

new wave taxidermy: novel techniques (and a recent fashion) for preserving the bodies of pets and people

niches: specialized markets, small groups with shared interests

nifty!: an exclamation of approval

Nigel: a slang nickname for a middle- or upper-class male

Nigerian fraud: an Internet begging letter intended to obtain money by deception

night owls: individuals who are active at night-time

nip-and-tuck: cosmetic surgery and body enhancement

NLP: an abbreviation of 'neurolinguistic programming'

no-gos: elderly consumers who are unwilling to embrace innovations

noise: the mass of (distracting) messages and data generated by the professional environment

noisy: grainy, fuzzy, visually indistinct

no logo: anti-consumerist, antibrand

no logos: anti-capitalist and/or environmentally aware, thrifty consumers

non-financial risk: danger (to an organization or brand) that cannot be directly quantified financially

nonlinear shopping: purchasing unpredictable combinations of products from more than one source

non-monetary: not involving cash or capital

non-substantive: unreliable, of questionable accuracy or authenticity

Normans: slang for customers

nostalgia foods: foodstuffs that evoke memories of youth or a sense of times past

not a happy bunny: an individual who is upset, disgruntled and/or disaffected

not on our radar: outside our field of interest, unworthy of our attention

not too shabby!: an exclamation of approval

noughties: the years between 2000 and 2010

nouveau niche: designed for consumers who have come to demand personalized, specialized provision

NRN: an abbreviation of 'no response necessary'

nu-austerity: a recent tendency to shun high spending and display of wealth

nu-post-punk: new versions of indie rock music styles of the early 1980s

nurdling: clever, confusing machinations

nutraceuticals: health-promoting foodstuffs enhanced with chemical additives or special treatment

nutty!: an exclamation of approval

occulture: New Age mysticism

odorizing: releasing perfumes into an environment

offer: (a range of) items or services made available to customers

offshore English: an English-based *lingua franca* used in international settings

offshoring: transferring activities to an overseas setting

off-sider: an assistant

okey-dokey, artichokey!: an exclamation of assent or agreement

old skool rare grooves: music recordings (especially of soul, R'n'B or hip-hop) from previous eras

olfactory signature: characteristic smell

online community: a group of Internet users with shared interests

online conversation: a dialogue or discussion among Internet users

online interrogation: checking a product or organization's credentials by cellphone or e-mail

on my watch: during my period of duty

onomastics: the study of names and naming

onomasts: specialists in the origins and uses of names

open editing: the unrestricted amending or rewriting of texts by anyone who wishes to

open-kimono philosophy: a policy of transparency

open-source: freely available to all

opinion-formers: individuals who are able to influence others in terms, for example, of consumer behaviour

ops: an abbreviation of 'opportunities', 'operations' or 'options'

Optical Illumination Enhancer: a pretentious title for a window-cleaner

optimalization: making the best (of)

optimization: making the best (of)

optimize: to make the best (of)

option paralysis: the inability to make decisions or exercise choice

orange squash: rhyming slang for 'dosh', itself slang for money

'orders of love': roles assumed or ascribed in emotional relations

organic architecture: building and design using natural shapes and materials

organigramming: constructing or using charts showing the disposition of roles in an organization

O/S: overseas

outreach: making contact and/or building relationships with external parties

outsourcing: delegating and/or transferrring activities to outsiders

ovenable: able to be cooked in a microwave or oven

over-claiming: exaggerating one's probity or compliance with good practice

overdetermined: reflecting several different origins, sources or theories at the same time

overscheduling: making too many demands on one's own time

over-spec: to incorporate more features, functions or power than are strictly necessary

package: a discrete part of a system

paid-to-play: (Internet users) receiving money in return for posting messages

pain-point: a source of distress or area of vulnerability

paint-watchers: idle and/or bored employees

pant: a trendy version of 'pants' in the sense of trousers

pants: (something) inferior, disappointing and/or annoying

papes: slang for (paper) money

paradigm shift: a fundamental change in thinking or approach

parameter: to set a limit or limits, define the scope (of an interaction or transaction, for example)

parameterizing: setting limits or defining scope

parametring: setting limits or defining scope

parked: set aside for possible later attention, delayed

particle: a discrete part of a system

partner learning: acquiring knowledge or skills in parallel and in collaboration with a fellow learner

partner up: to get together, form a partnership

passive users: those who access electronic media but don't send or exchange messages

pay-per-click: charged according to the number of times accessed

pear-shaped: in disarray, dysfunctional, distorted

pelf: slang for money

pencil you in: make a tentative appointment with you

penny-boys: menial, low-paid employees

percussive maintenance: striking or kicking a device in order to make it work

performance: the (efficient) execution of tasks

performance enhancement: improving the efficiency and quality of work

performance-related: connected with the (effective) carrying out of workplace tasks

performative: efficient, effective, dynamic, or bringing about by stating

perk: a work-related incidental benefit

perma-youth: prolonged youthfulness

personalization: adapting to individual needs or preferences

pervasive networks: wide-ranging electronic communications systems

pet therapy: spending time in proximity with tame animals to relieve stress

phishing: illicitly accessing personal data stored electronically

phone rage: a bout of fury occasioned by use of the telephone

pick-and-mix: selecting and combining from a variety of sources or options

PICNIC: an abbreviation of 'problem in chair, not in computer'

piece of kit: item of equipment, machinery or other hardware

pig: a population bulge rendered in graphic form

piggybacks: attaches itself (to), takes advantage (of)

pikey: slang for a member of a social underclass

PIM: an abbreviation of 'personal information manager', handheld electronic data-file

pimp my ride: slang for customize my car

pink ceiling: a barrier to professional advancement based on homophobia

pink pound: spending by gay people

pirating: illicitly copying or imitating (a product for example), infringing copyright

pitching: making a persuasive presentation

Planet B: a hypothetical new home for humanity

planned spontaneity: acting partially on impulse, 'quasi-impromptu' behaviour

planogram: a graphic representation of an arrangement of items for sale

plastic surgery vacation: a holiday, part of which is spent undergoing cosmetic enhancement

platinum circle: one of an ascending order of honorary memberships or a hypothetical very high ranking in a sector

playa: a successful male (such as a seducer)

play hardball: to adopt aggressive tactics and/or an unyielding stance

plus-one: an assistant, second in command, subordinate

PMG: an abbreviation of 'personal mobile gateway', multi-function electronic handset

pod: a capsule, oval container or object

podcasting: creating downloadable audiofiles resembling radio broadcasts

poddies: owners of iPods

podsters: owners of iPods

POG: an abbreviation of 'planogram'

POS: an abbreviation of 'point-of-sale'

poison pills: stratagems, typically setting traps for investors, used by vulnerable businesses to prevent takeover or buy-out

polyattentiveness: paying attention to several sources of information or performing several tasks simultaneously

pomosexual: an individual with progressive and flexible sexual attitudes and/or behaviour

poo-flinging: directing insults (at someone), denigrating

portfolios of purchases: personal selections of items from different sources

portfolio working: incorporating more than one professional role and set of tasks into one's work schedule

poshos: (over)privileged individuals

poster boy: a male person who embodies a cause or project

poster girl: a female person who embodies a cause or project

posters: those placing or exchanging messages at Internet sites

post-humanists: those who envisage a future in which humans will merge with or be replaced by machines, and/or will be transformed electronically

post-minimalism: a reaction to, or successor to, the trend towards austerity and simplicity in design

post-nationalists: individuals without allegiance to or residence in a particular country

post-PC computing: electronic communication based on technology too advanced for desktops

pound in your pocket: the personal spending power of UK citizens

pov: slang for a member of an underclass, poor person

power nap: a brief restorative sleep or rest

predatory lending: advancing funds or credit at punitive interest rates or on unfair terms

predatory reconstruction: regional aid schemes which enrich or favour the providers rather than the recipients

pre-installed: built in before purchase (by the end-user)

prepone: to bring forward (an appointment or arrangement) to an earlier date

preprogramming: organizing in advance

pre-scrutiny: checking a system before it is operational

presenteeism: spending excessive time at one's workplace

presentism: judging the past by present-day standards, believing that only the present has relevance or exists

price-gouging: overcharging or applying extortionate terms

price points: places in a retail outlet where typical prices are displayed

prioritize: to treat as most important or put in order of importance

privates: customers or clients

proact: to take initiative, initiate action

proactive: showing initiative, willing to act

probs: a short form of 'problems'

proctocracy: a regime in which fools set the standards

product incidents: damage, malfunctions or recalls associated with items sold

professoriat: the body of professional academics

programmable brick: a learning toy designed to impart some engineering principles

project life cycle: the entire duration of a project

props: decorative objects placed around products to enhance a retail display

prosthetic enhancement: improving physical appearance and ability by means of surgery or mechanical aids

prosthetics: using artificial aids to replace or repair living body parts

provisional storage virtualization: (the creating of) electronic models of industrial storage and retrieval systems

P2P: an abbreviation of 'peer-to-peer'

puckered-ups: sycophants

pull a Leeson: to take an action (typically a financial speculation) so risky that it threatens the future of one's organization

pulling a shen: committing a practical joke

pump and dump: to talk up a share price, then sell out (before the ploy is discovered and the price drops)

puppy-pile: a heap of strangers engaged in non-sexual physical bonding

push the peanut forward: to progress an arduous and delicate task

put it/him/her back in its/his/her box: to return an object or person to an environment in which they can do no harm, render safe

qpq: an abbreviation of *quid pro quo*

quality: positive attributes such as efficiency, integrity or high value

queer theory: an academic approach that seeks to interpret the hidden sexual aspects of texts and cultural practices

radicals: devotees of progressive ideas and/or 'alternative' or environmentally aware lifestyles

rainmaker: an employee able to achieve success by charisma and/or clever manipulation

ramp: to boost, increase, promote

ramp and de-camp: to talk up a share price, then sell out (before the ploy is discovered and the price drops)

ramp up: to boost, increase, promote

random: an all-purpose slang term of disapproval

rate tarts: debtors who switch credit sources according to best rates

Ratner moment: a momentary indiscretion with disastrous consequences

rattles sabres: adopts a threatening posture

RDC: an abbreviation of 'responsive digital concept'

re-branding: changing the name and/or public image (of an organization, product or service)

received over the transom: arriving by an unusual route

recessed: placed into a hollow space

re-colonization by stealth: covert (re)imposing of political and/or economic control

reconceptualizing: finding a new way of understanding, rethinking

reconfiguring: adjusting one's lifestyle

recreational shopping: purchasing for enjoyment of the experience rather than from necessity

redistributionism: channelling resources to new and deserving destinations

red buttons: stimuli provoking anger

red-top: a downmarket tabloid UK newspaper

re-engineerable: possible to redesign or reformulate

re-envisioneering: thinking creatively anew (about)

refocusing: giving new or renewed consideration (to something)

reimagine: to think in a new and creative way (about)

relationship managers: employees responsible for cultivating and ensuring positive links with clients

release management: supervising the issuing or installation of new products and systems

relocating: moving one's base, finding a new site

remote gaming: online gambling

rep: an abbreviation of '(sales) representative' or 'reputation'

repurposeable: potentially usable for different functions or objectives

re-recruitment: taking back former employees

resistant consumers: potential customers who are difficult to persuade, typically because of their entrenched ideas

resolution: fine detail, sensitivity

resource optimization: reduction in personnel

rest management: the control and monitoring of sleep patterns and relaxation

retail therapy: pleasurable shopping

retrenchment: drastic reduction in staff or reorganization

retro: evoking the styles or behaviour of an earlier age

retro-modern: (reflecting) a modernist design style of the past, typically of the early 1960s

reverse engineering: reducing (an object or system) to its formative components

reverse googling: entering minimal data into an Internet search engine such as Google in order to access fuller information

rhino: slang for money

right-sizing: adjusting (a workforce or organization) to optimum limits, invariably by reduction

ring-fencing: protecting from possible access, interference or amendment, safeguarding

Rio trade: an investment or speculation that risks disaster and may necessitate flight

roadblocks: obstacles to progress, which may be due to inhibitions or misunderstandings

road rage: a bout of fury occasioned by or while driving

road warriors: employees who spend much of their time travelling

robot rage: a bout of fury occasioned by automated telephone responses or call-centre practices

rogan josh: rhyming slang for 'dosh', itself slang for money

ROI: an abbreviation of 'return on investment'

role-sitter: an employee who substitutes temporarily for an absent colleague

roll back: to retreat, or curb, reduce

roll down: to reduce a number of debts by settling one by one

roll out (vb): to release (sometimes gradually or in stages)

rollout (noun): a staged release, an extendable platform

roll over: to carry forward (a financial commitment), to overwhelm, to surrender

ro-ro: short for 'roll-on, roll-off (vessel)'

routing: influencing the movement of buyers through a retail outlet

ROW: an abbreviation of '(the) rest of the world'

rump shares: stock held by a minority who have yet to commit to a change in status

runway: a fashion show catwalk

Rupert: a slang nickname for a 'posh' or upper-class male

sachet: a small (and, typically, cleverly designed) package

Saga-louts: boisterous elderly tourists

salariat: the body of salaried employees, white-collar workforce

salaryman: a middle-ranking corporate employee or white-collar worker

sales-in: (recorded as) having been received and/or paid for

sales loading: inflating periodic sales results, such as year-end figures

sales-out: (recorded as) having been dispatched but not yet paid for

sales-through: (recorded as) in the process of being sold/dispatched but not yet paid for

satisfaction: contentment (that basic or initial needs have been met)

scalable lifeskills: personal capabilities that can be assessed in order of importance

scamsters: swindlers or tricksters

scanning: reading electronically

scavenging: collecting from un-intended sources

scenarios: hypothetical situations

scope: (to assess) extent or limitations

scrapbooking: storing and retrieving memories and memorabilia

scrutable: possible to interpret or assess

seed money: funds to enable a startup and/or expansion

selective extravagance: indulgence in a limited range of luxuries, moderated excess

self-branding: putting one's own brand on goods from elsewhere, marketing oneself (as if one were a product or service), making individualistic consumer choices

self-diagnosing: judging one's own medical condition(s) without professional intervention

self-focused: self-centred, selfish, self-aware

self-medicating: administering drugs or medical treatment to oneself without professional intervention

self-treating: indulging oneself (in luxuries for example)

sense of entitlement: a feeling that one has an automatic right (to advantages or privileges)

sensograms: devices designed to measure tastes, smells, sounds and/or textures

sensor telemetry: measuring and monitoring environments with reactive electronic technology

sensory audits: reviews and assessments of tastes, smells, sounds and/or textures

sensory augmentation: extending the range of human sensation by artificial means

sensory branding: selling by using sounds, smells and/or feelings

sensory clubbing: frequenting clubs which enhance music with atmospheric effects and built-in tactility

sensory sells: selling by using sounds, smells and/or feelings

shakeout: the sorting and discarding of employees

shared wisdom management: developing expertise and skills through collaboration between provider and customer

sharing economy: a social and financial system based on free exchange rather than buying and selling

shark-jumps: instances that signal the imminent decline of a media series or sitcom

Sharons: slang for working class and/or uncultured young females

sheeple: gullible, conformist consumers

shelf optimization: the most efficient, profitable choice and arrangement of retail items

shepherd: to gather together and sort, collate

shock and awe: (the experience of) overwhelming and incapacitating force

shoot the breeze: indulge in casual conversation

shoot the dog: to do the unthinkable, take extreme action and/or terminate an unacceptable situation

shopaholic: an obsessive shopper

shop-droppers: infiltrators who covertly introduce their own items into a retail outlet

shopgrifters: customers who buy a product to use and return for a refund

Shoreditcherati: innovators and adepts of new technology based in East London

short and distort: to talk down a firm's reputation in order to profit from its shares

short selling: disposing of overvalued stock in order to buy it back cheaply later

silent commerce: controlling movement and sale of goods by electronic surveillance

silent funds: financial schemes that have been closed to new business

SillyValley: a derisive nickname for Silicon Valley, itself a nickname for the concentration of IT-related facilities in California

siloing: compartmentalizing, and impeding the free flow of, data

silver bullets: supposedly infallible, usually ingenious and dramatic, solutions

silver ceiling: a barrier to professional advancement based on ageism

silver circle: one of an ascending order of honorary memberships or a hypothetical high ranking in a sector

silver surfers: elderly Internet users

single households: private homes containing only one resident

singletons: unmarried people (living alone)

singularity: a unique event involving dramatic expression or breaching of natural laws

skate to where the puck is going, not where it's been: look to the future rather than dwelling on the past

skills-mapping: reviewing and assessing employees' capabilities

skin: an intermediary which attracts clients for a(n Internet) gambling enterprise

skin operator: an intermediary which attracts clients for a(n Internet) gambling enterprise

skip-licker: a forager for free (waste) food

skirt-length indicator: a supposed means of assessing economic well-being according to changing skirt-lengths

SLA: an abbreviation of 'server log-analysis'

Slaptops: laptops or palmtops ill-treated by enraged users

slash and burn: (to adopt) indiscriminate and destructive tactics

sleep economy: commercial activity based on sleep and its implications for work practices and lifestyle

sleep market: (the potential for) commercial exploitation of sleep

sleep solutions: means of providing rest

slipperiness: ease of access to and negotiation of a website, site user-friendliness

Slow Food: prepared food of good quality that demands to be savoured carefully

small cultures: localized or common-interest groups with shared values and behaviour

smart: equipped with sensors or otherwise able to interact electronically

smart dust: sensitized interactive particles

smart mobs: leaderless groups who exhibit collective intelligence because they are linked to electronic communication networks

smart objects: objects able to interact electronically and/or equipped with sensors

smoochers: sycophants

SMS: text-messaging

SMS spam: unwanted text messages

social bottom line: (a measure of) the impact of an organization and its activities on society (and sometimes vice versa)

social capitalism: commercial enterprises designed to benefit society

socialized enterprise: an organization in which members can interact freely and on an equal basis

social marketing: selling in ways that benefit society or take account of social imperatives

social (re-)engineering: intervening to change a society or economic and/or political system

social risk: danger of social instability or harm to social relationships

social sparks: progressive, influential consumers

soft-edged: using curved forms and yielding surfaces

soft-skills-enhancement: improving interpersonal communications and psychological tactics

soft-spot: period of (relative) inactivity, short recession

solution (vb): to solve, resolve, find a means of dealing with

soup-to-nuts players: providers or enterprises that cater for a complete range of activities

space burials: disposal of human remains in inner or outer space

space management: the (effective) arrangement of objects in a physical environment

spam: unwanted electronic messages

spec: an abbreviation of 'speculation' or 'specification'

specificity: detail(s), definable nature or attributes, essential quality

speed-dating: seeking a romantic partner by a staged encounter with several strangers in quick succession

spend peaking: interspersing controlled spending with extreme extravagance

spide: slang for a member of a social underclass

spidered: searched or scanned selectively and/or by criss-crossing

spillage: deprivation experienced by those excluded from aid or reconstruction schemes

spim: unwanted messages received through instant messaging systems

spin doctor: a manipulator of public relations and/or the media

spit: unwanted messages received via Internet telephony

spitting the dummy: having a tantrum, expressing fury

splurge generation: an age group given to extravagant spending

spon: slang for money

spondulicks: slang for money

sponsor: the person or organization paying for someone to undergo coaching

spotting a fin: detecting the first sign of an imminent decline in a television series or sitcom

Springer crowd: a social underclass, trailertrash

sprinkling: urinating as part of sex play

squeaky wheel gets the grease!: a vocal individual will gain attention

squids: slang for money

SRDS: an abbreviation of 'sudden reputation death syndrome'

stabilization: restoring (or enforcing) normality after a disaster

stags: opportunist and/or speculative investors

stakeholder-based: giving consideration to all interested parties, especially those previously excluded

stakeholders: those parties having vested interests in a project, system or entity

stalwarts: consumers who hold to a preference for high-quality and/or traditional products

stand-alone: separate(d), self-contained

stats: an abbreviation of 'statistics'

status anxiety: worrying about one's relative wealth and social standing

stay-and-delay: putting off the time at which one leaves the protection of the family

steek: slang for a member of a social underclass

step-change: a significant transformation in quality or quantity, a move to a new level

stitch 'n' bitch: sewing or knitting and exchanging malicious gossip

stock overhang: excess in stock held, resultant surplus

stooze-pot: a cash surplus resulting from clever manipulation of personal credit rates

stored-value cards: debit cards issued to employees or members by reputable organizations

straight from the box: (ready) for immediate use

strategize: to achieve through or formulate a strategy

stray: a heterosexual who behaves like a homosexual

stromo: a homosexual who appears heterosexual

stuffing the channel: deliberately oversupplying and/or offloading surplus on customers

subtle shoppers: discerning, sophisticated consumers

successful child has many parents: a positive outcome depends upon a number of factors or contributors

suits: white-collar employees, managers

sunset clauses: stipulations that a contract or regulation will lapse unless renewed

sunset industries: economic or business activities (such as the manufacturing sector) that are or appear to be in decline

supersavers: consumers who are intent upon and successful at economizing

supertarting: switching personal credit sources to get the best going rate(s)

surface web: the easily accessed resources of the Internet

sustainability: avoiding depletion of (natural) resources and environmental damage

sustainability accounting: financial reporting which takes account of environmental responsibility

swallow their own smoke: to take responsibility for and suffer the consequences of one's misdeeds

swarm factor: the effect(s) of collective decisions or preferences

swarm logic: imperatives imposed by the workings of collective intelligence

sweatshop economy: commercial activity based on exploiting underpaid workers

sweet-on-book: a small irritation which impedes or destabilizes on a large scale

swirling: enrolling in several institutions simultaneously or in succession

syndicating chameleon: a boss who succeeds by adopting different stances or roles and coordinating multiple interests

synergizable: with potential for development through collaboration

synergize: to achieve successful collaboration

systemic constellations: (networks of) personal interrelationships within families or organizations

take a bath: to suffer a financial loss

takeaway: insights or information resulting from a meeting or interaction

takeaway nuggets: insights or information resulting from a meeting or interaction

take-back: (accepting responsibility for and) receipt of (for recycling or disposal) a product sold previously

take on board: to take into consideration, include or accept

talent management: nurturing special skills and expertise possessed by one's employees

tanking: facing imminent failure, showing signs of rapid decline

tanks on the lawn: evidence of an imminent attack, signs of an opponent's intentions

targeted-but-holistic: aimed both at specific and generalized (consumer) needs and preferences

Tarquin: a slang nickname for a 'posh' or upper-class male

tart alert: an updated notification of latest credit terms

tarting: switching credit sources to get the best going rate(s)

task (vb): to assign (a responsibility) (to)

task-oriented: exclusively focused on immediate needs

TATT syndrome: a state of constant fatigue

teardown artists: specialists in dismantling

techie: a devotee of new technology

technofood: foodstuffs enhanced with additives or special treatment

technophobe: an individual who is resistant to and/or intimidated by new technology

technorapture: a time of transcendence when humans and technology will merge

technotoilets: toilets which can monitor and/or react to users' state of health

techno-savants: bosses who rely on specialist knowledge of advanced technology

technostalgia: fond memories of the gadgets, appliances and machinery of the fairly recent past

technotrash: discarded machinery, appliances and related waste products

tech rage: a bout of fury associated with technical equipment

tech-savvy: adept at handling and understanding new technology

tech-wreck: the collapse of enterprises based on new technology

teflegation: the effortless offloading of responsibility

teflegram: a message informing that a responsibility has been offloaded onto the recipient

teflicon: an emoticon attached to a message delegating responsibility

Teflon manager: a senior employee who tends to offload responsibility and avoid blame

telecommuting: working electronically from a remote office

terrans: humans who refuse to endorse the rise of non-human intelligence and its implications

test-drive: to experiment with, sample

textual harassment: oppression by an excess of e-mails and/or text messages

thin: employing or favouring simple technology or simplification of systems

thin client: a simply equipped dependent (or dependant) terminal

thinking outside the box: adopting a creatively unorthodox approach

thin solutions: systems using complex central hubs and simple terminals

third-agers: middle-aged and/or elderly people

third mode: the third and latest incarnation or version (of capitalism), based on information exchange

3BL accounting: financial reporting that seeks to take account of social and environmental factors as well as finance

3BL investment: (making) financial decisions that take account of social and environmental factors as well as profit and loss

3BL management: business operations that take account of social and environmental factors as well as finance

3BL reporting: reporting that seeks to take account of social and environmental factors as well as finance

thrift economics: avoiding overspending or display of affluence

thrifters: consumers who are unwilling to indulge in luxuries or spend on novelties

thrifting: practising careful unostentatious spending

throwing a sickie: taking time off (perhaps illicitly) from work as a result of illness

throwing his toys out of the pram: having a tantrum

throwing teddy out of the pram: having a tantrum

time-barred: subject to a time limit (after which it cannot be dealt with), ruled inadmissable

time-poverty: (having) insufficient time to complete tasks and/or relax

tip-from-a-dip: a piece of informal investment advice from a private source

tipping point: the point at which a state of affairs or system begins to transform, pivotal moment

title-creep: the tendency for employees to assume more and more grandiose job titles

title-morph: the tendency for employees to assume more and more grandiose job titles

TLA: an abbreviation of 'three-letter acronym'

TMC: an abbreviation of 'too much choice'

TMI: an abbreviation of 'too much information, or input'

TMT: an abbreviation of 'too much technology'

Toby: a (street or covered-)market boss

toileting: failing irrevocably

toiling midgets: overworked and/or oppressed menial employees

tontine effect: (the collecting of) (extra) benefits for those who have remained in a financial scheme until it is closed

too much input: (a complaint of) superfluous information

top-down: imposed by those in authority (on those below them)

top-line: a best offer

touching base: contacting briefly (to maintain a relationship)

townie: a member of an urban underclass

Tracies: slang for working class and/or uncultured young females

trade-loading: inflating sales results such as year-end figures

trading up/trading down: combining cheap items with luxury items in the same set of purchases

trailertrash: (members of) a US underclass, uncultured, unsophisticated individuals

transition: to change form, status or position

transitioned: made redundant, dismissed, ousted

trans-monetary: based on values other than money or only partially on money

transparency: open and visibly fair dealing, accountable behaviour

trash cash: money generated from recycling or waste disposal

travelling cultures: (behaviours or beliefs shared by) mobile populations or travellers

trawled: searched or scanned gradually and systematically

treasure hunting: seeking out and buying a permutation of desirable items

'treps: entrepreneurs, especially younger creators of Internet-based businesses

tribal chiefs: bosses who dominate through charisma and patronage

trickle down: to influence or be adopted by successively less privileged individuals

triple bottom line: a reporting model or approach that seeks to incorporate social and environmental as well as financial factors

triple play: (a package) combining three separate electronic functions in one

Tristram: a nickname for an affected and/or self-satisfied media employee such as a television producer or director

TROIKA: an EU designation of an international collaborative group

trolley rage: a bout of fury experienced while shopping in a supermarket

troubleshooting: dealing decisively with difficulties as they arise

trying to nail jelly to a tree: attempting an (almost) impossible task

TUNIC: an EU acronym for a collaborative research group

turbulence: disruption and/or instability (in an organization, market or sector, for example)

turnkey status: the capacity for immediate use or implementation

tweenagers: pre-teens or teenagers affecting the behaviour of an older age group

the two and twenty crowd: a nickname for hedge fund managers

TYFS: an abbreviation of 'thank you for sharing (that) (with us)'

über-model: a most impressive and/or prestigious product

über-nerd: a gifted, successful and/or extremely dedicated technical specialist

übersexual: an individual who is successful and self-assured in sexual matters

u-commerce: (successfully) selling a very wide variety of goods or services in a very wide variety of settings

ultra-HNWs: wealthy individuals who are more than affluent but not quite super-rich

underbanked: enjoying or requiring only minimal banking services

under my radar: having escaped my scrutiny and/or taken me by surprise

undertime: (time spent) doing something else while supposedly engaged in paid work

undocumented features: unpredicted defects or malfunctions

unforch: a short form of 'unfortunately'

uninstalled: removed from one's post

unwaged: unemployed

up: a customer who is on the spot (and ready to buy)

upcoding: electronic interaction between consumer and provider, sometimes involving the creation of personalized product codes

upgradation: an upgrade or upgrading

uplinked qualification: an ascending order of educational credits or awards

upscale: (among) the more expensive, prestigious or extensive of a range of possibilities

upstarters: creators of new businesses, (young) entrepreneurs

uptitling: conferring or assuming more (and more) grandiose job titles

upward mobility: (the potential for achieving) increased wealth and/or higher social status

urine drinking: the imbibing of urine

urine therapy: the use of urine to improve health and wellness

urophiles: devotees of urine drinking and/or other urine therapies

user-behaviour management: directing and/or monitoring the way customers interact with a site, system or product

user-centric frameworks: system components whose form and function are dictated by usage

user-created: originating from unofficial sources, generated by users rather than providers

user-driven: based on the desires and needs of users rather than providers

user-query: demands of access or questions posed by potential users

utopian space: an environment offering unlimited possibilities, ideal setting

utterance without language: a message, sign or gesture that is not interpretable in linguistic terms

value: genuine benefit, intrinsic worth

value-add: extra quality, additional benefit or enhancement

value-audits: reviews and assessments of the positive attributes of and/or prevalent beliefs within an organization

vamp (up): to make fresher, better, more powerful; concoct or confect

vanity sizing: pretending that a garment is smaller (or occasionally larger) in order to flatter the wearer

vehicle dismantlers: car breakers, scrap dealers

vertical infohubs: facilities or tools able to process both easy-access and hard-to-find Internet information

vinyl junkies: enthusiastic (gramophone) record collectors

viral marketing: selling by making use of online word of mouth

virement: transferring a financial transaction or amount to a different account or category

virtual angel: a (philanthropic) financial backer operating online

visibility-providing infrastructure: an internal arrangement whose structures and workings can be inspected

visionaries: inspired, gifted and/or far-sighted leaders

visual merchandising: techniques whereby customers are enabled to view items for sale

vivisystems: networks of living entities

vlogs: blogs featuring video technology

voice-lifts: surgical procedures to create a younger-sounding voice

VoIP: an abbreviation of 'voice-over Internet protocol (telephony)'

voodoo economics: ingenious and little understood financial manipulations

VPL: an abbreviation of 'visible pantie-line'

VS: an abbreviation of 'voluntary separation'

wad: (a handful, pile or large amount of) money

walk-away position: the terms and conditions under which, or point at which, a negotiation will be broken off

wantrepreneurs: innovators who cater for those who hope to sample new lifestyle choices

warez d00dz: illicit copiers and distributors of protected software

washes its face: justifies or pays for itself

watersports: sexual practices involving urine

wave-forms: undulating curves, peak-and-trough patterns

Wayne: a slang nickname for a lower-class and/or uncultured male

waystage monitoring: periodic checking

wearies: customers or clients

web concierge: an intermediary who assists in selecting and using online services

weblog: an updatable online journal

wedge: money, wealth

WEEE: an abbreviation of 'waste electrical and electronic equipment'

weekend warriors: individuals who pursue dangerous or strenuous leisure activities at the weekend or in spare time

welfare bargain: the provision of state support providing taxes are paid

wellness sanctuaries: health farms and/or spas

wet room: a domestic space containing ablution facilities

wheels come off the wagon: the enterprise encounters problems and/or fails

whistling past the graveyard: affecting cheerfulness in the face of disaster or danger

white knights: investors who are willing to rescue or assist an endangered venture

whitelist: a register of favoured or commended individuals or organizations

wifi'd: connected by means of wireless technology

wikis: online information sources that can be edited by anyone who wishes

WiPhishing: using illicit wireless hotspots to entrap users or disable their devices

wild-carding: adopting unpredictable tactics, trusting to chance

window-licker: a sycophantic and/or gormless individual

wipes its face: covers its costs and/or makes a profit, justifies its existence

witch doctor: an employee entrusted with finding ingenious, unpredictable solutions

wodge: money, wealth

wolf nearest the sledge: the most immediate threat

wombat: an abbreviation for '(a) waste of money, bandwidth and time'

workaholic: an individual who works to excess

worklessness: unemployment, redundancy

work–life balance: (adjusting) the relative amounts of time spent in work and on leisure

wunch: a pejorative collective noun (for bankers)

yatties: (over)privileged and/or spoilt young women

yawn factor: the degree of boredom (induced by a talk or text, for example)

year of the zombie: a year (supposedly 2005 in the USA) in which zombies enjoyed a particular vogue

yeppies: an abbreviation of 'young, experimenting perfection-seekers'

yuppies: young(ish) ambitious and affluent professionals

zapper: a remote control device for a household audiovisual appliance

zoomorphic: using shapes inspired by animal life

zootropic architecture: design and building using shapes inspired by animal life

Zopa: an abbreviation of 'zone of possible agreement'